A HEADBANGER'S BALL

Real Family Life with a Disabled Daughter

Sandra Murphy

First published in Great Britain in 2008 in Hardback by
The Book Guild Ltd
Pavilion View
19 New Road
BN1 1UF
ISBN 978 1 84624 224 3

Paperback Published by Sandra Murphy in 2015
ISBN-13: 978-1512317022
ISBN-10: 1512317020

Author's Note

All opinions and inclusions shared and expressed, and interpretations of or from information, research or conversations, are entirely my own and are not representative of any other person or organisation. Any errors are entirely mine. The names of all professional people have been changed to protect their identities and no locations given other than Great Ormond Street, King's College and St George's Hospitals, London.

For Raymond, Clare and Ben
With all my love

Special Acknowledgements

First and foremost my love and a huge thank you to Bill for his love, friendship and support and for never tiring of my endless unpredictability! Thank you to my wonderful children for keeping me on the straight and narrow, especially Raymond for his help and guidance, and for telling me what I can and can't do with 'English'! Clare, Patricia, Ray, Jill, Christine and Dave, Mick. Cheryl, Lesley and the little owl – thank you so much for all your help. Ming, for always being close by, and the Make-A-Wish Foundation. Thank you. Amberlie's consultant, doctors, nurses, physio and portage ladies – you know who you are – my endless gratitude, we were so lucky to have such a great team. And my biggest, biggest thank you to Amberlie for coming into my life and for all the love and happiness you brought with you.

A HEADBANGER'S BALL

Prologue

The conversation had dried up and my aunts dispersed to organise the afternoon's high tea. I noticed the local paper on the table next to my chair, picked it up and casually flicked through the pages, glancing momentarily at the headlines.

At the bottom of one of the last pages, there was a large boxed advertisement about a little boy who had been put into care. He was nine months old and disabled. His name was James and the authorities were trying to find a family to foster him.

'Bless him,' I said. 'How can people do that? He's only a babe and I bet he's gorgeous... I'd have him.'

'Here we go,' said Bill, my husband. 'As if having two kids and one on the way isn't enough!'

Someone, somewhere, was listening to me that day.

1

I gasped as the cold gel was squeezed out onto my belly and spread around by the radiographer.

'Here we are!' she said, and started to measure cursor points on the screen. 'A foetus of seven weeks and everything looks good.'

I thought for a long moment and said, 'That doesn't match my dates – it should be ten weeks.'

The radiographer shrugged her shoulders and explained that according to the measurements it was the right size for seven weeks. I assumed it must be a small baby.

At the regular 20-week scan, I was given yet another, even later expected date of delivery, which, by my calculations, meant that I would have missed two periods before discovering I was pregnant. I pointed out that this couldn't be right as I always had a totally regular menstrual cycle, but they insisted their interpretation of the evidence on the scan was correct. I left the hospital confused, dismissing their dates and summarising that the baby would be early then.

At my routine 36-week check at the hospital, the doctors found that my blood pressure had rocketed. I had been on medication to control it for a fair while and they were very worried. They did another ultrasound and explained that I would need to stay in hospital because there was evidence that the baby had not been growing so well and was less active. I had noticed over the last couple of days that the number of kicks and movements the baby made had slowed down. A midwife gave me a tablet to bring down my blood pressure and moved me to another room while they sorted out a bed on the ward. I was warned not to move off my trolley for any reason, not even to wee, and I wasn't to worry! I asked what was going to happen and they explained that my blood pressure was now dangerously high and the baby was now at risk. They were going to put me under observation for a while and probably induce the baby within forty-eight hours. We didn't know how long we would have to wait so Bill returned home to check on our other two children and to collect a few things for me.

I was soon moved to the ward and a nurse wired me up to a blood-pressure monitor and a cardiograph to check the baby's heart. The midwife studied the reading and bleeped for the doctors. She explained that there was an unusual dipping in the baby's heartbeat.

After much activity and various examinations, the registrar said they suspected the umbilical cord was around the baby's neck, which was making the heartbeat drop and consequently weakening it.

'We must deliver the baby straight away,' she said. They explained that to give the baby every chance to be born naturally and quickly they would start by breaking my waters. If the labour didn't progress as expected they would have no option but to do an emergency caesarean section. I grabbed the phone next to my bed and told Bill to come back to the hospital fast.

I was still not allowed to move and I lay there completely dazed, trying not to panic and wishing Bill would hurry up. Everyone had disappeared to organise things and I could hear the clattering and dashing about down the corridor.

I felt so alone. There was only one other person in the ward and she was being sick all the time.

The midwife put her head round the door. 'Try to rest,' she said with a sympathetic smile.

Rest! I thought. *Jesus*!

Bill arrived within twenty minutes just as they were moving me to the delivery suite. Before I knew it and while the registrar was explaining what she was doing, my membranes were ruptured with what looked like a giant crochet hook and the water gushed

2

out. There were two midwives scuttling in and out of the room preparing for the birth and I felt the twinges begin. They went on building for the next forty-five minutes or so, and the worried midwife said that if it didn't happen in the next few minutes they would have to do the caesarean. I then had a massive contraction, so strong, powerful and excruciatingly painful it nearly threw me off the bed! The monitor alarms all went off as the baby's heartbeat sank and my blood pressure went through the roof. The doctors dashed in just as the baby's head appeared.

'Don't push! Don't push!' they shouted. 'If you do the baby will die!'

'Strewth!' I shouted, desperately trying to hold everything back.

The cord was tightly wrapped twice around the baby's neck and needed cutting while it was still inside me. Seconds later they grabbed the baby and rushed it out for resuscitation.

Bill and I looked at each other. Everyone had disappeared outside with the baby and there was silence.

'Did you see what it was?' I asked him.

'I think it's a girl,' Bill said, gobsmacked.

It seemed like an eternity as we waited, listened and hoped for any sign that she was alright. There was not a sound. Then the door opened slightly and we heard a baby crying, then the midwife with a big grin all over her face poked her head in and announced, 'It's a girl!'

The door closed again and a few seconds later she reappeared with the baby tightly swaddled and yelling away at the top of her voice. It was a wonderful sound and an enormous relief!

'She's fine,' said the midwife. 'She arrived at 10.58 pm and your labour was only fifty-four minutes. Well done! What are you going to call her?'

We had waded through hundreds of names looking for something different and pretty for a girl. Amberlie Rose was perfect – modern, with a touch of the 'old fashioned', and it flowed so well off the tongue.

It was the first of April.

'You know what today is, don't you?' I said to Bill. 'It's All Fool's Day ... It would have been nicer for her birthday to have been tomorrow.'

Amberlie settled straight into a breastfeed. She was so tiny – 2160g (4lb 12oz) – and so blue. No meat on her at all. I noticed the little toe on her left foot was very large so I mentioned it but was told it wasn't anything to worry about. The paediatrician thought that although the baby was very small, the foetus was older than 36 weeks, nearer 39, so she was a bit bemused. I told her there had been some confusion over my dates all along. She explained that they would be keeping both of us in for a few days to make sure the baby fed well and kept a constant temperature, and also to make sure that my blood pressure settled down. After three days we were allowed home.

We arrived outside our house and Ray, Amberlie's 5-year-old brother, was waiting on the doorstep with Auntie Pat. Bouncing up and down with excitement at having a new baby in the house, he shouted, 'Have you got Elmer?'

We all laughed. He couldn't say 'Amberlie' to save his life!

Within a few days Amberlie developed a cold and really nasty sticky eyes, so I took her to the doctor, who prescribed antibiotic drops. By her fifteenth day her weight had increased to 5lb 6oz and her head was growing well, at 32 cm. She continued to gain weight beautifully, sometimes a pound per week! Her first smile came for Ray at twenty-one days old. The cold and sticky eyes persisted and after eight weeks and another two bottles of antibiotic drops, a midwife suggested I try a few drops of breast milk into each eye three times a day, which I did, and amazingly that solved the problem!

At Amberlie's six-week review, I asked the doctor about the large little toe as it looked odd and I was still concerned about it. He told me that approximately one in every two hundred babies had an odd little toe, or a finger, and occasionally an additional one. He said that sometimes they grew to be a bit unsightly but were not usually anything to worry about, and if Amberlie was concerned about it later on or it became a problem with shoes or whatever they would be able to sort it out for her.

Amberlie was an absolute delight to have around. She was such a contented and docile child. The nights were good, with regular four-hourly feeds, and she was always happy and smiley whenever she woke. She had a very infectious hearty laugh, which was reserved for her dad only, and she always knew when he was due home from work as she would get really excited a few minutes before he walked in the door. She was such a sweetie. Our only concern was that her immunity seemed to be virtually zero. Every germ that came into the house Amberlie got. She was never without a cold.

2

We enjoyed the summer holidays that year. The weather had been great and we had a lot of days out. Everybody was happy and it had been a lot of fun. Then Amberlie got colic.

I assumed that introducing her to formula milk, as my breast milk supply didn't seem to be keeping up with her demand, had caused the colic. The crying started each day between 4 and 5 p.m. when Amberlie seemed to be in agony with tummy pains, bringing her legs up towards her chest and shouting out. She would bang her head on my shoulder and then nuzzle her mouth into it, so I presumed she was also teething.

These sessions would continue for two to three hours, sometimes longer. Neither Bill nor I could settle her and she eventually cried herself to sleep. I tried the usual remedies available at the chemist but things did not improve. Sometimes during the day, I noticed Amberlie pulling a few strange faces while looking at her baby gym. These only lasted a few seconds and I put them down to wind.

After another dreadful evening, I called the doctor. He suggested I bring Amberlie to the surgery the following morning so he could check her over.

A couple of hours later, Amberlie was sitting in her bouncing chair looking at the toys hanging from her baby gym. As I glanced at her she went totally still. Her eyes were fixed and she looked just like a doll. It was as if the whole world had stopped for a single moment. Then her little head shook, her face contorted and she was alive with little twitches, and her eyelids were flickering at an astounding rate. I panicked. I just knew this was a fit of some kind and belted out the door to phone the doctor, who arrived about half an hour later. In the meantime there had been no recurrence and Amberlie had gone off to sleep. The doctor examined her and took her temperature and said that on the face of it everything appeared to be fine. However, he wanted us to bring her to morning surgery the next day just to be sure.

Bill and I put Amberlie in our bed that night so we could watch and be close to her. I felt very agitated. Something was very, very wrong. I could feel it.

In the early hours she had another two of these episodes and during the second one her body shook all over. I felt the panic surge again, woke Bill and rang the doctor. Again he told me to bring her to the surgery first thing. I couldn't wait to get through the night. I was scared and panicky and thought if she got any worse I'd take her straight to the hospital. I was so worried that I dared not sleep. When I did feel my eyelids close I wrenched them open again. The feeling of dread was overwhelming; I just wanted someone to say that this was just a fluke and she would be OK.

Our usual GP was away, so we saw a locum doctor. I would much rather have seen the doctor who came in the night.

I explained all that had happened and she said it would be best to get Amberlie to hospital so that they could observe her for a while. She rang the ward and we went straight there. About halfway there Amberlie started to stiffen and her eyelids flickered as if something had gone into her eyes.

We were shown to the doctor's office and explained all that had happened again. They wanted to know all about her birth and how she had been progressing since. They said she was small in size for a baby of four and a half months but was obviously thriving.

A nurse took us to a small room in the baby area of the ward. It was very bland in colour, sort of a pale grey with a couple of Disney stick-on pictures on the wall and a clock. In the middle of the room was a high steel cot that looked more like a cage than a bed. A fold-up bed already made up with crisp white starched sheets was positioned under the large window beside a cabinet with a television on. An oxygen and air point was situated on the wall behind the cot along with other medical equipment. It was very small and claustrophobic.

Within an hour of being admitted, Amberlie had another episode and luckily this time, the doctors were there to witness it. Several tests were taken: blood – which took an eternity to get because she was chubby and her veins were small and hidden – urine, temperature, anything and everything. All the results came back quickly and were normal.

The episodes were becoming more frequent now and much harsher. Amberlie would clench her fists tight and curl her toes and feet. She brought her arms and legs steadily and stiffly upwards towards her chest and her expression was fixed and red. She would release this position in an instant and then repeat it over and over again. She was getting so upset in between each episode and seemed very frightened. So were we. I was becoming very frustrated that this was being allowed to continue without someone doing anything about it. The registrar explained that this was definitely some sort of epileptic seizure pattern that Amberlie was in and they needed to find out what was causing it before they started her on medication. They took more of her blood and Amberlie screamed. It was horrendous. Her blood just would not run freely from her veins. They had to keep pricking her in different places and squeezing her hands tightly to get more drops. Poor Amberlie was becoming more and more distressed.

'Why do you have to do it that way?' I questioned, letting them know my concern. The registrar explained that to use a syringe on a baby would cause the veins to collapse and this was the only way. They also decided to do a lumbar puncture in case she had contracted a brain virus such as meningitis. They thought it best we stay where we were as it was not a pleasant experience for anyone. They left the room while I was in mid-protest, and Bill and I were left biting our nails in terror and exasperation.

They weren't long and Amberlie was quiet – too exhausted to complain. They handed her to me and said the results would be back quickly. They were. They were normal.

The next stage was for Amberlie to have an EEG (electro-encephalogram), to see what her brainwaves were doing. The nurses explained that Amberlie would have little electrodes put onto her head. These picked up the electrical signals made in her brain and fed the information into a machine, which would then print out a graph showing the pattern of her brainwaves from each section.

Amberlie was taken on her bed to the neurology department along with an oxygen tank and other bits and pieces on a tray. A doctor and a nurse stayed with us all the time. When we arrived a technician was waiting for us and began attaching the electrodes to Amberlie's head using a type of glue. There were wires everywhere, each colour coded and linked to a relic of a machine. They were all placed in a specific pattern on her head. It took an age for this woman to complete her task. She apparently was not used to babies and nervously got herself into quite a state, making the whole process seem quite brutal. I don't think she appreciated so many people watching her do her job.

The machine started up and was noisily producing reams and reams of paper. By now the consultant neurologist was in attendance and studied the graphs being drawn. He was mumbling away to himself and then calmly said:

'Part of the brain is missing.'

There was a huge pause as life stopped in the room. I sat staring at him, open-mouthed and totally dumbstruck.

'What?' I spoke directly to him. I couldn't believe what I had heard. I looked at the nurse. She was stunned. I had visions of half-brains and weird mutations. I burst into tears.

The consultant explained that the brainwaves were forming a constant but abnormal pattern, showing that part of the brain was missing. He was sorry.

'Missing? Missing? What do you mean missing?' I blurted out.

'We will need to do a CT scan now to see what the actual problem is before we can tell you anymore.'

There was silence. I just looked at Amberlie. It couldn't be true. No, she was just a baby. She looked fine. The technician removed the electrodes in the same brutal way she had put them on. The nurse started to gather our things together and moved Amberlie's bed towards the door. The tears were pouring, I couldn't hold them back. The shock had drained every bit of colour from Bill's face and I knew he was staying silent in an attempt to keep controlled. Everything was blurred. I could see everyone busily moving around trying hard not to look at us. No one knew what to say. The nurse had taken my hand and was squeezing it. I could see the worry and shock in her eyes as she tried to stop her own tears from falling. I was still and unable to respond. I couldn't think. We started to move. I don't remember getting from there to the ward, I only remember Amberlie, my baby, lying on this white bed in her white all-in-one baby suit with this awful sticky glue in her hair that I was going to wash off as soon as possible. Wash away what it had found.

Everything seemed far away and removed, almost as if we had watched a television programme about somebody else.

The nurse made Bill and me a cup of tea and Dr Thomas arrived to talk to us. The nurse had complained to him that the neurologist should not have told us the news in the way he had and Dr Thomas apologised on his behalf. I did not react. He went on to say that he needed to organise the CT scan (computer assisted tomography or CAT scan).

'And what's that?' I interrupted.

He went on to explain that the machine would take images of Amberlie's brain. It dissects the brain into slices in different directions and would show which part of her brain was not normal.

They were now going to start Amberlie on an antiepileptic drug called carbamazepine to try to stop her seizures. She would also need to be sedated for the scan because it was imperative that she remained still throughout, otherwise the pictures would blur.

We had to wait ages outside the scan room in this white corridor with windows all along one side. The sun was shining straight through and the glare was irritating the massive headache I had developed. We had another nurse with us now who seemed to find it difficult to talk. I tried to make conversation with her just to make the time pass but gave up in the end, thinking she was a lousy addition to a children's ward. Amberlie was still having a fit. The seizures were so strong they were overriding the sedation. I wished the doctors would hurry up.

Eventually a woman came to collect Amberlie, saying that only one parent was allowed to be present during the scan.

'I'll go,' I said.

I had never seen a CT scanner before and this awesome cream-coloured machine with a dark tunnel through it was very intimidating. My insides felt empty, and as the panic started to rise and my chest tightened, fear set in, fear of what it was going to find. Pictures of half brains were still dancing around in my head while a reasoned voice kept saying, 'Calm down and wait.'

The scan took forever. Amberlie's seizures kept coming and they had to keep stopping the programme until she settled. I spotted Dr Thomas in the computer room concentrating on the screens. At last she went to sleep and they completed the job.

On our way out of the room we got caught up in an onslaught of doctors dashing into the developing room. I felt a cold fear instil itself deep into my bones and a chill ran over my skin, making the hairs stand on end. I could hear myself breathe. I knew this was bad. Doctors don't get excited for nothing.

The nurse with the personality by-pass was mute and ignoring the commotion. No surprise there.

We went up to the ward and had a short but agonising wait for Dr Thomas. He put up a scan of Amberlie's brain onto the light box in our room. They had found in the first instance that her brain looked normal. Then came the 'but'. On closer examination they could see that part of the surface looked a little smooth and that the ventricles (brain cavities) were on the large side. They could not be absolutely sure, as the radiographer had never seen this before and it would have to be referred to experts for confirmation, but if their initial diagnosis was correct, Amberlie had a malformation of the outer layer of the brain called lissencephaly.

He explained:

'Our brains - normal brains – have bumps, valleys and mounds over the surface called gyrie. Lissencephaly means there is an absence of gyrie so the brain is smooth. This, because it is an abnormality, causes the electricity in the brain to divert from its normal patterns and bounce around incorrectly inside Amberlie's head. This is why she is having seizures.'

'Is that epilepsy then?' I asked. 'Can we make her better?'

'No,' he said, sighing and wincing at the same time. 'It is epilepsy but a complicated form.'

We were now going into the summer bank holiday weekend and the expert they needed to verify their findings and guide them was on holiday until Tuesday, so in the meantime they would be endeavouring to get Amberlie's epilepsy under some sort of control. Dr Thomas said this could be extremely difficult with this type of brain abnormality.

We learned that antiepileptic drugs work for some and not for others. It would be a case of finding which drug or combination of drugs would work for Amberlie, starting with the best first-line drugs. It was all going to be trial and error.

I asked if there was anything that could be done to change her brain or make it right. He explained that once the brain had developed in the womb it did not change.

'It does not grow and change in the same way as the rest of the body and nor can it be replaced. It is therefore a matter of dealing with the symptoms rather than the cause ... and that is the seizures.'

Bill and I were so stunned and upset that our emotions entered a state of paralysis. There was so much to take in and so much to understand. I was petrified Amberlie's condition was terminal and could not think beyond that. Dr Thomas said, 'It is not like a cancer and to my knowledge, not terminal in itself.' He did not know what might have caused it and the only information available was one line of text on lissencephaly in a huge reference book on paediatric medicine, and all that said was what the definition of it was. It was an extremely rare abnormality.

We were left alone with Amberlie, who was still fast asleep. I held her hand. There was nothing to say. The silence was deafening and the agony deepening. It was very frustrating having to wait for this specialist to see her. There were so many questions banging around in my head and all the answers I did have were floating about in a jumble of confusion.

The seizures were not improving. If anything they were worsening. The medication was doing nothing. It felt like we were going round in circles, so much happening but nothing changing Amberlie's predicament.

The poor little soul was going from one seizure to another, following the same pattern as before but with her head now turning towards the left. Sometimes her knees would be up to her stomach and her left arm bent into her chest with the right arm totally straight and pointing at a forty-five degree angle. Her breathing would pause during the more severe ones but thankfully they were not making her blue in colour (cyanosis – caused by lack of oxygen around the body), something we were told to look out for.

By Sunday she was still no better. The fits often occurred at the beginning and end of feeds, so the doctors rechecked her blood-sugar levels. They were still normal. In desperation I decided to change her formula milk to another brand, hoping that the root cause was an allergic reaction to that particular brand. I had it stuck in my mind that weaning her off breast milk had triggered her fits and the doctors agreed that this was possible, though unlikely. I was scratching around in the dark looking for a simple answer. Deep down I knew I was clutching at straws. We would never know what had started them, only that she would have started fitting at some stage whatever we had done. Dr Thomas told us that when there was a brain abnormality, it was usual for seizures to start at around four to five months of age. That was because the normal development of children accelerated at this time and babies progress from the sleepy, sucky and dependent stage, into becoming aware of and responding to their surroundings. The brain therefore becomes more active and more electricity builds up and bounces around in response to the increased amount of information coming in. A normal brain copes easily, but a malformed brain goes awry.

Every time I looked for a ray of hope, I was given a logical explanation. I struggled to take it all in. Eventually the questions started to sort into a pattern and each time I saw a doctor or a nurse I was ready to ask the next batch. Not that I got anywhere much – no one knew anything about lissencephaly, and nothing helped my swelling frustration. Most of the questions were shots in the dark, but everything had to be worth asking.

'It's just one of those things,' Dr Thomas kept saying. I couldn't accept that. I had to have done something wrong. After all, I had two other perfectly healthy children. I went through the whole of my pregnancy as best as I could; I was searching and searching for reasons. I'd eaten all the right sorts of foods – lots of fruit and vegetables, suffered through the hay fever season by not taking antihistamines – I didn't even take a paracetamol for a headache. I got my potatoes delivered weekly and there had been lots of green-tinged ones among them ... it might have been them ... I should have thrown them away and not cooked them. I did go to the dentist very early into the pregnancy and forgot to tell her I was expecting before she X-rayed me ... perhaps it was that? The doctors dismissed them all. We would probably never know.

The nurses were so patient with my constant questioning and pleading for answers. I was so persistent, even possessed. I suppose it was an attempt to try to accept it all amongst a pain that I could not share or explain. I was withdrawing into my shock, devastated with disbelief and misery. On top of that Amberlie was not getting any better.

The seizures were now extremely severe, one after another and Amberlie was not getting a break. Some of them were twenty-five minutes long with Amberlie coming through intermittently, crying and shouting out. Some lasted only five minutes.

Bill and I were very worried about the length of time she was in a fit and asked it this would be hurting or damaging her. Dr Thomas told us that fits lasting under half an hour were fairly safe, but beyond that there was a possibility that some damage would occur, especially if they kept following on one after the other. He said:

'This situation is known as "status epilepticus" – seizures occurring so close together that one seizure runs into another, without the recovery of normal cerebral function and consciousness between them.' There was a pause, then he continued, 'It really is essential to get her under control as soon as possible before this happens.'

We were beginning to grasp some of the language of epilepsy and noted that there can be many different types of seizures that are categorised under different headings.

'So what are tonic-clonic seizures?' I asked, trying to work out which ones Amberlie was having.

He explained that it was a seizure where stiffening and jerking occurred throughout the body.

'So which has Amberlie got?'

'Infantile spasms,' he replied.

We were at our wits' end and unable to comfort her. We kept begging the doctors to do something, anything, to help her, and all we kept hearing was 'they're doing all they can' and 'we need to wait for the expert'.

The drug wasn't working so Dr Thomas decided to give Amberlie a loading dose of another antiepileptic (phenytoin): a strong drug that would knock her out and give her some rest. It needed to be administered by a drip to get it into her bloodstream quickly so that it would hopefully take immediate effect. Evidently, when this particular drug is given orally, it can take up to two weeks to get to an effective level in the blood. There were some risks in giving this in such a large and fast dose as it could cause her blood pressure to rise suddenly and sharply, putting a lot of strain on her heart. She would therefore have to be carefully monitored.

My heart sank. I was trying to keep cheerful and remain optimistic. They had to do what they had to do. I just wanted Amberlie safe.

The nurses wheeled in the monitors. One was for the drip, to measure the timed dose accurately, one was a heart monitor, because the seizures would already be having an effect on her heart, let alone the risk involved in giving the transfusion of medicine; and one was a high-tech blood-pressure gauge.

The drip was inserted into her left wrist. Yet another needle in her ... They still had difficulty in finding a decent vein. Eventually the line went in and we hoped we would soon see some relief for Amberlie. The nurse said it would take twenty-five minutes for the medicine to get into her system. She did not leave Amberlie's side and watched the monitors the whole time. The blood-pressure gauge was programmed to take a reading every four minutes and we never took our eyes off Amberlie and the monitors. When the drip finally bleeped its end we jumped, startled in case something had gone wrong. The nurse smiled and said, 'That's it done. Now perhaps Amberlie will get some peace.' They were going to leave her on the monitors for the time being to make sure all was well.

Amberlie had been lying on an apnoea cushion in case she stopped breathing. (Babies show their breathing in different ways according to whether they are asleep or awake. While awake their stomachs move in and out, and when asleep you see their chests move. An apnoea cushion monitors this and alarms if breathing stops.) As Amberlie was so unstable in her seizure pattern, trying to sleep off the effects of the fits and then being jolted awake by another one, the apnoea cushion was constantly alarming. I would sit or lie down thinking she was resting only to jump up a minute later to check that she was still with us. After doing this incessantly for twenty-four hours I was exhausted and my nerves shattered. The nurse said it wasn't fair to any of us to have this going on the whole time and took the cushion away, saying there was no need for it with Amberlie being linked to all the other monitors.

The hours passed and we waited and waited, hoping and praying, but there was no change in Amberlie. The phenytoin was not working. Her fits were continual. Dr Thomas had gone home but left instructions to ring him if needed.

By now I was at the end of my tether. I was so desperate to see Amberlie seizure free and settled. The more upset she got, the more upset I got. Nobody seemed to react when I said I thought the drug was useless. I kept saying it to different nurses but didn't get any response from any of them. They just looked at her, crying, fitting and suffering. Then suddenly I broke. Enough was enough. I went berserk.

I demanded something was done immediately. Amberlie was suffering so much.

'Sod the bank holiday! I'm not interested in bloody doctors being on fucking holiday!' I screamed. 'This bloody man can't be the only paediatric neurologist in the whole damn country! Find somebody and find somebody now! I am not going to stand here letting Amberlie fit until bloody Tuesday!' Tears were streaming down my face. I was fraught, absolutely livid and sobbing uncontrollably.

The nurses were panicking and the doctors were 'bleeped'. I was going mental and the whole ward knew it, and my Amberlie was still fitting.

One of the lady doctors arrived straight away. The room was now full of nurses. She tried to explain their difficulties, all of which I had already heard. I was having none of it.

'I'm not interested in your excuses! Amberlie is my only concern, nothing else. Bugger your administration. Bugger the lot of you! You're supposed to be fucking doctors. Do something! This child is suffering and has been for the last four days. Sort it!'

She decided it would be best to phone Dr Thomas.

Dr Thomas came immediately. He said that he had hoped the phenytoin would have worked but Amberlie was obviously in very serious trouble now and on the brink of going into status. The only option now was to put her out entirely on a general anaesthetic type of antiepileptic called heminevrin to try to give her some rest and gain the chance to administer oral antiepileptics to attempt to bring her seizures under control.

'This will stop them, won't it?' I asked.

'We hope so,' he said.

'Hope so? Is there a chance it won't?' I fired back, feeling my heart rise into my throat.

He sighed and looked at me. I could sense his reluctance to answer but I was looking straight into his eyes; I was determined to know. He said, 'In some circumstances, status cannot be controlled. There comes a point of no return where the brain thinks it is normal to fit rather than the other way round and will fight all attempts to reverse it.'

I closed my eyes.

'Jesus,' I mumbled to myself. My whole body was shaking. I was trying so hard to keep it together and not cry. I couldn't speak.

'We have lots of hope at the moment, Sandra, and if we act quickly we should be able to control her seizures,' Dr Thomas reassured. 'Amberlie will need to have a ventilator at hand, though, because this drug can suppress her respiratory system and stop her breathing. This hospital does not have a suitable ventilator for a baby and we will need to transfer her to Great Ormond Street Hospital where they will be better equipped to deal with her problems, plus there will be experts on hand to sort her out. OK?'

I nodded. He left to phone them.

He returned a few minutes later, saying we would be on the next emergency ambulance that arrived at the hospital. I was relieved but felt nauseous. I knew we were going to the best place in the world to help my baby.

I threw all our belongings into bags while the nurses kept an eye on Amberlie. I then rang home to let Auntie Pat know what was happening and to check on Ray and Clare. The adrenaline was pumping.

Dr Thomas said that Dr Simon Pagett would be waiting for us at the hospital. Carla, the doctor who took the brunt of my anger and Sam, the night sister on the ward, would be coming with us in the ambulance just in case Amberlie needed emergency medical assistance during the journey.

Bill was going to take his car and was warned not to try to follow or keep up with the ambulance. The doctor told him we would be travelling very fast with blue lights flashing and it would be extremely dangerous for him to be behind us. Also he did not need to be stopped by the police, arrested and delayed in getting to the hospital.

Twenty minutes later, we were ready to go. Bill stayed with us while Amberlie was secured onto the bed in the ambulance and the emergency equipment prepared. The doctor and sister sat opposite her so they could watch her and I sat on a seat at her feet. One of the paramedics sat by her head. Bill took our bags and left. Amberlie was still fitting.

The ride in the ambulance was very rocky and bumpy. The heat was stifling and I felt very sick all the way. I couldn't tell if it was the journey, the worry or both. The paramedics were very jovial and cracked lots of jokes. I didn't understand some of them, as they were medically orientated and mostly about a large shovel hanging on the door beside the doctor. Apparently used for scraping 'messes' off roads! Yuk!

3

It was difficult to see out of the ambulance's smoked-glass windows to judge where we were on route, but thankfully it wasn't too long before we were reversing towards the hospital doors, where a ward sister was waiting with a security guard.

The entrance to the hospital was beautiful, bright and spacious and scrupulously clean with a stunning royal blue and white marbled floor. There was nobody about, the whole place seemed deserted. Still, it was well past 11 pm on a Sunday night.

The sister guided us quickly down the corridors. Amberlie was nestled safely in Sam's arms. I wanted to carry her but I didn't say anything – I guessed it was their responsibility to make sure that Amberlie arrived safely when transferring to another hospital.

It was so strange and eerie waking through the barren corridors with our footsteps echoing and rebounding unpredictably off the walls, making us all turn around to see if we were being followed. No one spoke. We arrived at the lift and were surprised to find an old dark wooden contraption, which could not have been more than a metre square in size, waiting to take us to the first floor. We all looked at each other, passing amused smiles between us, and crammed into the small space. It was just like having a ride in a moving wardrobe – it creaked and groaned all the way.

The doors opened and a young chap in intensive care uniform was waiting for us. He led us down an old cream-coloured, very enclosing corridor. At the end was a darkness broken by the warm glow of a single lamp. As I focused my eyes, I could see a group of women sitting around a table having tea and cakes. They looked up and smiled as we passed. We were shown to the far corner of the room where a cot had been prepared for Amberlie. As the lights were switched on I could see a very full high-dependency ward. We were introduced to Doreen, who was a specially trained intensive care nurse who would be staying with us on a one-to-one basis for the whole night. A doctor with a very strong Irish accent rushed in and Amberlie was quickly undressed. Our doctor handed over Amberlie's CT scans and her notes. They whizzed through all the details of the last few days and Amberlie was examined.

In walked Bill, looking windswept and flushed. The ambulance was waiting downstairs to take Sam and Carla back, so they had to rush. They hugged us both tightly and wished us all the best, saying they would ring every day to see how Amberlie was getting on. We were all caught up in the emotion of it all and Sam scrambled in her pocket to find some tissues. I don't know why but I had assumed in my disturbed mind that once we were at Great Ormond Street Hospital (GOSH), they would sort Amberlie out one, two, three – in an instant – and we would then take her home and that would be all. It was at that moment I realised I was very wrong.

Poor Amberlie needed to have more blood tests, which proved to be just as difficult as they had previously been. They ended up putting a line into the crease in her arm because she had run out of decent veins. The monitors and alarms were all switched on and as the heminevrin was administered she immediately began to relax. As Amberlie drifted off to sleep, fit free, I felt a very strange mixture of relief, worry and insecurity. My whole mind had gone blank and I couldn't even consider the next five minutes.

By now Dr Pagett had arrived and sat us down to talk. He needed the full story plus any odd things that had happened and could be relevant. He asked if our other children were well and whether they had been ill recently. I said they had both had a virus a week or so ago and a slight rash had appeared on their skin. He thought that interesting because sometimes a normal virus can enter the brain and cause serious problems. We explained that Amberlie had already had a lumbar puncture and it had proved normal. He felt it would be best to give her two courses of antibiotics, one through her line and the other orally to be on the safe side. He was also going to start her on phenobarbitone, another antiepileptic, to try to bring her seizures under control so that they could get her off the heminevrin as soon as possible. Another EEG was also planned, but as it was a bank holiday we would have to wait until Tuesday for that. Bill and I both sighed. I was not quite so irritated this time because Amberlie was now peaceful. Dr Pagett justified the delay by saying that Amberlie was totally exhausted so a restful day just sleeping would be good for her.

Bill and I were urged to get some rest and we were shown down an offside corridor where the nurses found us a mattress and a trolley to sleep on. It was now 5 am and it hardly seemed worth it, and anyway I didn't want to sleep or be away from Amberlie. They assured us that Amberlie would be safe with Doreen and that if anything happened they would come and get us.

We both lay there. We didn't talk much. There didn't seem to be much to say apart from being relieved that at last Amberlie had settled, albeit into an artificially induced sleep. It was very chilly, and the room had obviously been unused for a long time. Bill and I were both dressed in summer clothes and the goosebumps rose high on our skins as I rummaged in the bags for our jumpers. From shoulder height the room was all windows on three of the walls and the last one was an icy pale green with a sink attached to it. The other side was attached to a total blackness and seemed to be a day room. It looked very forbidding so I didn't bother to try to see anything through the windows. I felt very vulnerable and cut off and was so glad that Bill was with me. I wasn't convinced that the thin blankets we had been given were going to do much in the way of warmth so neither of us bothered to undress. I stared at the ceiling, cold and uncomfortable on the trolley, and started to worry about Ray and Clare and whether it was possible for Auntie Pat to stay to look after them while we were away. I must have eventually dozed off.

At 7 am I awoke, startled by the hospital cleaners bashing their buckets and mops about. Trolleys were being moved around and nurses were busy doing their early observations. It all sounded like pandemonium. God, it was cold! I ached in odd places and was glad to get up. Bill stirred.

We hurried to wash and change our clothes so we could get back to the ward to see Amberlie. It was quiet in there, and she looked very settled. She was such a beautiful baby with her features full and rounded, such innocence dressed in pure white.

Doreen was sitting beside the bed filling in various forms and she greeted us, saying Amberlie hadn't murmured at all and that she needed us to answer a few more questions. She then went off duty but said she would be back for the night. Our day nurse was to be Noreen. We smiled – Doreen/Noreen!

Amberlie was too sedated to be able to feed and a nasal gastric tube needed to be inserted into her nose to maintain her nourishment. The first tube they tried was too large and made her gag as it passed into her throat. They were surprised, as this was the usual size for a baby. They then tried a smaller one and it went in just fine. Once the tube was in place it was taped to her face to keep it secure. An acid test was taken each time before feeding to ensure that the tube was well into her stomach. This was done by syringing a small amount of fluid from the tube and testing it on litmus paper to make sure it was hydrochloric acid and therefore in the right place. this was essential as it was possible for the tube to move during a seizure and end up in her lungs instead – the last place anyone would want to put a bottle of milk.

It was all a bit awesome and the nurse told us not to worry and that we would soon be used to doing it. We raised the top of her mattress to aid gravity and inserted a large syringe into the end of the tube. We gradually poured in her usual quantity of milk. The tube was then flushed through with water and a stopper put in to avoid any leakages. We kept to her daily feed times.

The ward itself was bedlam, busy beyond belief and the noise level was incredible. All the other children seemed to be having a bad day and three were having seizures, all related to different conditions. Amberlie was resting well considering, and other parents had started to approach us to chat and investigate.

One mum explained that her little boy had caught encephalitis (a brain virus), leaving enormous damage and he was now severely handicapped. Another boy had been born with terrible head/brain abnormalities together with intestinal deformities. He was recovering from his umpteenth operation and they were hopeful he would now be able to start to take some food orally.

A thirteen-year old girl had developed a rare allergy to copper. She had lost her balance, coordination and control of her body functions. I was amazed to learn how many things contained traces of copper and how impossible it was to avoid it. She was trying a new drug to control it and through it all had managed to draw and colour in a 'Bravery Award' for Amberlie, which she gave to me to stick to the bed. I was really chuffed.

Every child had massive problems, and together with coping with Amberlie's condition, I was rather shell-shocked by it all. I was soon even more amazed by just how used to it I became.

Bill went home that night to see the kids. There had been a lot of arrivals at the hospital that evening, children and parents who had come to stay overnight before day surgery. All the offside rooms were now full and the mums from our ward were worrying about where they were going to stay that night. By the time I decided to look for somewhere to lie down there were no blankets, no pillows no anything. The nurses insisted we leave the wards for a while to get some rest so I eventually spent a few hours tossing and turning on a green trolley at the far end of the corridor in the freezing cold, wishing for morning to hurry up and come. The woman snug in her bed in the adjacent cubicle was snoring for England. I was glad someone was comfortable.

The EEG machine rattled on its metal trolley down the corridor at bang on 9 am. The technician soon had the probes on Amberlie's head, done in a much more gentle and expert way than the woman had done at the other hospital. The machine etched its large complex patterns for about ten minutes and Dr Munroe, Amberlie's consultant, arrived. He had a quick look at the printouts and acknowledged our existence. He said, 'I'll be back for a chat later.'

It was late afternoon when Dr Pagett and Julie, the staff nurse, asked Bill and me to join them and Dr Munroe in one of the interview rooms. We looked at each other. Here we go. We both sighed deeply.

Dr Munroe explained that he was retiring that very day but wanted to talk to us about Amberlie's condition.

He said he had looked at her file and examined the scans and EEGs and from their results it was conclusive that Amberlie had lissencephaly. He continued to say that this meant she would be slow to develop and to what extent they did not know. He estimated it would be around two years before they would get a clearer picture concerning her development. It was a possibility that she would be mentally handicapped but more likely that she would be 'slow' or even somewhere in between. The condition was rare and there was virtually no knowledge or information they could pass on to us to give any precise prognosis. They could only make an educated guess, a case of waiting to see. As Dr Thomas had previously explained, the main thing was to control the fits, then Amberlie would stand a greater chance of developing. We were also made aware that there was a possibility that the fits would not ever be fully controlled or eradicated with this type of condition.

I listened but did not take it all in. It was all very carefully and technically worded and everyone seemed very relaxed about the whole thing. I questioned him as much as I could and was left feeling that Amberlie was likely to be slow and I could manage that. It was so strangely calm that I left the room almost relieved. Bill and I walked down the corridor with Julie and we talked about the meeting. I think we all expected there to be more bad news than there was.

We returned to Amberlie feeling that at least we now had a formal diagnosis, and knowing that the main task was to control her seizures we could now start to accept the situation and deal with it. We had every confidence in the doctors and felt very safe and secure in Great Ormond Street. Amberlie was in the best place in the world, after all.

Julie suggested we get some fresh air.

'It'll do you good,' she said.

Reluctantly we went out and walked the streets for a short while. We didn't know where we were going and didn't really want to be out there anyway.

Amberlie was due to have an MRI (magnetic reasonance imaging) scan the next day. She had already had her heminevrin slightly reduced as she was responding well and the other drugs were now establishing in her system. As with the CT scan, children are usually given a sedative in case they move and smear the images, but as Amberlie was already heavily sedated they just moved her along with her drip.

We were taken to a very 'space-age' room that was segregated underground away from everything else. A technician explained this was because the hospital floors could not withstand the size and weight of the magnet used to power the scanner. It was also a very vulnerable machine. We were shown to an anteroom, which had nothing but two black chairs in it that were a stark contrast to the clinically white walls. The atmosphere had completely changed – it was like being in a fridge. Chilled air swirled around and we all shivered with cold. The technician asked us to remove our jewellery and any metal objects such as keys, credit cards and metal buttons, because anything that had a metal component would blow the magnet as we entered the room. Unfortunately, Amberlie too had to be disconnected from her drip because the monitor was metal.

I was concerned about that, but Dr Pagett assured me she would be OK. We were then led to a huge room where the temperature dropped even more. In the middle was the machine. It was immense and stood from floor to ceiling. It was colourfully decorated with Disney's 101 Dalmations, even on the inside of the tunnel. There were large dark, heavy curtains on either side, hiding the monster magnet at the rear.

Amberlie was placed onto a pillow on the long conveyor belt leading into the tunnel. The technician adjusted her head into padded supports to hold it firmly in place. Amberlie didn't much like that and wriggled to try to free herself. A plastic helmet was then lowered over her head. Once she was ready, the technicians started to set the machine, and then the poor little mite had a seizure.

'Well that didn't take long did it? She's only just come off the drip!' I said in horror and disbelief. Her agitation at being put in the head support probably didn't help.

They had to reposition her again and as she settled she was moved along into the tunnel. Through the smoked glass of the little room opposite the machine, we could just see all the screens and monitors with what seemed like millions of tiny red lights on them. Simon Pagett was in there with three or four other doctors and technicians. A nurse sat with us and communicated with them through a microphone.

Bill and I sat on either side of the tunnel entrance. We were both in awe of the technology and the situation. We watched Amberlie, so tiny in this monster's mouth and worried for her.

They told us what they were doing, stage by stage. First they programmed the machine to pinpoint the areas they wanted scanned and then there were lots of mechanical clicks over a period of minutes. As it started, a deafening dreadful racket overtook the whole room and continued until the programme was complete. All in all they did about four separate programmes, each one looking deeper into different parts of Amberlie's brain. The noise changed for each one, getting louder and louder as they progressed. The last one was like having the QE2 pass through the room. It was so loud it penetrated Amberlie's sedation and she jumped out of her skin. Irritated, she wriggled continuously through the rest of the programme and the last part was lost.

They paused, hoping that Amberlie would settle so they could get a chemical picture of her brain. There was no way. Amberlie was distressed now and crying. As the doctor came out and opened his mouth I said, 'That's it, enough is enough. You've got your pictures, I'm not putting her through any more.'

Simon accepted it and said that the scans had proved interesting. It seemed that in addition to the lissencephaly, both halves of Amberlie's brain had not fused together properly and were slightly askew. The scans were very difficult to analyse and they still needed experts to look at them. The lissencephaly seemed to be mild but extensive and we would again have to wait to find out more details. They now knew enough though to deal with her immediate problems.

We returned to the ward and the doctors decided not to put Amberlie back on her drip, hoping that the other drugs would now be strong enough to compensate.

Amberlie had an awful evening. Bill had very reluctantly gone home and it was murder being there alone. She was awake enough to no longer need the nasal gastric tube and had guzzled a large bottle of milk as though it was the best she'd ever tasted, and on top of that was experiencing sudden and massive withdrawal from the heminevrin. The doctors were called to see her amazingly distended, grossly uncomfortable belly and they examined her thoroughly. They said it seemed that she had taken in a huge amount of air while feeding and that was obviously causing pain, and as far as the withdrawal was concerned, they said she would soon settle. There were no other problems they could detect and said she was a perfectly healthy baby apart from the lissencephaly.

It took about four hours for Amberlie to eventually settle. I had walked her up and down the ward, the corridors and the playroom over and over again to try to stop her crying. When she finally passed out I sat down exhausted and a nurse brought me a cup of tea.

Amberlie's case was being taken over by Professor Robert Jamieson, in allegiance with a French doctor who was a world authority on brain malformations. We met both men and their awestruck entourages during the next ward round the following afternoon.

There were the formal introductions, then 'how is Amberlie?' Simon explained to the professor that the fits had improved but she was still having them fairly frequently.

'Have we started clonazepam?' he asked, and I watched Simon write it down. I guessed this was another antiepileptic. He looked at Bill and me and asked if we were first-time parents and if not, why had we not noticed any problems? Slightly ruffled at his tactful accusation of idiocy, I explained that we had two other 'normal' children and that as Amberlie had been born at 36 weeks, we were told to expect some delays in her development. She fed well. Her health visitor and GP checks had all been fine and she had smiled before six weeks of age. She also responded visually and physically when she saw us and when we spoke to her. What was so strange about that? There was no comment.

Amberlie's pink and white toy bunny that Bill had bought her when she was born flashed into my mind. It was on a ribbon and just the right size to hang on her pram so she could see it. She never took any notice of it at all. I had thought maybe the colours weren't vivid enough for it to catch her eye. I had shrugged it off as nothing to worry about at the time.

I remembered that Amberlie would also sit in her bouncing chair looking at her baby gym, never attempting to touch the hanging toys. She was still very much a newborn baby at four months old. I should have worried more. Had I not been told to expect delays I would have worried.

The professor returned his attention to his audience and began his lecture. He was in full flow about 'these such cases' and 'the problems and severity of the mental and physical handicap' and that was when my world came to a grinding halt.

I was no longer listening to him. All I could hear were the words 'mental and physical handicap' filling my head. I remember staring at him but I don't remember his face. I looked at Simon, who was looking at me. I became aware of the mumbling in the background and was immediately irritated. I felt panic oozing from every part of me, hollowing and emptying every space, every sense, apart from the deep penetrating pain manifesting itself in my chest ... tightening, constricting and rising into my throat. Everything became larger than life, people, cots, moving equipment, loud voices, crying children, walls closing in, a pounding, thumping whirling chaos.

The words spewed out...

'Mentally and physically handicapped? You mean not slow but mentally and physically handicapped?' My eyes fixed on the professor.

He looked stunned. The colour had drained from his face.

'Yes,' he said. 'Mentally and physically handicapped.' He slanted his head to one side with a slight questioning frown. He suddenly realised that we had not been properly informed about Amberlie's condition. Looking distraught and like a fish out of water, he continued:

'The extent of the lissencephaly covers most of Amberlie's brain. I am afraid the outlook is very bleak.'

Everybody was silent. The whole ward was silent. The sea of faces blurred as I looked down at Amberlie lying there, watching us, happily kicking her legs and blowing raspberries ... totally oblivious to this dire prognosis of her life.

I was frozen, unable to move or look at anyone. I could still feel the panic surging deep inside me, searching for a place to go. My breathing was heavy and fast. Stinging, burning tears began to flood, cutting like knives as they spilled down my cheeks. I couldn't speak. There were no words. My teeth sank deep into my bottom lip in a vain effort to stop the overspill. I couldn't take my eyes off Amberlie. I heard the professor say how very sorry he was and his entourage departed in silence.

My head was spinning. All the happenings of the last few days whizzed round and round in my mind trying to sort into some order.

'But yesterday they said she would probably be just slow.' I said, still watching Amberlie. 'How the hell did I get it so wrong?' I looked up at Bill who was shaking his head.

'Go get some air,' Jo said, 'I'll look after Amberlie.' Jo had become a good friend; her little boy was in the next bed to Amberlie.

Deeply shocked, we numbly walked down the corridor, Bill holding onto my arm. I was so full of tears I could hardly see at thing. We didn't want to go out so we headed for the refuge of the parents' room.

Looking out of the window, I noticed how awful the scenery was. The bare brown brick walls of the back of the hospital. So depressing, it looked like it had been raining for days but nothing was wet. How fitting I thought, dull, dismal and depressing. I could see all the intricacies of the brickwork. So close, if I leant out I could touch the opposite wall.

'The irony of a brick wall,' I said.

My panic then rushed and erupted, and the torrent of tears burst though. I was shouting, 'Why, why, why?'

Bill was crying too. We couldn't believe that this could have happened to our beautiful Amberlie. She was so innocent, so pure, and so precious. What had I done to her during pregnancy? Was it my blood pressure, the dentist, potatoes ...?

Oh my God what had I done?

It then struck me what Amberlie would never do. No school, no work, no friends ... she would never marry or have children ... her life ... no choices. All gone.

'You bastard!' I screamed looking upward for God. 'How can you do this to a child? What gives you that right? You're a bloody joke!' I was seething. I felt sick, so sick. 'I need the loo!' Then as I opened the door the nausea gave way to anger. I was so bloody angry. I turned to Bill and ranted, 'First they said slow and now they say mentally and physically handicapped. Are they on something? It's not a game, messing about with people's lives!' He just looked at me. His face wet with tears and his eyes etched with pain.

'I'm going to sort this out!' I stormed out of the room with Bill following in close pursuit. I tore into the ward. The doctors were all swarmed around another child.

'I want to see someone and I want to see someone now!' I shouted. Everything stopped and everyone turned to look at me. I didn't care. Simon intervened between the shocked professor and me and was given permission to leave by a wary nod of the head. He quickly guided me back to the parents' room, and as soon as the door was shut I bellowed,

'What the hell's going on? Why are you messing us about?'

Simon sat down. I refused to. Calmly he explained that they now knew more about the extent of the lissencephaly than Dr Munroe had known the day before.

'So you wait for a ward round to tell us?' I snapped.

Simon did not reply.

'So what does this mean?' I went on. 'Is she going to be in a wheelchair or what? I need to know what's coming!'

'We don't know,' he said quietly.

'Don't know!' I retorted. 'You know enough to tell us that she's going to be mentally and physically handicapped!'

Simon sighed and keeping his calm, doctor-like disposition, continued. 'Amberlie will have her own individual responses and capabilities. She will develop to her own peak and some aspects of her ability will be more affected than others. She will have a potential and she will reach an optimum level, but we are unable to say what that will be. All humans have different talents and different capabilities. No one's brain is the same. The brain itself is so complex that we do not understand enough of it. We cannot tell how the lissencephaly will affect Amberlie's abilities compared with other children with the same condition. We can only give an educated guess based on evidence and limited research. We hardly know anything about it because it is so rare.'

'How rare?' I asked.

'About one in two million,' he replied.

'Jesus!' I said and paused. 'Will she die?'

'No. We have looked for tumours and other terminal problems and all her tests are clear. She is perfectly healthy apart from the lissencephaly. Much does depend, however, on how or if her seizures are controlled. You must realise this type of epilepsy is extremely difficult to manage, and we need to wait and see how she responds to the medication.' I spotted his warning but shook away the little voice trying to speak in my head. I also remembered Dr Thomas said the same thing.

He would not be drawn any further on her potential handicaps. And said he could not offer us any more information. I was too stunned and exhausted to persevere. I then wondered if he now knew what might have caused it. He said they did not know, but he would arrange for us to see the geneticists who would run some tests to see if there was any possibility it was genetic or to shed some light on any possible causes. Simon left us to talk. I had calmed down enough to listen to reason but the panic remained and the pain just grew and grew.

There was some solace in that I wasn't going to lose her. I was bereaved though. I had lost the Amberlie I thought I had, and now I was going to have to get used to a different Amberlie who was not going to grow and develop in the same way Ray and Clare had.

It never occurred to me when I was pregnant that all might not be perfect. I always took it for granted that my babies would be fine. When I thought about it, I realised there was so much that could potentially go wrong when a human being developed in the womb, and the real miracle was to give birth to a 'normal' child. This sort of thing only ever happened to other people or on television, though. I cried for hours until, shattered and drained, I had no more tears left.

Amberlie was a very much-wanted third child and loved to bits. Bill and I felt very protective of her, and all that had happened made our love for her far more intense. We had been given a very special, precious gift and she was going to be treasured. She was going to have everything we could possibly give her to make her life as good as possible. It was so hard to come to terms with the fact that our child was handicapped, but Bill and I knew that we would have to deal with our pain and accept it, and to a large extent put it to one side in order to give Amberlie the best chance in life.

After our talk with Simon we decided to go out for some fresh air. We thought a walk might help us to think logically as well as calm us down. We walked the streets surrounding the hospital virtually on automatic pilot. I could sense people looking at me. I looked an absolute wreck – it never occurred to me to make myself presentable before going out. It seemed odd being amongst people on the street, all going about their business as usual. No one knew what had happened to us. It was just a small incident in a big world. There was no sympathy out there. It was just another day – the same as every other. We were going through hell and everything else was carrying on as normal. How could that be? I wanted to get back into the hospital.

On the way back to the ward we bumped into Professor Jamieson on the stairs. He looked embarrassed but kindly said, 'Hello ... Are you OK?'

I felt a tinge of forgiveness for him ... just a little, as he had no idea of the conversation we had had with Dr Munroe. Obviously there had been an enormous and embarrassing breakdown in communication, not that it provided any excuses for letting us know in the way they did. Bill and I had been wrongly and insensitively informed about Amberlie's condition and I imagine someone was hauled over the coals for it. I make no apology for my reaction. I felt we had been originally misinformed because the doctors did not wait for all the results to be in before making their formal diagnosis. As a result of that we ended up being brutally told in front of the whole world ... and we were just expected to accept it. All I wanted was some consideration, especially under such circumstances, and of course for the information to be delivered in a caring, sympathetic way, which I was entitled to. After all, my heart had been shattered to pieces.

I didn't have a problem with the doctors from then on as I had earned their respect ... and they mine, for I had no complaints about the wonderful care and attention they gave to Amberlie. During many subsequent conversations they said how sorry they were because they really do worry about 'newly diagnosed parents' and like to give as much support as they can.

It was during one of those conversations that I remembered Amberlie's enlarged little toe. They immediately examined her foot and both doctors looked at each other.

'Well?' I asked.

Professor Jamieson said that in a lot of instances where there is a brain abnormality, a child has an extra toe or a finger, or more than one, sometimes an extra one on both hands and feet.

'As you can see, Amberlie's toe is very wide and has two nails,' Simon said.

I could never make out whether it was two nails or one long one but it definitely had a line down the middle. He did not say for certain if it had two bones in it or one large wide one but that the extra toe had not fully separated. He said that they did not need to confirm it with an X-ray. It was one of the few possible features expected in a case like Amberlie's.

Professor Jamieson said that also some of Amberlie's facial features were consistent with having lissencephaly, such as her slightly indented temples, the absence of a bridge on her nose and her full upper lip. I couldn't say anything unusual struck me. The professor, seeing my blankness, said, 'It takes a trained eye.'

Bill and I looked at each other and raised our eyebrows in unison.

Amidst caring for Amberlie I spent a lot of time talking to nurses and other mums. It was a strange world in the ward – everybody knew everybody and I got very enclosed in our own situation and theirs. Being there twenty-four hours a day, we mums became very dependent on each other for support and little babysitting duties while we nipped to the loo or grabbed some coffee.

The nurses were highly trained in paediatrics and their knowledge was vast. They were used to dealing with very distressed parents and could give informed and accurate answers to the often very difficult questions presented to them. It was so much more reassuring than someone constantly saying, 'I'll have to check that with the doctor.'

For my part, I didn't know whether I was coming or going and I must have repeated the same questions time and time again in an effort to find a reason, any reason, for Amberlie's condition. I would even rephrase questions to try to catch them out if I felt they were not telling me everything. They never lost patience but they must have thought I was round the bend. I also told them all about

Ray and Clare, which they seemed to enjoy. They saw so many very ill children that they often forgot there were normal children outside. As most of the children were there on a long-term basis and came back frequently for short stays, they couldn't help but get very attached to them.

The only time I needed to leave the ward was to eat or shower. Tea and coffee was always available in the kitchen and there were no restrictions on bringing refreshments back to the bedside. We used to look forward to the nurses' break at around midnight, as they used to join us for tea and cakes and a good old gossip.

There were various parent suites around the hospital where parents could get a decent bed and a night's sleep if they wished. There was a waiting list, though, because the mums used to hang onto their beds for dear life, and when one became available the promise was usually only for one or a few nights. Long-term parents were given priority. The nearest suite was on the floor above our ward and it was handy for a shower and brush up each evening. I did not want to be separated from Amberlie in a bed that was miles away, so I didn't bother to put myself on the list. Most nights I camped wherever I could and spent some in the chair beside Amberlie's cot. Sometimes there was no chair so I huddled into the corner on the floor. I guess I was tired but was on some sort of automatic pilot that kept me going, and I got used to being uncomfortable. The nurses used to worry about the lack of rest I had and nagged me all the time, eventually insisting I spend one night in a proper bed, which they went and organised, but that was on the other side of the hospital and I wasn't happy.

Bill, in the meantime, had been ordered to return to work by his boss. Being a conscientious and reliable employee of a well-known high street bank, Bill had religiously kept them informed about Amberlie, and was devastated that this man was being unsympathetic. He said that he had been off work long enough and that was that. Bill couldn't believe it.

'How would he feel if it happened to him?' Bill said.

He felt so let down. He had worked for the bank since he was 16 and had only ever taken time off for a few days once or twice for illness, and had even suggested he take the time as unpaid leave. I was fuming. Now he also had to deal with the stress of feeling there was no support from his employer.

The practicalities were so difficult to organise. How was Bill supposed to cope with a full day's work, support the kids and travel backwards and forwards to the hospital to support Amberlie and me, let alone deal with his pain of learning that his little girl was handicapped? The poor sod was worried sick and I was worried for him.

'Tell them to stuff it,' I said. 'Talk to head office!'

He was too loyal though – the sort of person who tried to please everyone all the time. In hindsight, we should have got him signed off by the doctor for stress, but it didn't occur to us at the time.

Every evening after work, Bill would come to Great Ormond Street for a couple of hours and then go home to see Ray and Clare, getting there just before their bedtime, which had moved to about 10 pm so that they could see their dad. He said the kids were being really good for Auntie Pat and she was keeping things as normal as possible for them at home. He said they were very worried about Amberlie and asked him lots of questions when he walked through the door. We had thought it best to be honest with them, so Bill explained Amberlie's day as best he could and then listened to what they had been up to.

I missed them a lot as I hadn't seen them for almost two weeks now. We had little conversations on the phone, but it didn't make up for a nice big hug! We felt at the time that it was probably best not to bring them to London as they would be upset at leaving us behind again, plus it wasn't strategically viable with Bill working all day. It would have been so late for them as well. Bill was already exhausted and I could see the strain engraved on his face.

Talking about his boss one evening, he said, 'I can't bring myself to be sociable to the bastard! Yes and no answers is all he gets.'

'Don't let him get to you,' I said. 'Just do what you need to and no more. Make sure you get your breaks and leave on time.'

I had never met his boss but hated him with an intensity I had never felt before. I'm not normally malicious but I believe what goes around comes around.

They say what you do in life comes back to you threefold.

Just after I had finished getting Amberlie washed and fed one morning, a lady dressed in a long beige skirt and a rust T-shirt peered around the door and introduced herself as the ward liaison sister. She said she was there to talk to me about any worries Bill and I had about returning home with Amberlie, and whether there was anything we needed at home to help. I was unprepared for her visit so I couldn't think of anything off hand, and to tell the truth, it had not occurred to me that anything would be any different – why should it be? She explained that she was available twenty-four hours a day and I could ring her anytime for anything. I thanked her but she left me unsettled.

A short while later, a medical social worker called Polly dropped by. She asked me about our family circumstances and was concerned how Ray and Clare would cope with our new life.

'New life?' I quizzed.

'Your lives will never be the same again,' she said. 'I know it's hard to understand ... but when you have a disabled child your life becomes dominated by them, and much of what you do and the decisions you make will be made around Amberlie.'

I hadn't once considered what would happen when we went home. My mind had blanked again. I looked at Amberlie. 'She's just a baby,' I thought. 'I couldn't see why it should make that much difference apart from her permanently needing medication. I was then agitated and felt this was just someone poking her nose into my family business. She was a social worker – why on earth did I need a social worker? My kids were all right. I started to only give basic answers to her questions.

I said to her, 'Thank you, but at the moment I think we are OK and have everything we need at home for a baby.'

'Fine, but please feel that you can ring if you need to. Once the shock of Amberlie's diagnosis has passed you will have some very difficult days when you will find it hard to cope. We are very good listeners, and care just as much for the families as we do for the patient. It is a shock for all of you and you will all need to adjust. We just want you to know that there is someone out there who cares.' She smiled, touched my arm and left.

I then felt guilty. Why did I have to put up a wall? She wasn't being pushy or interfering and I did listen, but I could not comprehend all she meant. I was having enough trouble thinking about now, let alone later.

After much deliberation on our conversation, I got an overriding feeling that I wasn't being told everything. I wasn't about to have another moan at the doctors, so I put it all to one side and carried on with the present.

I learned later that the standard procedure was to give parents information gradually and in stages. Parents were allowed to get used to the situation before the next load of grief was to come and hit them in the face. They were probably right in what they did and how, but it rankled at the time because I felt entitled to know everything about my child.

I also guessed that we were about to be sent home, and Simon later came by to say that now Amberlie was much more stable, they would be transferring us back to our local hospital. He said our consultant would be fully informed about Amberlie's medications, which would be easily managed by him. As far as Great Ormond Street was concerned, they would always be available if we needed them. They would be sending us a follow-up appointment with Professor Jamieson, and the geneticists would contact us in due course. It was now Friday and Simon said he was off duty for the weekend so he probably wouldn't see us before we left. He was arranging for an ambulance to take us back on Monday morning.

I asked him about Amberlie's eye, which had swollen up to the size of an egg overnight. He explained that it was probably due to pressure from the head supports when she had had her MRI scan and that it would fade quite quickly. I thanked him for all he had done. I was delighted to be going back as I desperately wanted to see Ray and Clare. I missed them so much, and it would certainly make life much easier for Bill.

Amberlie's appetite had blossomed incredibly and she was guzzling milk bottle after bottle. The nurses told us to monitor this carefully because the seizures she had before coming to Great Ormond Street may well have caused some damage, and she now might not know when she had had enough. I sighed, closed my eyes and rubbed my forehead hard with the tips of my fingers. I needn't have worried. Over the next few days she started to slow down and soon returned to her normal feeding routine.

It being Friday, some of the children were being discharged. Jo and I were offered vacant cubicles off the main ward. These were furnished comfortably with a cot and a proper bed where we could stay with our babies at night. We both jumped with excitement and grabbed the opportunity. It was sheer luxury – we could even close the door!

Jo's little boy had idiopathic epilepsy and they had been in the hospital over two weeks already. He was the same age as Amberlie and was also having infantile spasms but the doctors could find no reason for it. He had gone for test after test and Jo wished they would find something so that he could be helped. They just could not find which part of his brain was causing the seizures, as everything appeared to be normal on the scans. If and when they did, they wanted to try a new operation, which would laser away the affected area to stop the fits. He was having steroid injections in an attempt to stabilise him.

The doctors had considered Amberlie for this procedure but too much of her brain was affected by the lissencephaly.

Despite having our own rooms, there was no such thing as peace and quiet! That evening a thirteen-year-old Indian boy was admitted to the next cubicle. He had a behavioural problem and was a compulsive swearer. The noise and fuss went on all night. I reckoned his whole family, grandparents, aunts, uncles, distant relatives and any old acquaintance, must have squeezed into that room, and those that couldn't wandered up and down the corridor for hours on end, as if they were enjoying a sunny afternoon in Hyde Park! A nurse popped her head round the door to apologise and said they couldn't wait to give him his pre-med in the morning!

Thankfully, the rest of the weekend was fairly sedate and restful. Amberlie's fits had averaged out to five or six a day, some lasting five minutes, the worst ones twenty.

Bill's mum and dad visited us on the Sunday. They had not wanted to come before because they hadn't wanted to see Amberlie with her tubes in – I wasn't impressed. To give his dad credit, he did help Bill by dropping him to the hospital every day and he sent in a beautiful pink and white cuddly horse for Amberlie ... but he never came to the ward.

I had tried lots of times to contact my brother Ray. He was on holiday in the Maldives and I couldn't remember the date he was due back. My parents had died before Bill and I married and Ray and I were very close.

We had visited the GOSH shop that morning and bought a few bits to take home for the kids. I was so looking forward to seeing them.

We had to be packed and ready early Monday morning because no one knew what time the ambulance would arrive. Once it did we would have to leave immediately. Our accompanying nurse came and introduced herself at around 8.30 am and was busy organising a car seat for Amberlie. We finally left at 10.30 am in a flood of emotion, with nurses hugging us and waving goodbye. Our gifts of chocolates to the nurses and the few pounds spent in the GOSH shop seemed such an inadequate gesture to express our deep gratitude to the hospital for saving Amberlie's life.

Despite wanting to go, I was really overawed and nervous at returning home. It was so safe and secure at GOSH and venturing out into what now seemed to be a strange world, not knowing what the future held for us, was scary.

The well-meaning ambulance men thought they would give me a sightseeing tour of London en route. I tried to get a word in edgeways to say that I was London born and bred and would rather just get home quickly, but they were overcome with their own excitement. Amberlie was already agitated at being tied into the car seat and I could see that the journey was going to be fraught. It took forever. They went all around the world and got caught in all the traffic hot spots and eventually even missed the right turn off from the motorway. Amberlie had started to twitch and I could feel my blood pressure rising fast.

I'm going to lose it in a minute, I thought to myself as I got hot and bothered and a bit panicky.

Once we were back on the ward, Martha, the house doctor, was anxious to get the update. The journey had taken its toll on Amberlie and her seizures had become frequent again. My heart sank as I realised we wouldn't be heading for home just yet. She wasn't able to settle and after a few hours Dr Thomas increased the doses of both her medicines and the fits went back to around five or six by the next day. This increase made Amberlie very drowsy and she slept most of the time, only stirring when she was hungry. Dr Thomas wanted to make sure that Amberlie maintained some stability before he felt confident enough to allow us home.

On the Monday I had at last managed to talk to my brother Ray. He was shocked and devastated at the news and visited us that evening. He said he felt awful that he was away when it all happened.

'Don't be daft,' I reassured him. 'No one could ever have expected this.'

4

It was so odd going home. I sat in the back of the car, suddenly feeling old and exhausted. I could feel new lines etched into my face, burrowing deep below the skin's surface, and I was sure I had spotted one or two grey hairs appearing at my temples when I quickly glanced in the washroom mirror. At that moment, I felt nothing, I was empty and devoid of any emotion; yet at the same time I could burst into floods of tears. I felt as if I had been in a time warp and had lost all concept of reality. There again, what was reality now if our lives were never to be the same again?

It was wonderful to see the kids again. They were totally surprised when we walked through the door. Bill hadn't told them just in case there were any last-minute hiccups at the hospital. For a split second they hesitated, double-checked that it really was us and both ran into my arms shouting, 'Mummy!'

They seemed to have grown so much in the two-and-a-half weeks I had been away. They looked so big in comparison to Amberlie!

Bill was delighted to have us all under one roof again. The past weeks had taken their toll on him and he was relieved that he wasn't going to be chasing all over the place each day any more.

We sorted out Amberlie's various medications and Bill put up a schedule inside the cupboard door so we wouldn't miss anything out. Amberlie had been given 'open access' to the children's ward, which meant that if she became ill or we were worried about anything, we could just ring and take her straight there, rather than have to go through the GP procedure.

While we were at GOSH we were told there was a Lissencephaly Society up in the north of England, and that they might be able to provide us with some answers to our questions and put us in touch with other parents if we wished. I was desperate for information but I wasn't keen to talk to other parents at the moment. I hadn't yet accepted Amberlie's plight, let alone have anyone else's realism to deal with. I only wanted to know the facts about lissencephaly.

I explained this to Professor Jamieson and he told Bill and I that the best thing for Amberlie was to bring her up in a normal environment because our other children would provide the best stimulation for her development. He told us we needed to take one day at a time and try to accept and adjust our lives before we talked to others with similar problems. He said that societies were a good thing and offered a lot of support when parents were ready, but, of course, not everyone wanted to use them. Some parents had found it rather an alarming experience and had felt more depressed after speaking to someone who was having a bad day, or someone with a worse problem than theirs. Whilst they were sympathetic towards them, it was very hard to cope with someone else's doom and gloom when they were already trying to deal with their own situation.

'Find out as much information as you can, but at the end of the day, it is you who have to take care of Amberlie, and you will need to be strong,' he said.

I saw a lot of sense in what he said and decided to see how things went.

I felt I needed to treat Amberlie as an individual to help her to develop her own special potential, and not compare her to others who could or could not do as much or more than her. It would have been easy to become depressed – I was halfway there already – or disappointed and write her off as a lost cause. I didn't want that to happen. She deserved the best life possible and I was never going to give up without a fight. It was not in my nature, and I wanted her to be happy.

After settling in at home, Bill and I felt we needed to tell the children properly about how Amberlie would be. We explained that her brain was not the same as ours, and it now made her have fits. Searching for an easy description, I said, 'It's a bit like when the television picture goes off and it's all fuzzy. It doesn't hurt her and she doesn't know anything about it.'

They listened intently, gently stroking Amberlie's head all the time.

'If you see her do little shakes or see her eyes flicker' – I blinked quickly to show them what I meant – 'then you must tell Mummy or Daddy and call us if we are not in the room, because it can be very dangerous for her.'

They wanted to know why Amberlie's brain was not like theirs and I told them we didn't know. 'The doctors tell us that something went wrong when she was growing in Mummy's tummy.'

We went on to explain that she would have lots of medicines to take every day to try to stop her having the fits, and that as she grew she would not be able to do the things they could.

'When she's bigger she can run round the garden and play with me, can't she?' Clare said.

'No darling.' I sighed. 'She probably won't be able to walk but we will have to see.'

We left it at that. It was enough for them to take on board for the time being. They were just so glad their little sister was home and OK. Straight away their observations were spot on ...

'Mum! Ambams is flicking!'

And she was.

I was very nervous being at home, unable to shout for a nurse when I wanted to. In the back of my mind I was fearful that Amberlie's fits would accelerate again and we would end up back in hospital.

Even the thought of everyday routine was frightening. How was I going to manage to cope with everything? The realisation of being on my own terrified me. Bill needed to go to work, Auntie Pat needed to go home and the kids needed to go to school. I couldn't begin to think how it was all going to happen. The biggest worry of all was 'What if Amberlie has a fit while we're out?' Every place entailed a longish walk and how was I to get home quickly? I was so used to being able to shout for someone when Amberlie had a fit. Not that they were able to do much, but it was a security for me. I felt myself start to panic and lose control.

'I've gotta sort this out!' I said to myself. 'I can't fall apart, I'm just gonna have to deal with it. What doesn't get done doesn't get done, and I'll just have to run the risk while I'm out, and run home fast if something happens. I want to take the kids to school myself. I don't want to be relying on anyone else, that's not right. Amberlie and I can't spend our lives cooped up indoors just through fear of a seizure happening outside.' I took a deep breath and braved myself for the morning.

The next day I dropped Ray off at school and Clare at playschool. A lot of mums stopped to ask how we were but a few looked our way and made their escape quietly. I knew they didn't know what to say to me but I'd rather they'd said the wrong thing than ignore me. Some stumbled through an apology for not being in touch or sending a card, all their reasons ending with a 'but'. Why did they feel that because there was something wrong with Amberlie's brain she didn't need a 'thinking of you' card? I appreciated that the 'get well' sentiment may have been partly inappropriate. They didn't want to look at Amberlie ... maybe they thought she had grown three heads. I couldn't be bothered and I didn't offer them anything to ease their discomfort. I was particularly surprised by the reaction of one good friend who I thought would be fine but she couldn't wait to dash off. Some people were very strange.

On no account was I ever going to be embarrassed or cagey about showing off my little girl. I was proud of her whatever.

I made my way to the surgery to tell our GP what had happened, and to organise Amberlie's very specific and regular prescription. He was very shocked when I told him Amberlie had lissencephaly; it was something he had never heard of, and he had not yet received any information from the hospital.

One of the medicines had to be made using a special suspension. Having got the doctor to write it all down formally, I then visited the chemist who was rather peeved that this would be a monthly order from St George's Hospital, London, because it only had a 28-day shelf life.

'Can't she have it in another mixture?' the chemist asked.

'No,' I said. 'This suspension keeps the medicine constant so we have accurate doses.' I passed on the information given to me by the hospital pharmacist so she could read it.

'It's expensive,' she persisted.

'Tough,' I said, shrugging my shoulders.

This is all I need, I thought to myself. *As if I haven't got enough to worry about, the bloody chemist has to be awkward.*

Each month I was to have the same trouble. On a couple of occasions they did not even have the suspension in on time and Amberlie's medicine was late. I kept explaining that Amberlie could not be without it, until one day when I finally lost patience and screamed, 'You had better sort this out and sort it fast otherwise I shall be taking this up with my GP, the hospital and your bosses. It's not your money, it is paid for by the NHS, and it is not your child that is fitting!'

They were embarrassed in front of the other customers who were in the shop and assured me one of them would go to the hospital and collect it ready for that afternoon. They treated me carefully for a while and I never had to complain again. As time went on they got to know us well and always made a fuss of Amberlie, holding her hands, stroking her hair and talking to her. They always showed an interest in her progress and supplied everything we needed and, often went out of their way to fulfil an urgent request.

The first few days at home were very stable and Amberlie's seizures had reduced to four a day. Unfortunately, though, she was very drowsy and it was becoming difficult to feed her. We really had to persevere. She had no energy. She couldn't even raise her eyelids when we spoke to her and her desire to feed had vanished. We missed her beautiful smile. We hadn't really seen it since she was diagnosed and now we weren't getting any responses at all.

It was very unnerving that Amberlie was sleeping all the time. At first we were all very quiet, tiptoeing around, and the kids tried hard not to make too much noise in case they disturbed her. We soon discovered, however, that even huge amounts of noise made no difference: she still slept.

Ray and Clare found it very strange because they had always been able to play and talk to her before she went into hospital, and in return she would giggle at them and blow raspberries! They kept asking why she was asleep all the time and were forever checking her. They desperately wanted their sister to wake up.

'Is she always going to be sleepy, Mummy?' Clare asked.

'I hope not,' I said, unable to keep the dejection out of my voice.

All the chores were getting done in the house because Amberlie was asleep, and I was also able to spend time with Ray and Clare. Amberlie was always in her bouncing cradle chair so it was easy to take her with me around the house and keep an eye on her. The only demands she made on me were her general care and feeding. I hated it. It was so quiet when the others were out – no baby noises or a gurgle or a chuckle. Nothing.

It bothered me so much because she hadn't been like that before she was on medication. I understood that there could have possibly been additional damage caused by all the seizures she'd had but most of the sleep state seemed to have been drug-induced. I also appreciated that her seizures had to be controlled. Her little life seemed to have been taken away from her already. I used to sit just looking at her. It was so difficult to accept there was so much wrong with such a beautiful baby. The sadness of it all was overwhelming.

Her seizures then started to increase in number and she was 'flickering' in her sleep between the larger ones. She was also very grumpy in the afternoons and early evenings again, just as she had been before her diagnosis. Luckily we were due in outpatients for an appointment with Dr Thomas. He immediately readmitted her for observation as he was worried that she might return to status, and we would have to start all over again.

By that evening her fits had changed their make up and she was now having classic 'salaam' seizures. Dr Thomas explained that they were called 'salaam' because her body jerked forward and was suggestive of the bow involved when praying to Allah. He said, 'This type of seizure is usually only seen when there is a brain abnormality and is also known as West's syndrome.'

It was so complicated and bewildering. I felt as if I had been knocked sideways again and the glimmers of hope and optimism I had been nurturing just ebbed away.

Dr Thomas thought it was time to give Amberlie a course of steroids that GOSH had recommended if she had a bad patch. He initially gave her a five-day course of prednisolone. He hoped this would not only stop the fits but, together with her other drugs, perhaps provide a basis for a fit-free period. We were warned that there could be side effects such as increased weight and a 'Buddha-like' appearance. She also might be a bit hyperactive.

I looked at Bill and said, 'Hyperactive! It's a bit difficult imagining that. Any response would be lovely.'

By the next day the fits had started to slow up and reduce again but Amberlie was still very sleepy. Things continue to improve and the following day she managed to be fit free for a whole twelve hours! Dr Thomas felt it was fairly safe to let her go home but to come for a review in a week's time. For the next three days she was fit free and then she settle back into her previous four-a-day routine. She was much brighter though, feeding properly again and spending some time awake.

At the next review Dr Thomas was very pleased with her improvement and noticed the difference in her awareness. Her 'sleepiness' had obviously been due to too many fits, and he said to keep raising the phenobarbitone would just make her more drowsy, so he gave Amberlie a further ten-day course of the steroid with only a slight increase in her other medications.

The steroids had really perked her up. Strangely, though, the fits had changed again and were short and sharp, only lasting a few seconds. There were the odd few lasting about two minutes that really upset her. I thought this was because they made her jump when they started, and frightened her. It was at these times that I could see real fear in her eyes, pleading for me to do something. I hated not being able to help her. I felt such a painful uselessness and wished that her fits would just go away and leave her alone. All I could do was sit and hold her with my arms wrapped tightly round her, rocking and staring out of the window, my eyes waterlogged and stinging, hoping and waiting for the fits to disappear.

'My God, didn't she have enough problems without these bloody fits?'

At the next review Dr Thomas gave us instructions on how to wean her off the steroids as he thought they had run their course for the time being. He was also worried that the longer she stayed on them the greater the risk of side effects. It took approximately two and a half weeks to get her off them and she stayed bright and attentive throughout.

In the meantime our health visitor had become very interested in Amberlie's case. Naturally, she was there to help us but felt inadequate because of the lack of information available. When she phoned me she said she had contacted Polly, our social worker and Simon at GOSH who had explained to her that Amberlie had 'agyria'. I was not familiar with this word and was instantly irritated. She had also been in touch with the Lissencephaly Society and had received an information pack from them. She said she wanted to come and talk about everything so we could go through it all together.

Having launched into a seething rage, I abruptly ended the conversation and immediately rang Polly at GOSH. I complained that I had not been told that a specific information pack was available to send for, and that I did not know what 'agyria' meant. I explained that I realised our health visitor was trying to help but I resented someone different ringing up telling me what I didn't know about my child. Polly apologised and said she understood what I was saying. She went on to explain 'agyria' meant the absence of mounds and bumps on the brain and that it was just another term used in explaining lissencephaly.

'Yes, but when my health visitor rings and tells me she has "agyria" and I don't know what the hell she's on about it is frightening. It's a term I am unaware of, and I thought Amberlie had something else as well!' I was so angry.

'Amberlie has one of the severest forms of the condition,' she said.

I felt that sinking feeling again and as I sighed long and deeply, the pain and devastation filled my head and chest once more. Polly continued, 'I gave your health visitor the number of the society and she assured me that she would bring the information round to you and your husband and you would all go through it together. I am really sorry.'

'Well you didn't give me the phone number while I was at the hospital and now I would like my own copy of the information, thank you,' I said. 'Anyway, I don't understand why it should be the health visitor. I know her, but only in a routine baby/child development way because she's connected to our surgery. Why should she be the one to go through the information with us? She won't be able to answer our questions properly – she obviously needed the information herself. This is just totally beyond me!'

Polly promised to get me a copy in the post that evening and also gave me the phone number of the contact lady at the Lissencephaly Society.

I stood for a while after I put the phone down, with my elbows leaning on the chest of drawers, rubbing my forehead with both hands, lost in pain, frustration and disappointment. I felt that despite well-meant intention, I had been let down and could feel myself lurching into depression. Although I was coping, I realised how much I was living on a knife-edge and something coming out of the blue like that was just enough to upset the balance and cause an outburst.

'Damn it!' I shouted.

My mind had been so involved in all the drama and devastation that it hadn't really occurred to me to ask what actually physically happens to cause lissencephaly. I think it was because every time I asked a 'why?' question, the only answer I ever got was 'we don't know', so I assumed the doctors knew nothing. The overriding impression was that Bill and I had to accept it all without question, and to a point, it seemed the doctors were avoiding the issue. From our perspective they were only allowing us to understand and deal with 'today and now' rather than open up any clues about the future. Why did they feel that we didn't need to know the ins and outs of Amberlie's condition, or was it that they didn't feel we were clever enough to understand, or did they just not have the time or bottle to confront us?

The envelope from Polly arrived next morning. Bill and I sat together and read it through.

The information was factual and to the point. In simple terms, it explained that lissencephaly fell into a group of conditions known as neural migrational disorders. 'Migration' means that the cells move from the central part of the brain (stem) towards the surface at around four months into pregnancy. This migration forms the bumpy surface of a normal brain (sulci and gyri), and is six layers thick. It is through these bumps and cells that information is taken in and stored in the brain.

It said that lissencephaly occurs when there is a disruption in the early migrational patterns of these neurons and subsequently they do not reach the surface. Thus the cortex (the outside covering of the brain) becomes only four layers thick, and those layers of cells are abnormal. This results in the cortex appearing smooth. Therefore a child with lissencephaly is severely disabled because it cannot receive or understand either physical or mental input. There were various degrees of severity:

- Nearly all lissencephaly children have seizures, which usually begin during their first year and vary from brief tonic (petit mal) lasting only a few seconds, to full tonic-clonic (grand mal) seizures where the body stiffens and there is rhythmic jerking of the head, arms and legs; plus other types of seizures falling between the two. There were many medicines available, some more effective than others, but it was rare to gain 100% control of seizures.
- Feeding was often problematical due to refusal, gagging and spitting up of food, so weight gain could be poor.
- Problems become more severe as the child grows and as spasticity progresses. Their bodies are sometimes floppy and a lot have arching postures.
- There could be lots of problems with aspiration and reflux. (Aspiration is when liquids or foods fall down the windpipe rather that the oesophagus. Reflux is when stomach acid shoots back up the swallowing tube and is similar to heartburn.) This increases the risk of repeated episodes of pneumonia as does being sedentary and inactive.
- There was some basic practical information on how to help with feeding to avoid some of the smaller problems occurring and how to make eating more comfortable for the child.

- There is always mental retardation and overall development does not generally exceed the ability of a 3 – 5-month-old baby.
- If they are lucky, some smile and have some head control.
- They may also be able to reach for things but not grasp them or be able to roll on the floor.
- All these abilities may be lost later because of size and degree of seizure control.
- Everything worsens over time.

The facts were all there, the condition, the syndromes (varieties of lissencephaly), associated problems, disabilities and in particular and above all, standing out like a thumping headache was the life span. The life span was much shorter than normal.

- It was expected that half of tube-fed children with severe mental handicap would die before adolescence. If a child could feed itself, its life span would be at least double.
- The lissencephaly syndrome that the child's diagnosis falls into also determines the expected life span. That is, the more serious and debilitating it is, the shorter the life span.

We did not know which syndrome Amberlie's lissencephaly fell into. The doctors hadn't mentioned anything beyond 'lissencephaly'.

It was all far worse than we ever imagined and we reeled back in shock. The words were stark in their message. There was no ambiguity. We had what we wanted ... the truth. We had it in all its glory. And it hurt ... it hurt bad.

I now understood why Polly had wanted the health visitor with us when we read it – not that it would have made an iota of difference to the way it hit us. It wouldn't have saved any pain. Beyond a cuddle, what could she have done? I had been brought up to take life on the chin and dissolving into floods of tears in front of another someone was not on in my head. I doubt I would have been able to formulate any sensible questions for her to answer right there and then, only ones that would cause fear and panic. Facts were facts at the end of the day and nobody could change that. Bill and I had to grieve in our own way and I was glad we were on our own.

I wanted to know all there was to know about my Amberlie regardless of the overwhelming pain the knowledge produced.

It was, however, too much to take in all at once, and I couldn't budge my mind beyond the fact that we were going to lose Amberlie one day. I was also totally disillusioned to think that the time between now and whenever that might be was to be filled with trauma, illness and milestones for Amberlie to reach. It was agony now and I couldn't file it into any logical order in my mind to help relieve some of the pain with sense. I decided I couldn't think about it anymore because today was what mattered, so I shut the future out. It was all so bloody unfair.

As I started to build protective walls around me my whole body became numb and I dragged it around with my heart sunk somewhere below my feet. No matter how hard I tried, I couldn't stop my brain being engulfed in a terrible darkness that I could not shake off. My every thought was Amberlie, I couldn't think of anything else and nothing seemed real. I was locked in a tunnel of doom, and to this day have no recollection of any events or things to do with Ray and Clare or anyone else during that time – I don't even remember taking them to school.

To cap it all, Amberlie's fits were escalating again and as a result she had become very drowsy and sleepy. All I could see was a pointless existence for her. What was she getting out of life? Little glimpses, that was all – a nice period when she was with us and alert ... then seizures, then an increase in her medicines, then too damn drowsy to even open her eyes properly. She just sat there sleeping, floppy and unable to do bugger all except fit. I couldn't stand it.

I was trying to keep going and carry on as normal so I started to redecorate the living room. The tears constantly welled up, and mixed with paint and the drips from my nose. My swollen eyes stung terribly as I struggled to see the paint going onto the walls and ceiling. I kept looking down at Amberlie asleep in her bouncing cradle under the ladder. I just couldn't understand how anything so beautiful and so innocent could have so much wrong. Why did it have to happen to my baby? I was inconsolable and totally disgusted with life, God, anything and everything.

We were due at GOSH that week to see Professor Jamieson. We knew what to expect now, no that forearmed or forewarned was any consolation. Amberlie was terribly drowsy on the day and the doctors said it was to be expected. Also her legs had stiffened up and they said we should expect a certain degree of spasticity as she had been so sedentary since birth.

'That's not true!' I said defensively, my nerves totally on edge. 'Before she fitted and before she had to take these awful drugs, she was happy, kicked her legs, chattered, smiled and was aware of her surroundings ... not since birth!'

There was no comment. It didn't seem to matter what I said. It's amazing how silence speaks reams.

'I'm only her mother – I couldn't possibly know anything. I must have imagined it all!' I sulked loudly so they heard.

Professor Jamieson joined us for his chat. I noticed he was a very tall, broad man probably in his late fifties. His hair was grey although thinning and he stooped very slightly. He was dressed in a starched white shirt and blue tie with dark trousers, which matched the jacket he'd slung over the back of his chair. He shook our hands, and said it was nice to see us again, and indicated chairs for us both to sit. The conversation was difficult and he was still avoiding our questions and giving woolly answers. We seemed to be going round in circles all the time with nothing of any relevance being said. Bill was fidgeting on his chair and I could hear him breathing heavily through his nose. I knew he was agitated. His patience soon wore thin and he blurted out the dreaded question.

'What is her lifespan likely to be?'

The professor moved uncomfortably in his chair and gazed up at the ceiling several times before taking a deep breath followed by a huge sigh. Then, with a fixed expression, he turned his swivel chair towards Bill and quickly said, 'Generally they do not reach adulthood, ten years on average.'

We both sat silent. I watched him. He did not once take his eyes of Bill. I knew he was refusing to look at me. He continued, 'Thirteen was the oldest I have known and she is now gone. You must understand that she was exceptional though.'

Amberlie was sitting contentedly on my lap looking at me. He eyes were shining brightly and she was blowing gentle raspberries. I watched her unaware that my bottom lip had my teeth embedded in it and was hurting badly. Without bothering to raise my head I continued to listen to the professor as he explained that a lot would depend on her seizures both in severity and control. He was sorry. Sorry. What an empty word.

'So,' said Bill. 'How long has she got?'

I looked up at him under my eyebrows.

The professor shrugged his shoulders and upturned his hands. 'We don't know. Her lissencephaly is severe. Two years ... maybe more ... and as I said, a lot depends on her seizures.' He obviously hated having to tell us, and I could understand that. His grey hair was now standing on end after he had run both hands through it and he fidgeted and squirmed in his chair.

The tears were brimming again. How could she die so young? She's so beautiful; it's not fair ... not right. Children should not be robbed of their futures – neither should parents be robbed of their children. You don't bring children into this world for them to suffer and die before you do.

The silence was deafening ... an awkward lull in time. I was holding onto my tears for dear life, frightened to speak in case it all blurted out in a sea of uncontrolled emotion and I tried desperately hard not to even sniff as I felt the water start to run down my nose. I did not want to break down in front of him. If I did I would lose it entirely and I wasn't going to give anyone the idea that I couldn't cope. There was no more to say. The professor came and shook our hands and stroked Amberlie's head. He wished us well and left the room.

I couldn't breathe. The air and the pain and the trying to hold it together was like a brick stuck in my throat. I gulped and sniffed, shaking uncontrollably as I gripped onto Amberlie so tight that Bill had to take her from me.

Through the torrents of tears now soaking my face, I regained my composure and took Amberlie back in my arms again and said to her, 'I promise you that you will have everything you ever need and more. I am going to make your life as happy and enjoyable and as special as I can. I am never going to give up on you. I am going to take you to Disneyland and all the places a child should go. I love you so much.' I hugged her tight, never ever wanting to let her go.

'Come on Sandra, let's go,' Bill said with bloodshot eyes, trying to move my rigid body from the spot I was anchored to. He was being so brave, trying to keep some control as well as needing to escape as fast as possible from the hospital.

As we left, I stood on the outside step and took a deep breath. I looked around at the buildings and melee of the traffic whizzing past in a chaos of colour and pollution, and at that moment accepted the situation. I made up my mind that I would never give up hope. How would Amberlie stand a chance of improving and developing if I did? I had to accept her problems in order to help her. Despite feeling a very physical pain knowing that I was going to lose her some day, I felt my depression lift as I lurched into the future with a new determination: the determination to keep her as long as I could.

Our journey back was in silence – neither of us remembers it. I don't know how Bill managed to drive that day ... I guess he was on automatic pilot. We went straight to my aunties' house to collect the kids. Naturally, they wanted to know what had happened and we told them. The kids as usual took it very well. There was no point in not telling the truth – after all, they weren't daft and they could see we were upset. We just said that one day Amberlie wouldn't be with us anymore and that she would be an angel up in the sky somewhere. They didn't cry. They gave her a hug and carried on with their game.

5

It was now November and Amberlie was nearly eight months old. She had suffered yet another cold and her fits had increased in number again. Dr Thomas decided that the mixture of phenobarbitone and clonazepam was not really working as well as he had hoped and that Amberlie remained too drowsy.

'She stands no chance of developing in this state,' he said. 'I think we should wean her off these drugs and try a "new wave" drug which has shown lots of promise in controlling infantile spasms and has reduced side effects, especially as it does not seem to cause so much drowsiness. Both the drugs she is taking at the moment are rotten for this.'

I felt quite excited by this and was willing to try anything.

'It's called vigabatrin and I want you to start straight away by giving Amberlie half a tablet per day for a week and then one whole tablet per day from then on. I have written down a reduction programme which I want you to follow to get rid of the phenobarbitone, and I want you to reduce the clonazepam to twice a day, OK? I'll see you in two weeks.'

After the first day the fits stopped.

'Maybe it's a fluke,' I said to Bill. 'Better not get our hopes up, we have to wait and see what happens when the phenobarbitone has gone.'

Each day we hoped and each day there were no signs of any seizures. I knew deep in my heart that she wouldn't have any more. We had found a little miracle.

Gradually Amberlie began to liven up. It was very slow to start but wonderful to see. Her eyes were bright and awake and her gorgeous smile appeared again, lighting up her face. She knew just how to mix it with a touch of shyness to make it totally endearing and irresistible. We were so excited to have her back. The kids' fascination with her was renewed and they bombarded her with all their toys. When we took her out she giggled excitedly at the trees swaying, cooed at all the different noises and kicked her legs vigorously as we went along. The kids were chuffed that she was so busy and noisy, and whenever the opportunity arose they held her hands so they could be close to her all the time.

Three weeks later she got a respiratory infection and stopped eating and drinking. I contacted the ward and took her in for Dr Thomas to examine her. He said he could hear a rattle in her chest and she also had a very sore throat. He wanted to keep Amberlie in for observation, as she had not fed for more than a day, and to make sure it did not develop into meningitis or indeed spur on any seizures. He asked the nurse to start Amberlie on antibiotics as soon as possible.

Poor Amberlie was so miserable, crying all the time and whimpering. She couldn't sleep, she couldn't drink and no amount of cuddles would settle her. She was very stressed and leaning over backwards all the time, which made it difficult and uncomfortable to carry her. The nurses kept pumping her with Calpol and I kept asking where the antibiotics were. After many fraught hours I grabbed the sister and asked, 'Why has Amberlie not been given her antibiotics yet?'

'Was she prescribed them?' she asked.

'Dr Thomas wrote them down on her notes. I was there when he did it.' I was anxious and baffled.

'I'll go and check,' she said on her way out of the door. Two minutes later she came back and said, 'The house doctor feels she does not need them because the infection she has is probably viral.'

'Dr Thomas prescribed antibiotics because of Amberlie's very inflamed sore throat and I am sure he knows more about what he is doing where she is concerned than a house doctor,' I said edgily.

'Well,' she said, 'I can't...'

'I'm not interested,' I said, interrupting her. 'I shall take this up with Dr Thomas or whichever consultant is on duty on the next ward round.' I looked her straight in the face then turned away.

Shortly after, the sister reappeared with a bottle of penicillin. Waving the bottle in the air and smiling broadly, she said, 'The doctor has looked at Amberlie's notes again and now sees that there was a prescription for antibiotics.'

'I guess he thought better of it,' I said wryly.

After two doses Amberlie was much better, and started to take a couple of ounces of milk regularly. In the morning when Dr Thomas came she had much improved and he said to the sister, 'I presume we have started the antibiotics?'

She said, 'Yes.' both she and the house doctor avoided my gaze. I grunted loudly in the corner.

We were discharged for Amberlie to recover fully at home. She was very washed out and tired but was getting better rapidly. I was amazed that through all the stress she still had not had any seizures. Dr Thomas was really pleased and amazed at this result and said, 'I will have to buy shares in vigabatrin!'

While we were in hospital, feeling a renewed optimism now that her seizures were controlled, I asked Dr Thomas for clarification of Amberlie's lissencephaly. I wanted to know his opinion and I was also fishing to find out what Great Ormond Street had said to him.

He said that he had found it difficult to spot on the CT scan, and looking with an inexpert eye, her brain appeared normal. The lissencephaly in terms of 'smoothness' was mild in that Amberlie had bumps but with the tops cut off. The problem lay in the extent being far worse than was originally thought. I asked if it was possible to have a totally smooth brain and he said, 'Yes, that would be the most severe form. Like most things, there are different degrees of severity.'

6

Bill and I decided we would like Amberlie to be Christened. Ray and Clare had both been Christened, and I wanted the same for Amberlie. I also very much wanted the opportunity to celebrate her birth and her future, whatever it held in store.

Although not a particularly religious person, I had always believed in God despite hating him intensely when Amberlie was diagnosed. Perhaps a convenient virtuousness it may have been, but I prayed and prayed that Amberlie's fitting would stop and that if there was a miracle going spare, could she please have it? I got my wish – but was it due to God or science? Who cares?

I suppose I prayed to God because it suited me ... but doesn't everyone when there's trouble? We will all receive our judgements I guess, but some people live them in life, not afterwards.

For whatever reason – fate, luck, hand of God – I felt that Amberlie was meant to be here: she survived my blood pressure and being strangled in the womb, she made it through her diagnosis and if she was not a bright shining light, I didn't know what was.

I made an appointment to see the vicar and told him all about Amberlie. I asked if there was a verse he knew of which would be poignant for the service. He said he wasn't aware of anything particular as the service of Baptism is fairly standard and special in its own right. However, since this was an unusual circumstance as Amberlie was a special gift from God, he would put together some words for us from what we had told him, and he would let us have a look beforehand. The Christening was arranged for 12 December 1993.

We felt it really important that we had reliable godparents who fully understood our situation. We chose my brother Ray,

Auntie Pat and my friend Jackie, who I had known for years and who had been there for me throughout the pain. I could always see sadness in her eyes when Amberlie was ill and pleasure and relief when she was OK. With children of her own she always compared it to how she would have felt if it had happened to her.

Having a celebration to plan gave me something else to think about and I enjoyed putting it all together.

Ray and Clare were very excited to be having a family celebration and were chuffed to have some special new clothes. Clare was especially pleased that Amberlie was to wear her Christening robe and she also wanted the same claret-coloured velvet dress I had bought for Amberlie, to wear after the service. Ray decided on a very smart outfit with a waistcoat and bow tie.

I spent ages trying to neatly embroider 'Amberlie Rose' on the inside of the gown, and managed to find a jeweller who could make her a gold rose pendant with a piece of natural amber in its centre. We thought this significant for her name and also because amber is said to have healing powers.

Close family and friends were invited. The service was lovely and Amberlie looked like a porcelain doll in her ivory satin and lace. She slept through most of it, only becoming agitated when she was passed from pillar to post for photographs. She then burst into tears and we made for home. It took a fair while to settle her again and she went back off to sleep. She enjoyed cutting her cake and opening her presents later with the eager and impatient help of her brother and sister. It was a lovely day and we all had a great time.

Amberlie's first Christmas was spent in the midst of a sickness bug. We had gone to Jackie's house Christmas Eve and it started there with a vengeance and went on throughout Christmas Day. Bill and I took it in turns to try to pacify and cuddle her, trying very hard to keep our spirits up so that Ray and Clare had a happy day. They were both busily enjoying all their new toys to worry too much. The sickness subsided during the evening and Bill and I finally collapsed into bed totally exhausted. Amberlie opened her presents on Boxing Day.

As the days went on Amberlie became more and more aware. Dr Thomas felt that since she had settled beautifully on the vigabatrin we should make an attempt to further reduce the clonazepam because she was on a relatively moderate dose and it was unlikely to be doing much at all.

After a few days we had got the dose right down to a tiny amount but noticed that her eyes had flickered. We put it up again to the next level, but I am not sure that the wean down was totally responsible for her reaction as she was teething and had a lot of irritating catarrh left from a recent cold.

At the next appointment, Dr Thomas was surprised that this had happened, since it was such a small dose, but said we probably knew best. He was delighted with Amberlie's progress and noted how smiley and enthusiastic she was at having discovered her voice!

During a visit to relatives, one of my aunts mentioned that she worked with someone who strongly believed in alternative medicine who had given her the name and phone number of a man who was a cranial osteopath. She had apparently already spoken to him about Amberlie and he was convinced he could help her. Being very open-minded about alternative medicine, I took the details home with me. I thought long and hard about it for a couple of days and being a great believer in fate – as the event had come to me and I had not gone looking for it – I decided it would do no harm to talk to him and see what he had in mind. I resolved that I was not going to allow anyone to alter her medication though, now that we had the fits controlled, as I was loath to risk any further trauma for her.

I rang his office and spoke to his receptionist. He had already told her that if I rang she was to give me his home number to call him in the evening. I asked her what cranial osteopathy was and she briefly explained that it was a gentle massage of the skull which makes the spinal fluid flow around the brain in greater quantity, stimulating and nourishing the brain cells. The osteopath can direct the fluid to specific areas so that certain aspects can be stimulated. She said the patient normally finds it extremely relaxing and enjoyable. It sounded pretty harmless to me so I called his house later and left a message on his answer phone. He called me that evening and explained his background and training, which also included traditional Chinese medicine.

I explained Amberlie's condition to him and he said that he obviously couldn't promise anything but would like to examine her. He had never dealt with such a severe problem before but did have children with autism, cerebral palsy and other developmental problems on his register. I asked him whether he had dealt with epilepsy before, and he said that some children he'd treated had managed to either stop or reduce their seizures and were now seizure free.

Bill and I went to his home the following week. I had visions of a big roaming house in acres of land but instead it was a two-up, two-down terraced cottage, painted totally white and about half an hour's drive away. We sat and waited in the tiny, dingy coloured dining room. An old orangey lamp cast a dull light in one corner and made the wallpaper, which was embossed with a gold bamboo grass design, glow warmly around the room. On the table centred in front of the window was a poor excuse for a Christmas tree with its needles shed below it on the cloth, and a strange mingling scent of Chinese cooking and incense hung in the air. A cream-coloured, very tall, carved mantelpiece was piled high with used candles and ethnic-looking knick-knacks. The heavy dark black curtains blotted out nearly all the natural light, and I thought there was no way I could live there.

It was deafeningly quiet apart from a few occasional creaky footsteps on the wooden boards upstairs. It was unbearably hot and stifling – the central heating must have been on at its highest level. Bill and I looked at each other.

'Bit weird innit?' I said.

He smiled. Amberlie was fast asleep and not in the least bit interested. After about thirty minutes my eyes were straining in the light and I was feeling very hot, uncomfortable and a bit nauseous. I thought, *If he doesn't hurry up I'm going to have to leave or he'll have two more patients to attend to.*

James then appeared. He wasn't how I expected either. A young Englishman (I thought he would be Chinese), tall, with loads of thick dark wavy hair that kinked upwards at the front, soft dark eyes and a thick pyramid-shaped moustache draped over full lips. He was dressed in a very creased, off-white laboratory-type coat with black trousers and socks. He had a totally relaxed demeanour – the lack of shoes illustrated it well! I had noticed a huge pile of heavily soiled shoes under a bureau earlier, all lace-ups. After a cheery introduction he led us up some lethally steep stairs. There was a room leading off either side of the top step and we entered the left one.

Immediately the abysmal lighting made me think of headaches. I peered up and a dull single bulb surrounded by a Chinese paper shade made me look away. The walls were adorned with posters of the brain, and a huge Buddha print showing which parts of the body relate to whatever problem dominated one end. Umpteen books on every subject of alternative medicine you could imagine, together with a section on the occult and books on Tarot readings, were piled on small painted shelves. The old cream-coloured mantelpiece over the black iron fireplace had dark brown medicine bottles full of aromatherapy oils, all labelled and haphazardly left. A dirty old net curtain was draped across the large window. I couldn't see much outside as it was late afternoon and dusk was settling but I was able to spot some slate rooftops glistening with dampness under the streetlights. At the end of the room was an old oak desk with absolutely nothing on it, and right in the middle of the room was an old stretcher trolley with floral sheeting tucked around it. It reminded me of the old-fashioned fabrics my mum used to use to cover the ironing board. There were two chairs, one a swivel, and both had seen better days.

The atmosphere was calm, almost esoteric. Amberlie was laid on the trolley and James sat beside her. He touched her head and chest with his fingers placed in a certain way. He had started treatment and it was so gentle we hardly noticed.

Amberlie was still asleep. Nobody said a word. As the time passed we saw Amberlie's body relax more and more. Her arms and legs were spread open like a star, and her breathing changed to heavy and slow. I noticed James also had his eyes closed; it was very much like faith healing.

Amberlie woke almost as soon as he had finished. She was noticeably bright-eyed and he said she would either be sleepy or hyperactive later. He asked if he could see her regularly and I said it would be difficult for me to get to him as I did not have a car, and to take Amberlie on a number of buses with Ray and Clare would be a nightmare. We had also not discussed the cost of her treatment, which might also be a consideration. James said he had friends living fairly near to us whom he visited regularly. He suggested scheduling our appointments to coincide with his visits so that Amberlie could be seen at home. He said he charged £25 per visit.

Certainly Amberlie seemed more alert each time he came. We weren't sure whether it was down to him or due to the reduction in her medication. We would have to wait and see.

We didn't hear from James for about a month but during that time Amberlie had progressed and was starting to show an interest in her toys. He then visited every week, taking her up to our bedroom for a more quiet, relaxed atmosphere. He concentrated on different parts of her brain each time to encourage her to do different activities. After each treatment we noticed more and more changes in Amberlie, nothing specific but very subtle differences. She was coming alive, like a rose bud, gradually but slowly opening up.

7

During Amberlie's appointment with Dr Thomas in January, he explained that it was now time to transfer Amberlie's care to Dr Eleanor Ramsay, a consultant neuropaediatrician, who was a specialist with unquestionable experience based at the hospital.

Now her seizures were controlled, Amberlie's development was of the utmost importance and Dr Ramsay was the doctor with the knowledge to guide us. Dr Thomas had previously warned Bill and me that this would be the case on a couple of occasions, but it made me very unsettled to say the least. I trusted him and now we were going to be under another doctor my security was wavering. He obviously sensed my unease and told me as much about her as possible.

I sighed heavily and thanked him for all he had done. His care, attention and expertise saw Amberlie through her roughest times. He was also too damn modest to accept our praise!

We met Dr Ramsay later on in the month. She was a northerner, and older than I expected, wearing a classically styled, non-dating floral dress. I immediately detected some eccentricity in hr manner – she reminded me of 'a professor at work' talking to us and thinking about a thousand other intensely important things at the same time, and it made me smile. When she spoke she was very down to earth, strong and forthright with caring soft touches peeping through every now and then. I liked her. Bill was not keen – he really couldn't make her out. He was still very disappointed that we were not under Dr Thomas anymore but accepted that Amberlie needed a specialist.

Dr Ramsay said that she had only known of one other case of lissencephaly in her whole career and that was years ago.

'It was very bad,' she said, 'couldn't do anything at all, too many fits and only lived about eighteen months.'

We both listened.

'Compared to that, Amberlie has lots of promise. A rarity ... never known a lissencephaly case where the fits have been totally controlled ... we're on a new ball game here ... development is the goal!' she said, with gusto.

We soon learned that Dr Ramsay literally spoke as she thought, and we had to concentrate hard to follow the conversation and where she was heading sometimes.

'We will now be able to see how far a child of this kind can develop without the inhibition of fits,' she went on.

I found I was becoming excited along with her, but felt cautious because under no circumstances was Amberlie ever going to be a 'guinea pig'.

She asked if I wanted to be involved in everything that was going on in the hospital for disabled children. I said I only really wanted necessary appointments because I had to think about my other children too, as I was determined that their lives should go on as normal. She understood and suggested physiotherapy, which I expected, as Amberlie would need to be monitored for any signs of spasticity and helped to develop physically. The doctor was pleased that Amberlie's legs had become supple and mobile again now that the fits weren't agitating her. There was also a 'baby playtherapy group' which met once a month to give ideas on how to get your child to do something new each time; and 'portage', which was a development/physio thing where someone comes to your home once a week. Dr Ramsay explained that there was a waiting list, but Amberlie's name would be put on as a priority. There were also various support groups for mums that I declined. I was, however, alarmed at the number of appointments we had thrust upon us and at first glance it looked as if it was all going to be a nightmare. We would be practically living at the hospital.

I was panicking as we left Dr Ramsay. How on earth was I going to be able to get back and forth to the hospital on the bus with Amberlie? Using taxis would cost an arm and a leg ... and the time involved ... *Oh my God!* And what about the schools ... how was I going to get round the schools? I would be juggling pick-up times from Clare finishing at midday and Ray finishing at 3 pm; and just to add salt to the wound, Bill piped up and said 'I can't have all that time off work.'

I was almost in tears. I knew it was unreasonable to expect him to be there all the time.

'I'll just have to have my own car,' I said with an arrogant resolve. Looking stunned, Bill said, 'And where do you think I'm going to get the money from for that?'

'Well I'll have my Invalid Care Allowance and Amberlie will be getting her Disability Living Allowance, surely that's what the money's there for ... to help with Amberlie's care all round,' I said.

'Yes, but it's the initial outlay to buy the car in the first place,' he said.

'Well I'll have to get a loan from somewhere, won't I?'

Bill sighed and said nothing.

I knew I'd put unreasonable pressure on him, which had now stressed him out. I was so worked up panicking and thinking of all the implications and impracticalities. There was so much involved in caring for a disabled child and I supposed this was what GOSH meant when they said it would be life changing. Also to a point, I resented what I saw as an encroachment on my life by the authorities, an interference with what I wanted to do with Amberlie. There was a route I was expected to follow, and whilst I didn't object to anything that enriched her life and was of benefit to her, I was anxious that Ray and Clare's needs were met as well. I wanted my family to remain as normal as possible and I meant it. As I calmed down I managed to get most of it into perspective and decided that I would of course attend for any medical or physiotherapy appointments but as for the rest we'd just have to see.

Luckily, my Auntie Pat came to the rescue about the car and lent me £1,500, for which I made monthly repayments from Amberlie's allowance. Two weeks later I had a little Mini Metro just in time for the start of the appointments.

Physiotherapy came first and Amberlie did not like being pulled about at all. I explained that she had a classical lissencephaly trait of lurching backwards and hanging her head at any available opportunity, but the physio was quite pleased with her generally and especially her head control. The muscle tone in her legs was good and she was able to do the basics of crawling on her tummy. Amberlie's left hand needed manipulating to make it open as her hand had remained closed in a fist since her seizures first started. Carol asked me to work on her thumb joint, gently pulling it outward each time we sat down together and that would encourage her hand to loosen. By the next physiotherapy session two weeks later, Amberlie's hand was open and supple.

The next thing to deal with was her arms, which were weak and she needed gaiters to help support and straighten them when putting her hands onto the floor in the crawl position. Carol also suggested a couple of toys which benefit special-needs children: one was a pop-up-peg-men set and another was a thing called a 'Skwish' (a construction of beads on sticks and threads with a bell – it looked a bit like a scientific molecular structure). I had noted that Amberlie had excitedly reached for a set of jingle bells that I had waved in front of her. I found the bells easily the next time we went to town but had a lot of trouble finding the other two items. The pegs I had to order and I eventually found the Skwish in a specialised toy shop. She absolutely loved the Skwish from the moment I put it in her hand and it went everywhere with us!

8

Our long-awaited appointment with the Great Ormond Street geneticists had arrived. It was very important to us to find out if Amberlie's condition was hereditary, as this could affect our other children in the future.

Having deposited Ray and Clare with the aunties for the day, we made our way to London.

We were shown into a huge playroom beneath the hospital to wait for the doctors. It was very lonely and deserted, with only one other child there at the time. Every word we said echoed loudly around the room. Even whispers were clearly heard. Occasionally a few doors opened and banged shut and footsteps came and went.

Eventually two young male doctors appeared and called Amberlie's name. We followed them into a small office where Dr Pearce was waiting. The doctor was a well-groomed man with a distinct aura of seniority. He greeted us informally explaining who he was and what he did, and also who the other doctors were and what their specialist areas of interest were. The atmosphere was very relaxed and informal, and he chatted away naturally and made us feel at ease. We didn't realise at the time that he was one of the top experts in genetics and was well renowned and respected all over the world.

He explained that Amberlie's doctors had diagnosed that she had the Miller-Dieker syndrome variant of lissencephaly. My heart sank. I knew this was one of the worst types.

'There are different forms of lissencephaly, and we can diagnose which form a child has by the symptoms and problems that it presents. We then group the similar traits together and put them under a syndrome heading and this determines which type of lissencephaly a child has.'

'So why is it called Miller-Dieker?' I asked.

'Simply because that is the name of the person/persons who discovered it,' he replied.

'Then how do you arrive at this syndrome for Amberlie?'

He perched himself on the corner of his table so he was close to Amberlie and explained, 'If you look at the shape of Amberlie's head you can see that her temples narrow in.'

As before, I still couldn't see anything different. He noticed my expression.

'It is difficult for an inexpert eye to see but if you look at photos of your other children at this age and compare them to Amberlie you will see that her temples indent slightly more than theirs. Her eyes are also slightly wider apart than normal and she has no bridge on her nose. Her mouth is shaped in a certain way with a thinner lower lip; he chin is also quite small.'

I studied her but was still none the wiser. She looked like a normal baby to me. Bill and I looked at each other and he shrugged his shoulders.

At least it's not just me, I thought.

The doctor also said that her arms were a little short in length. I had noticed that before and nodded.

'Unfortunately,' he went on, 'this particular syndrome is one of the severest and does affect life expectancy. It is also genetic.'

'Go on,' I prompted, needing to know.

'Most affected children do not survive for more than a few months, especially those with heart abnormalities … and nearly all will have passed away by their second birthday. Others do live beyond that but not normally beyond adolescence.'

Silence fell.

Never gets any better, I thought to myself. This time, though, I felt no pain … in fact, I felt nothing. My brain was in total control and I had subconsciously set up a protection barrier in order to shut out the hurt. It wasn't intentional – I supposed I was getting used to the constant blows. This ability was to become my defence mechanism and saviour of soul and sanity.

The doctor then asked if we had any family history of disability. I said, 'My uncle on my mother's side had been what they called 'spastic'. He had seizures from birth and severe learning difficulties, and died when was seventeen during a fit. There had been no formal diagnosis of any condition apart from 'spastic', which I understand was just the way it was in those days.' The doctor nodded his agreement. He explained that there was not the diagnostic medicine and machinery we have today, so they used to pile a lot of disabilities under the same hat and that was that. I said, 'I do not think it was at all related to Amberlie.' And neither did he. 'About it being genetic,' I went on. 'Does that mean it could affect my other children when they have families?' He explained that it was usually genetic, but that there could be other reasons why Amberlie had lissencephaly.

'If it is genetic, it would mean that one or both of you carries the defective gene.' There was a pause while he let us mull it over.

'Either one or both of us?' I asked, prompting a deeper explanation.

'Yes,' he said. 'One of you may carry the dominant gene or both of you carry the recessive gene.'

'So, what's the difference between dominant and recessive?' Bill asked.

Dr Pearce smiled.

'Genetics are horrendously complicated, but to make it simple … If one parent has a dominant gene, an overpowering one, the risk of you having another lissencephaly child would be fifty per cent. Where there is a recessive gene, the weaker one – it sort of works in reverse – it would need to be matched by the same gene in the other parent … meaning two recessive genes getting together to activate a recurrence. The risk would then be twenty-five per cent. We cannot confirm that a gene is recessive, though, because they cannot be seen under a microscope. The other factors we could consider are that you had a virus when you were pregnant, there was something in the environment, or an interruption in the blood supply to the baby; or, as research has found in America, some link to binge drinking of alcohol in early pregnancy … or an unknown cause … a blip. There is still much to learn about this condition and we are researching all the time.'

The doctor asked if I had been ill or binged on alcohol, or whether I had noticed anything strange or unusual about the pregnancy. I said, 'No, apart from high blood pressure all through the pregnancy.' With his lips pursed, he nodded thoughtfully but said nothing.

I wasn't a drinker – in fact, we hardly ever went out because we couldn't afford it, but if we did, I liked to have a glass of wine. I told him that we had a family party around the time I conceived Amberlie and I did have rather a lot to drink; I was merry but not paralytic as such. I shuddered. 'Oh god, what … it could be my fault?' I felt all the guilt in the world crush down on my shoulders. The doctor just shook his head. I have never been able to reconcile the possibility, and to this day I can still come up with possible reasons why. It haunts me constantly … when I let it. It was and is an unbearable consideration and if I was responsible in whatever way, then I deserve all I get that's bad in life.

Later I remembered a persistent green vaginal discharge that came and went several times during the pregnancy. I had spoken to my GP about it and he hadn't felt it was anything to worry about unless it became smelly or troublesome. I wished I had remembered it to tell Dr Pearce.

The doctors went quiet for a while – a natural time out while the information sank in.

'About this recessive part … you mean the coming together of Bill and me,' I said. 'Are you saying that we shouldn't have met?'

'Errmmm … mmm … one-in-a-million chance that two people with the same problem meet and have children,' Dr Pearce said cagily. Bill looked horrified, and the colour drained from his face. I held his hand. 'A microdeletion, a tiny chip off Chromosome 17 in both of you.'

'How can that be if we have two other normal children?' I was confused.

'Fluke,' he said. 'Twenty-five per cent risk – one child in four – could have been any one of them.'

'You mean that they could have probably had lissencephaly?' I mocked with a slight grin. I was trying to sort this out in my head.

'Yes, in a way,' he replied.

'No … that can't be … I'm sure you're wrong,' I said resolvedly, not accepting any of it.

'Do you intend to have more children?' he asked.

I looked at Bill and said, 'Well, we haven't ruled it out … not really thought about it … I guess it's a possibility.'

'Then we need to take some tests so we know what the recurrence risks are,' he said. 'We will need to take samples of blood from both of you and also from Amberlie. This will also provide confirmation of her diagnosis.'

One of the doctors took a large syringe full of blood from each of us but as usual there was huge difficulty in finding a decent vein on Amberlie. Dr Pearce said they would have to take it from her groin. He explained this could be a little dangerous and much preparation took place to avoid any problems. They said it would hurt a little, but Amberlie took it well with just a grimace and we held her hands and talked to her. They gave us some instructions to follow for the next twelve hours to ensure the wound healed properly, and if not we were to take her to hospital promptly. Luckily, she was OK.

'You still haven't said about the kids,' I reminded him. He explained that we would need to wait for the results, but if the tests were clear, there would be no reason to worry. It would be some weeks before we had the results.

I had many mixed emotions when we left. I felt dirty and contaminated, almost as if Bill and I were flawed and not the best bred of human beings. And as for the chances of us meeting … well … Jesus!

We were devastated to think that Ray and Clare would be affected if it turned out that one or both of us carried the defective gene, and at the same time I could not accept that they were possibly biological flukes! Bill said, 'I just know that if there is a defective gene it will be me.'

I couldn't be of any comfort to him. I decided it was best not to think about it too deeply until we knew. I already felt guilty enough about what happened to Amberlie, let alone contemplate Ray and Clare and whether or not Bill and I should ever have met. I didn't want to accept that Bill and I were a biological meeting that shouldn't have happened, and if that was the case then what was that going to do to our relationship? I couldn't begin to consider that our whole married life had been a mistake. The last thing I wanted was for a big rift, and I was already aware that many marriages fall apart when a disabled child is born. I dismissed it away. Anyway, Ray and Clare were normal, lovely kids … something else had to have gone wrong for Amberlie.

Regardless of whether one or both of us carried the defective gene, it couldn't change what had happened so I couldn't see the point in worrying over something I couldn't change. Letting it prey on my mind would just depress me more. Bill was already blaming himself and I could see he was terrified that his whole world was dissolving before him. I had no intention of blowing our family apart and said, 'We'll get through it … I think they're wrong anyway.'

We both thought the whole genetics thing was an awful lot to take in and neither of us could piece together the entire puzzle from memory. We needed to go over it again and again to make sense of it. With the help of a book and the information sheets from the Lissencephaly Society, we eventually sorted it out in our minds and understood a bit more about the human biological process. We then marveled at what an amazing thing the body is and that it was a miracle achievement to give birth to a normal baby.

It didn't make us feel any better for Amberlie though – for my part it made me feel nauseous. I still couldn't see why it had to happen to her.

A note to explain the genetics of lissencephaly:

Each of us inherits two copies of almost all genes, one from the father and one from the mother. The exception is the male chromosome in males. Chromosomes are numbered in order of size, 1 is the largest and 21 and 22 are the smallest.

Lissencephaly is caused by a missing part of one of the two No 17 chromosomes. Variants in the location of the missing parts determine the lissencephaly syndrome.

In most families the missing part is caused by a copy error – similar to a smudge on a photocopy. This means that the chromosome in both parents was normal but when they were copied to form the egg or sperm cell, one of the No 17s was not copied correctly and a tiny piece was missing.

Occasionally, as in the Miller-Dieker syndrome, one parent has a complex rearrangement of chromosome 17, and this means the tip of No 17 and the tip of another chromosome have switched for some reason. The parent is normal but is considered a 'carrier', and can therefore pass on an abnormal 17 to their children. This is uncommon. If a parent is a 'carrier', the risk of having another Miller-Dieker syndrome child is 25-50%. If neither parent carries, the risk is as low as less than 1%.

If a chromosome is reversed in its make-up (recessive gene), this cannot be seen under a microscope, so the given recurrence risk is 7%.

About two months later the letter arrived on our doormat:

'… Amberlie Murphy's Chromosome and DNA studies do not confirm a diagnosis of Miller-Dieker syndrome. She certainly seems to have lissencephaly and I did quote a recurrence risk of 7% …'

It was the best news we'd had in ages! Not identified … a blip … the kids would be OK … providence and recessive genes allowing.

It was April 1st and Amberlie's first birthday, and she woke with a beaming smile and a giggle then rolled herself right over onto her tummy, managing to get her hands out from beneath her! I couldn't believe it! I shouted for everyone to come and see, hoping I hadn't imagined it. I turned her onto her back again and we all watched in thrilled anticipation to see whether she would do it again. She looked at all our faces, smiled, and then over she went! The kids jumped about cheering and Bill had a grin wider than his face!

'Wow! What a clever girl and on your birthday as well!' I said, excitedly.

Amberlie knew she had been clever and the delight radiated all over her face. Her blue eyes sparkled and her mouth formed into a self-satisfied coy smile. She was so pleased with herself, loving all the praise, and we were just over the moon!

We had already had a small miracle earlier that week when she had managed to pull herself up to the sitting position with a beautifully straight back, and we certainly weren't expecting another one quite so soon! Up until then, she had only raised herself slightly from the floor, and that had taken an enormous effort – it was just enough to stop her nose from being squashed against the floor. We could see it took a tremendous surge for her to do it, and bless her – she wobbled a lot, trying hard to keep her balance, and each time she started to go down again she used her arms to push herself back up!

I think Amberlie enjoyed her birthday, although she slept for most of the day. She seemed to do this on special-occasion days and quite often ended up being sick. I felt this was down to the change in her daily routine and being handled by relatives who she was not used to seeing regularly. She would never feed properly and loathed other people feeding her. Her grandmother, who loved her to bits, used to like to try but despite constant reminders could never quite grasp the fact that Amberlie couldn't deal with spoonfuls of food being shoved into her mouth at a fast rate. This caused Amberlie to panic because she could not coordinate her swallowing (swallowing problems are rife with lissencephaly). Bill would then take over so Amberlie could finish her meal calmly. She loved her dad feeding her – his strong arms and gentle manner made her feel secure.

Ray and Clare had a great time helping Amberlie blow out her candles and open her presents. She seemed to love them being involved in her day – any day, and became excited along with them. I loved to watch them altogether – helping, playing, talking – it was amazing how Ray and Clare just accepted the way Amberlie was.

It was always a problem to know what to buy Amberlie, so I appreciated other people's difficulties. However, some were quite unable to use their logic due to Amberlie's handicaps being stuck at the forefront of their minds, which I found irritating. She didn't always need a toy especially for disabled children – a basic colourful, noisy, even musical infant toy would have been useful and gratefully accepted. She did have most of what she needed and I was often stumped for ideas myself but I was actually rarely asked for any suggestions. Clothes were always nice – she often needed changing many times in a day, hence the washing machine was always on – but even those were a problem for some.

'Well what sort of clothes and where do I get them – is there a special shop?'

She was not a funny shape, she had all her bits and pieces and she wasn't allergic to any particular designs. I really did wonder sometimes. What did they expect her to wear?

Amberlie always knew when she was wearing new clothes and reacted much like any other little girl would. She always looked at her arms to see what she had on and would try to pose herself to say, 'Look at me!' her shy smile told the whole story. Sometimes the presents weren't wrapped. Sure, she couldn't open them herself but if they could only have appreciated the wonderment in her face when she looked at a beautifully wrapped present, the way she banged it and listened to the paper rustle and crunch, perhaps they would have made more of an effort. I couldn't understand why her disabilities should have affected people's common sense. I used to feel so sad and dismayed that some of the people closest to us really didn't have a clue.

It didn't seem like a year since Amberlie was born. It had gone so fast despite all the dramas and we were different people now. Bill said, 'It's been the longest, saddest and even one of the happiest years of my life … I hope we never have another one like it.'

I sighed … the worst had to be over considering the progress our little sweetpea was making.

Bill had become a real family man. Before we were married he was sport-mad and one for being out with the lads. After Raymond was born he started to settle down and enjoyed spending time with him. He became a totally changed man after Amberlie was diagnosed and hated having to go to work in the mornings, always petrified that something would happen while he was out. Working in London meant he wasn't right on the doorstep, but he took the car every day so he could get home quickly if there was an emergency. I worried about him journeying to and fro and told him that he would have to train himself to relax and put it all to one side – after all, Amberlie had settled and was fine most of the time.

The last thing I wanted was for him to end up having a heart attack because he lived every day on a knife-edge.

He used to dash in each day, rush upstairs to change out of his suit just so he could snatch Amberlie from me as soon as possible … and she was always delighted that he did! It was nice for me too, as it meant I could get on with the dinner and spend a little time helping Ray and Clare with their homework. The break was especially welcome if Amberlie had had a rotten day.

Bill was also good at helping with the housework, trying to take the pressure off me in any way he could. We were real good mates and supported each other by talking about things for hours on end and working out ways to overcome problems. I would say the last year had aged him considerably and the cute laughter lines around his eyes had now become well engraved in his skin; but he was a calmer person who had worked out what was and wasn't important in life.

'Made me put things into perspective,' he would say.

9

Carol, the physio was very pleased with Amberlie's physical progress. Her sitting was coming along and she tried hard to use her muscles to balance herself. Amberlie didn't have any 'falling reflex' (instinct to put her hands out to save herself), and it was important to plant this idea in her head to help her stay in the sitting position. We used huge gym balls for her to lie across so that we could move her easily to give her the sensation of falling and hopefully help her grasp the idea of saving herself. This also gently built up the strength in her arms. It worked well, and as time went on her hands started to go towards the floor as she saw the carpet approaching. She also loved whooshing towards the floor and the faster we went the more she giggled – it must have been much like being on a mini roller-coaster for her!

It was now time to concentrate on her legs and feet. Her toes, like her hands, needed uncurling and the tendons down the back of her calves to her heels needed stretching as she was reluctant to fully place her feet onto the floor. It involved lots of hands-on stretching and Amberlie hated it. Carol explained that she wanted me to do this physio at home as often as possible to encourage Amberlie to push down with her legs onto her feet to facilitate standing. She said Amberlie could have a standing frame but in her experience it often proved very stressful for children because they were trussed up and tied in, so she was keen to avoid it for the time being. Another thing was for me to make Amberlie aware of her feet by getting her to touch them. This would make her rock her back to use more muscles to aid her sitting.

To help support Amberlie's arms during physio sessions, she had been measured for some gaiters that had not yet arrived. To avoid wasting precious time Carol lent us a pair. When Amberlie put weight through her arms she held her fists to the floor rather than opening her hands. Carol said the gaiters would support the elbow and therefore encourage the hands to open. She explained that for Amberlie to have to concentrate on both things without the use of gaiters was unfair. She didn't mind them at first but when her nose itched, which was a regular thing, she couldn't control the speed of her arm and ended up hitting herself in the face with the hard gaiters. She worked out the cause and effect there and each time I strapped them on she became agitated and wouldn't do her physio.

Throwing herself backward into an arched position was still quite a problem and Amberlie could do it with real force. Carol suggested I try dressing her on my lap as a starting point, as she would not be able to do it in that position. To me, not being able to do it and learning not to do it were totally different things so I wasn't sure this was going to solve anything.

I was elated when Carol commented on how aware and smiley Amberlie was. She said, 'Something must have happened to trigger all this progress – a bit like a light being switched on in her head. A trigger that has opened new doors for her.'

I was now looking forward to Amberlie's portage sessions beginning. I attended the baby playtherapy group but found it to be essentially a coffee and chat time for mothers. Also, when I spoke to the psychologist who ran the group, I was rather disappointed that she seemed not to have grasped Amberlie's condition. She said my target for the month should be to encourage Amberlie to hold her own bottle at feed times!

'What planet is she on?' I said to Bill later. 'Maybe she hasn't received her notes yet.' He just laughed. I never went again.

A lady from the portage service called in one evening to discuss what support Amberlie might need. They hoped that they would be able to start her sessions within the next few weeks.

At last I received a call from June Collin, who would be her teacher. When she arrived, I recognized her as one of the health visitors from our surgery. She explained that she did portage on a voluntary basis. We sat having coffee whilst wading through reams and reams of charts, discussing all that Amberlie could and couldn't do. June summarised by saying Amberlie's motor skills needed the most encouragement and that she, thankfully, had most of the 'infant skills.'

June started with her hands. The idea was to show Amberlie stage by stage that she could hold an object with support (it had to be something she liked), and then pass it to the other hand again with support. She started by showing Amberlie her jingle bells. June placed them in Amberlie's hand, folding her fingers around them, and then shook them so Amberlie could hear where they were. This was to encourage her to turn her head to look at them in order to prompt some hand-eye coordination. She then moved them from one hand to the other in a single movement, hoping that Amberlie would look and follow them. She did.

Amberlie was not always happy to hold things, so repetition and perseverance were essential. It she didn't want to know, I would leave it and try again later. It gradually began to work because she would open her hand to receive a toy but would then grasp her other hand instead. This was a tiny part of progression … a hope-filled stepping stone to the next level. Clever girl!

Amberlie was still having her cranial osteopathy either fortnightly or monthly, depending on when James was in the area. As time went on we noticed that the sessions became less and less fruitful, and other than providing a nice massage, made very little difference to her. Initially there was evidence that they settled and nourished Amberlie's brain and certainly encouraged her awareness and development. It had definitely been an extremely worthwhile treatment but it now seemed that its usefulness had peaked. (I wondered whether that was related to the lissencephaly itself, being that development is not usually more than the ability of a five-month-old baby.) Amberlie certainly enjoyed the massages, but where that was concerned I produced the same effect on her that James did. Bill and I now felt the money would be more worthwhile invested in new toys and equipment to promote more development and stimulation.

James had made such a difference to Amberlie, and I was more than a little cagey about stopping the sessions for fear that she might go backwards. He said of we needed him again at any time, he would be happy to hear from us. He also said that he wasn't sure how much more he could have helped Amberlie as he had never dealt with a child as disabled as she was, and thanked us for giving him the opportunity.

'She has given me a lot to think about. Perhaps I can help others with similar problems.'

10

Amberlie was a very mixed bag of emotions when her teeth were pushing through. Each eruption took weeks to break the gums and the pain and soreness brought nothing but misery. Paracetamol only worked to a certain degree and the teething gels made her gag. Despite daily intakes of vitamins A, C and D, a cold and runny nose always accompanied the teeth, and she dribbled profusely all the time. When it was getting her down most she would push her fist hard against her mouth, wince and let out a frustrated 'Mmm' followed by a shout, as she tried to fight the pain away.

Times of persistent stress made Amberlie hang her body backwards more, and keeping her upright was almost impossible. She used enormous thrusts to force herself back and I had to use all my strength to hold on tight (this backward position is known as 'extension' and is a lissencephaly trait). As uncomfortable as it seemed (and was for me), it somehow placated her. She never wanted to be put down, preferring to be carried in that position, and each time I tried to sit down with her on my lap she would go berserk until I stood up again. I had to carry her and walk round with her hanging over my arms like a heavy shopping basket so that she wouldn't scream her head off for hours. When I was able to eventually put her down, my arms would be numb and shaky and my shoulders ached like hell.

Despite all this, one day she accidentally found that banging her hand on her mouth while moaning made Red Indian 'woo-woo' noises. This changed the moans into entertaining giggles and the spell was broken for a while. At 3 o'clock one morning, she was lying in bed laughing hysterically at the 'woo-woos', thrilled that she was making such a racket! I sat watching her in the dim lamplight, amused and fascinated that she was having so much fun at such an unearthly hour. Amazingly, the other kids always slept through any noise she made at night.

Amberlie's personality was now developing and she was blossoming into a very charming little girl. She particularly learned how to let us know when she didn't want to do something. Whilst she didn't mind having a nappy change, she decided that being washed and having her clothes changed was not a desirable part of her day. She learnt that stiffening her limbs made it difficult to get trousers and jumpers on and off, and that grabbing her sleeves meant I couldn't pull them up her arms. Sometimes she would be even more adamant, and would moan and shout as well; at other times there was a real glint of mischief in her eyes daring me to try. Occasionally I could distract her by blowing raspberries onto her tummy and chatting to her – she loved to hear an expressive conversation. She would then go all soppy and giggle and forget her plan. There were times when I just had to hold my breath and brave the oncoming grief, especially if we had to go out! Her determination was so strong that every now and then it just wasn't worth it, and I would leave it rather than have her inconsolably upset. Generally by the time she'd had a nap and some food she had forgotten about it and I could try again. I found that introducing a massage into the procedure helped a lot and she decided that it really wasn't so bad, and sometimes she relaxed so much she fell asleep midway!

Amberlie was showing me that she was a person in her own right, able to make decisions and skilful enough to make herself understood – teaching me that I shouldn't take anything for granted. I was very proud of her.

Carol had provided Amberlie with a special corner seat and table to encourage the use of her torso muscles to aid her balance while sitting without too many straps as a restriction. She had just one strap around her chest and a block between her legs to stop her bottom slipping forward. The table was just the right height for her to rest her arms on and see her favourite toys. Amberlie was a bit unsure of it but seemed to like the freedom.

At first she just sat for a few minutes looking around the room, checking that everything else was still the same and that I was still there. It was also the first time she had sat without anyone being close to her in case she fell. Gradually, four little fingers appeared resting on the edge of the table. After a while I took her hand and rested it flat on the surface so she could feel the wood. Her eyes searched for her toys and she tried hard to move her hand towards the one she fancied. With help, she felt it gently, and slowly, much like a blind person would, her eyes widened in pleasure and surprise as she grinned from ear to ear. I folded her hand around her chosen toy to see if she would hold it but most of the time as she tried to lift it, it dropped straight away. We practiced day in and day out over many weeks and finally she managed to form a decent grip, and provided the toy wasn't too heavy or cumbersome she held it well. The Skwish was the real aid in her grip development. Its strings caught in her fingers and almost unwittingly got her hands used to weight bearing because it didn't fall away easily. Once she had hold of the Skwish, Amberlie soon realised that letting her hand fall heavily on the table banged the Skwish and jangled its bells. Finding this totally hysterical, she bashed it harder and harder, laughing more and more, and kicking her legs like crazy under the table. She had such an infectious laugh! We had a ball watching her – it was great to see her having such fun!

Every day Amberlie soon searched out her Skwish and grabbed it straight away, playing for ages and ages, enjoying all the noise. She even taught herself how to swap it from one hand to the other just by having both hands on it on one occasion. It was incredible to see her watching what she was doing – working it all out and making it happen.

I was so over the moon I could have had a party on the spot! Lissencephaly children can usually reach for things but not grasp them so this was a real bonus, and the fact that she was also coordinating her hands was an amazing and terrific achievement – more than I'd ever hoped for!

The Skwish also proved to be a good distraction for Amberlie on bad days. I would sit her in her chair whilst she was in mid-tantrum and within a couple of minutes of grabbing it, tiny giggles would ooze from her lips as the tears disappeared. She also liked the noise of a small tambourine she had but when she tried to bang it with her hand she often missed it and hit the table instead. Frustrated, she soon worked out how to push it off the table to get rid of it.

Amberlie preferred noisy toys and remembered which ones made the best noises. If something had a large bright face, though, she would coyly make eyes at it, unsure about whether or not it was real, and if it talked or sang, she would look amazed and tentatively feel it with one finger first before risking her whole hand.

We bought her several textured fabric toys but she was quite fussy about them and the ones she didn't like the feel of she would pull away from and ignore, never to acknowledge them again. She always resisted someone trying to control her hands such as by playing 'pat-a-cake', and would instantly pull them away and hold them tight to her chest, and if we sang too many nursery rhymes she'd start to rub her eyes and yawn!

In portage we were monitoring Amberlie's eye tracking. It always took a little while for her to focus on something and then she would be unable to follow its movement consistently. She kept looking away and catching up with it. We used mostly noisy toys, but found that a brightly coloured or black and white toy could be just as effective. A lot of emphasis was put on whether she moved her head in the right direction or not, scoring a point if she did. Amberlie would sometimes move her head in one direction to follow an object but only use her eyes to follow it back. I made the point that she was still tracking it, and that when we (normal people) watch something we don't always move our heads to follow it, and that perhaps watching the same object move from side to side several times was pretty boring. In my mind she had achieved the goal. June smiled at me. I got used to being smiled at without comment.

Amberlie was now thirteen months old and Dr Ramsay wanted her to have a hearing test at the hospital. I never had any worries about her hearing so felt this was rather a waste of time, but Dr Ramsay was curious and wanted to rule out any problems.

As Amberlie was unable to respond with language or specific reactions, the audiologist wanted to wire her up to measure the electricity from her ears. I knew Amberlie would hate that, and if they upset her they would not get any viable result at all, so I suggested that she might react to a normal distraction test. They looked at me as if I was nuts, but said they would try. One lady sat in front of Amberlie and the consultant stood behind her making a variety of sounds, from loud noises to soft whispers, in all directions. Amberlie responded by either turning her head towards the sounds or moving her eyes in the right direction – and bless her, she passed with flying colours and was discharged. She knew she had been a clever girl and we left the hospital with her happily kicking her legs in her new buggy. She adored being out in the warm, sunny weather.

11

Prompted by the good outcome of the genetics testing, Bill and I talked about having another child. We had never decided on how many children we intended to have and in the past finances had been a major factor. It had been a big decision for us to try for Amberlie but this time the decision seemed easy. We both felt an overwhelming desire to have another baby. Part of me wanted to prove that Amberlie's condition was a blip but I felt deep down that another baby was the right choice and was meant to be … and that it would be a boy.

We, of course, discussed the possibility that it could be another lissencephaly baby and what we would do if that was so. I had never been a great advocate of abortion for abortion's sake but did see the case for termination if there were problems. Whilst I could always reason anything, I also knew myself well enough that regardless of whatever was found, the question of whether I would actually go through with an abortion was another thing.

It was virtually impossible to diagnose lissencephaly through ultrasound scans and if it wasn't genetic, a sample of the baby's fluid (amniocentesis) wouldn't prove anything either. With a 7% risk factor, I reckoned it was worth it. I didn't feel in the least bit worried.

The only other factor Bill was concerned about was my blood pressure, which had been awfully high last time. I wasn't worried about that either. I was somewhat concerned about making sure Ray and Clare got the time and attention they were entitled to and resolved to make sure they did. We talked about the prospect to them and they were all for it because they adored babies.

I knew I would be able to cope. I couldn't see that there would be much difference in looking after four children compared with looking after three, especially when I was used to being flat out anyway. I knew this was totally right for Amberlie as well. I conceived the first time we tried!

'I never get much practice do I?' Bill laughed.

I thought it best to register my pregnancy with our GP as soon as possible. I was glad I did because he said I needed to take folic acid for the first three months, as it had been proven to help the development of the central nervous system to prevent things like spina bifida.

I think he was a bit surprised though, and immediately asked if I wanted to keep the baby.

'I do,' I said. I wasn't offended – maybe a little taken aback, but I understood where he was coming from. He said, 'I'm going to arrange for you to go to King's College Hospital in London to see a specialist professor at the Harris Birthright Research Centre. They will do an early scan of the baby at about ten weeks' gestation. There is a sac at the base of the neck which should fall within certain measurements. This will help to check if the baby is OK. You are thirty-four years old now Sandra, and because of your age there is an increased risk of having a baby with Down's syndrome. King's College is the best place to go for prenatal scanning.'

Now I feel like an old lady, I thought!

'They will contact you with an appointment and when they've seen you, come back and let me know how you got on. OK, Sandra?'

'Err, yeah … thanks … see you!' I replied. Well I didn't expect that.

Having half-expected the need to qualify my sanity, I was surprised to be let off the hook by not having to explain myself at all. I was really going to be well looked after through this pregnancy. 'This is definitely meant to be!' I said out loud to no one and was as pleased as punch!

The appointment came through quickly and they requested that both Bill and I attend when the baby was at 9.5 weeks' gestation.

My aunties offered to look after Amberlie; they were less worried about looking after her now that her fits were controlled.

It was like a cattle market at the hospital. People were squashed either side of a narrow corridor with others clambering over pushchairs as they made their way to the end in answer to their names being called. There was no one there unaccompanied, and all the faces were taut with concern, all either holding hands or with interlocked arms. It was hot, sticky and stuffy and hardly anyone spoke. Some had needed to bring their children and their noise seemed horrendous. It was in stark contrast to the adult silence and I guessed the kids sensed the stress. Some of the women had appointments but most had been for their routine 20-week scan that day at other hospitals, and were told to immediately make their way to King's College for further diagnosis as there may be a problem.

The wait was like an eternity. The doctors were obviously completely out of synchronisation with their appointments, having had to fit in all the emergencies which arrived all the time. It was so stifling, claustrophobic and uncomfortable.

'Thank God we didn't have to bring the kids!' I said.

The scan showed everything to be OK and my risk factor was reduced to that of a 20-year-old. They asked me if I would like an amniocentesis test or a test that takes a small sample of tissue from the cervix to test for genetic problems. I knew both tests ran the risk of miscarriage, especially the second one, and I refused on both counts. They were a little surprised but I said the result from the sac at the base of the neck was encouraging and I wasn't about to risk it when there was only a 7% risk of recurrence of the lissencephaly.

The professor came in to meet us and I explained my decision. He understood and suggested we attend for ultrasound scans at various intervals so they could keep an eye on how the baby's brain was developing. He explained that their scanners were the best in the world and sometimes instances of lissencephaly could be detected, especially the more severe. That sounded more reasonable to me and we went home with an appointment for a 19-week scan.

12

Some days Amberlie was very drowsy, so I guessed that there must be a few fits happening. I used to ponder whether her medication masked rather than stopped all her seizures.

We noticed that her right side seemed less responsive than her left, and she generally did everything on the left first and the right caught up later. There were also days when she found it very hard to concentrate and stay interested in any activity. It was difficult to tell if this was down to seizures or the onset of illness. It was always a warning, though. After a long session in physio one day, I noticed that Amberlie seemed more tired and uninterested than usual. She'd had a slight cold that seemed to be worsening, and by Friday her chest sounded awful. I took her straight to the doctor's and he gave her antibiotics.

I had become a little concerned about the amount of activity in Amberlie's eyes. Sometimes they turned deep into the corners and shook like a jelly. She had also started to cross them and leave them crossed, even to the point that one eye would move left then the other would follow seconds later, or one would move and the other would not. I used to go quite giddy watching her, but it must have been far worse for her … or maybe she wasn't aware.

I told Dr Ramsay about it and she asked me to bring Amberlie to see her. Although she knew of children having eye shakes before, she didn't know what was causing Amberlie's. She said it could be an eye problem as quite a lot of handicapped children have difficulty seeing and need glasses, and thought it worth referring her to the eye clinic. I wasn't convinced this was the answer to the activity but I could see that it was worth the investigation as I had been a little worried about her short-range vision anyway, because she didn't seem to take much notice of things that were placed right in front of her. I knew Dr Ramsay was concerned about Amberlie's general health and would rule everything else out before having to increase Amberlie's medication. It was also possible that she was just in an unsettled phase that would sort itself out naturally, making any increase unnecessary and difficult to withdraw.

Amberlie was always weighed before each hospital appointment to check she was thriving and still within her medicine dosage range for her weight. She was 10kg and doing well. Dr Ramsay still wanted to persist with reducing the clonazepam as it was probably ineffective now; her aim was to have her on the least amount of medicine possible … just above fit point. We informed Dr Ramsay of Amberlie's chromosome and DNA results and she was very pleased for us. Amberlie's Disability Living Allowance was also due for renewal and she signed the forms, anxious that Amberlie should get all she was entitled to.

A few days later, following the reduction in medicine, Amberlie's eyes were rolling more than ever. I hoped this was just a temporary reaction and that things would settle down, but after a couple of days her arms started to raise and occasionally her legs. I had no idea how quickly the eye appointment would come through and I worried about things deteriorating in the meantime, so I contacted Dr Ramsay and the clonazepam was put up again to its previous level. A week later, with things still worsening, I rang her again and this time she increased Amberlie's vigabatrin by 100% so that she had one tablet in the morning and one in the evening. This stopped her raising her limbs but the activity in her eyes persisted, although not as often.

The stress of Amberlie's teething was probably responsible for restarting the fits, which had obviously initially presented as activity in her eyes. Getting her upper canine teeth had been particularly bad for her and the more she jumped, winced and rubbed her mouth, the more her eyes moved. She also seemed to be absent at these times. I think the reduction in her medicine was at the wrong time and opened the gates for the fits to come through. The situation could then not be reversed, so the vigabatrin had to be put up.

After I mumbled my thoughts within earshot, it was pointed out to me that it was likely that the fits would have resurfaced at some stage anyway as the drug had been ineffective for a while.

I knew that. It was just hard to take. Dr Ramsay was doing her best for Amberlie – trying to keep her awake and alive so that she could have a chance to develop. All that the seizures had needed to recur was the trigger. I knew the deal and the risks but there had to be a happy medium somewhere because she wouldn't stand a chance of developing if the seizures ruled.

Amberlie's original and natural alertness had been reinstated in the first place not by reducing medicines but by changing the type. Realistically, Amberlie needed her medicines and would always need them and now things had been triggered out of hand again and double the original dose was needed to regain control of her seizures.

The other disturbing part of the situation was that we had become very used to Amberlie having lots of good times and had enjoyed seeing her develop and have fun. Things had been nice and relaxed and we had all adapted well to the changes. It was quite a shock to realize that we were tinkering so close to the borderline between lots of good times and the really bad ones.

The corner seat was proving to be a real asset to Amberlie's physical development and her muscle tone was now very good. Her torso was more reflexive and she could balance herself steadily in the sitting position. Her legs were well toned and she kicked them alternately and so energetically for such long periods it was a wonder they didn't ache! They were strong and straight and the push she had in them was brilliant.

Amberlie had got into what she thought was the hilarious habit of kicking down stacked displays in shops! Her face lit up with mischievous excitement when she tenaciously spotted a beautifully arranged tower of items and aimed her legs ready to kick it! The instant it all crashed to the floor, she pulled a straight 'who did that?' face with her mouth formed into an 'o' and then burst out laughing! I couldn't help but grin tongue-in-cheek along with her – after all, it was an intended act! The shop assistants would always tell me, 'Not to worry dear, I'll do it.' And I would smile to myself and whisper in Amberlie's ear, 'What a clever girl!' It was good to see her being naughty.

Dr Ramsay was always delighted to hear about Amberlie's physical achievements but seemed unconvinced when we told her that Amberlie kicked her legs alternately. She explained that because of her seizures, Amberlie was more likely to just throw them down stiffly and straight, and together all the time, and of course Amberlie would never perform to order. It was so difficult when we only had 30-minute appointments every two to three months and of course that was just the system - but if Dr Ramsay didn't see any evidence, then what proof did I have? If Amberlie did perform, the doctor was over the moon and excited by the progress! I often wished I had a video camera so that I could have shown her much more. Always, always was Dr Ramsay on Amberlie's side, especially if I made a negative statement, when she would say, 'Of course some of the things Amberlie will do will be normal. We must never underestimate the brain.'

And when I was being over positive she would remind me not to expect too much!

The physio decided that it might now be worth trying a standing frame so that some weight could be put through Amberlie's hips to stop them dislocating in the future and to avoid other possible problems developing over time. Amberlie hated it and I was appalled by it. We were given an old, decrepit wooden contraption that looked as if it had come out of the Dark Ages. It had a couple of snagged black plastic cushion pads attached to it and two Velcro and buckle straps which were well worn. It certainly looked more like a torture frame than a physiotherapy aid.

Amberlie was rigidly strapped into it so that her feet were accurately supported and positioned on the pedestal. Carol had made her some plaster soles in the shape of her feet for her to stand on and these were strapped onto her feet and placed inside her socks. I wasn't convinced this was going to be a good idea as Amberlie immediately started to push hard against the straps to try to release them.

I begrudgingly loaded it into the car and took it home. I thought I should give it a go and after much perseverance over several days and the fluke positioning of the frame in front of the television, the distraction of Wimbledon tennis (she loved the colour green) made her forget where she was and we got her to spend 10-15 minutes per day in it. It seemed to have the right effect and I could see her pushing down on her legs and straightening them.

Amberlie's body strength was growing immensely and, put together with the push she now had in her legs, it was quite incredible. Unfortunately, one day while I was sitting beside her, while she was in the standing frame, there was an enormous ripping sound and before I realised what was happening she had fallen to the floor in a heap. Luckily she was fine, just a little confused as to why she was on the floor! The Velcro straps were no longer strong enough to hold her so I told Carol that she wouldn't be going in it again and she promised to organise a replacement as soon as she could. Dr Ramsay was concerned and asked whether I would sue! Seeing that she was serious I said, 'I guess it was lucky that Amberlie wasn't hurt,' and I smiled at her.

One morning Amberlie spotted her set of wooden peg men for the first time. They stood with their coloured heads sticking out of a wooden block to one side of her and she knocked them over. Being unsure whether or not this was a deliberate act, I put the block back. She kept knocking them down. I wondered if she was actually trying to grab hold of the men so I stuck the block to the table to see. She started to hover her hand over them and then let it fall hitting them on their heads so they popped out of the block! She was delighted! I was jumping up and down because Amberlie was learning that she could cause something to happen. She smiled broadly as I clapped my hands and said, 'What a clever girl … what a smart baby!'

Well, it didn't stop there – my girl was on a roll! I sat totally amazed as I watched her control the speed of her left hand as she started to move it towards her chosen peg man, hover over it and slowly lower it, close her fingers round it and then pick him up! Well, I almost had a party! The excitement was too much and I jumped around the room shouting, 'Yes! Yes! Yes!'

Two days later she even managed to pick it up *and* put it in her mouth! I was so chuffed, I grabbed and hugged her and we danced around the room as she chuckled and laughed. We were both thrilled to bits!

When Amberlie achieved something, it was better than winning the lottery! I used to spend ages showing her how to do things, stage by stage, never really getting anywhere much. Then all of a sudden the penny would drop and it would happen and the smile on her face was worth everything and more! The lesson was to never give up and I started to appreciate what an incredible thing the brain is – so much more complex than I could ever have imagined, it capabilities infinite – even when it is malformed.

My mind often used to wander off laterally in all directions as I pondered life and what knowledge was already present in an egg or a sperm or learned in the womb. Whether much was down to instinct, or maybe even from past lives. It was incredible that despite the severity of the malformation of Amberlie's brain, she knew things. There was a light on inside her head burning very brightly, beaming out love and endearment, showing us that she could do things, albeit small, and that she was aware of us and her surroundings; and was very much a person with, and entitled to, a life.

Bill and I had attended King's College for the next baby scan and were told everything so far was fine. The scan picture was so clear, the detail astonishing, and I asked if I'd seen what I thought I had, and they laughed and confirmed that indeed it was a little boy!

Dr Ramsay was thrilled with Amberlie's progress, especially as the return of the fits could well have slowed her down. She was still having one or two five-second episodes but I didn't feel these warranted any further adjustment medicinally. I didn't want her drowsy again. After much deliberation we eventually agreed (sigh) to try to reduce the clonazepam again. Amberlie was obviously very addicted to it and the plan was now to reduce it in tiny, tiny stages over a long period so that she would not miss it.

Before we had a chance to begin, Amberlie became ill with a virus and this, coupled with her teething, lurched her into another bad time. There was no way I was going to attempt any reduction while this was going on.

Amberlie spent three days and nights crying solidly and then developed a rash all down her body. Luckily it disappeared as quickly as it came and she seemed to perk up. We gave her a lovely warm bath and she drank a full bottle of milk in a leisurely way. We started to relax, thinking the worst was over, but she suddenly deteriorated and sank into the dire throes of a chest infection. We called the doctor out and he gave her antibiotics. Amberlie's continual crying resumed and she locked into her ever-strengthening extension position, stretched out to peak point backwards and totally rigid. She wanted to be carried, so that was what we had to do. After a couple of days she improved but then relapsed, so we went back to the doctor's. The doctor said the chest infection was still there and it looked as though the antibiotics hadn't worked, so she was given another type.

Four days later, Amberlie was a different child, she was bright and breezy and everything was making her laugh. She giggled at all her toys as if she had never seen them before and I wondered whether there was something in the antibiotic spurring her on in an odd way. Certainly some of it was a little disconcerting, even sinister, but we couldn't help but join in with her infectious laughter. Some of it was genuine though, because she laughed at things that had always made her laugh, so there was obviously some control somewhere.

As Amberlie was much better and the weather gorgeous, we decided that we could all do with a bit of fun so we took a day trip to the Isle of Wight. She cooed and laughed at the swaying trees all day. She always adored car journeys, sitting next to Ray and Clare listening to their chatter and watching the world pass by. On the ferry she dozed off, soothed by its lilt on the waves. We were often out very late and Amberlie never slept in case she missed something, unlike Ray and Clare, who soon snuggled up to sleep. At night she was amused by the street lamps and bright headlights that caught her eyes as they zoomed past, making her chuckle softly to herself. The faster her dad drove, day or night, the more she liked it. She had such a charming aura about her, a mix of sheer happiness with a hint of wild child, and she made us fall in love with her more and more every day.

The last remnants of the chest infection finally went away and things returned to normal … except at night! This illness had gone on long enough to entirely mess up her routine and she hated being put to bed.

Amberlie's evening energy levels were amazingly high and her bedtimes ranged from around 10 p.m. to whenever. Giving her a warm, milky drink around 11 p.m. relaxed her but didn't often persuade her to sleep! If (and it was a big if) Bill and I managed to get her to sleep before we went to bed, and she was put between us, she would generally have a peaceful night; but if she was put in her own bed she would wake, or if she was put in ours while still awake, she would cry and cry for hours. Once this happened she would be totally inconsolable and nothing we tried would work. Nothing was guaranteed and it became a gamble every night to find some way of getting some sleep. When the screaming started Bill and I took it in turns to walk the house, walk the garden, cuddle her, feed her, and change her. Nothing would work and when everything else failed, we used to sit her in her chair with her toys and turn on the TV or radio, hoping that a change of noise or atmosphere would work, and tell her to get on with it! Eventually she would start to get drowsy and her eyes heavy, and we would be totally soul destroyed to notice the dawn light peering through the windows. It was just before 6 a.m. every time and we had to be up again at 7 a.m. to get the kids to school!

We couldn't leave her to sleep uncomfortably in her chair so we placed pillows and cushions beside it and slid her out slowly and carefully onto them and covered her with blankets. We found that if we took her up to bed, the minute her head touched the pillow she would be off again! We became totally paranoid about moving her at all once her eyes were closed! One of us always stayed with her and dozed on the sofa until it was time to get up.

I felt that as miserable and trying this situation was, somewhere along the line it was progress. After all, most children go through a stage of complaining when they are put to bed, not as extreme as this, but then we couldn't make Amberlie understand that there was a difference between night and day.

Bill and I then gave up trying to put her to bed and let her play and do whatever she wanted, but found it didn't make any difference to the crying. After a short while she would start and there would be no stopping her – it seemed that going to bed was irrelevant to the upset. We didn't have clue what was causing it so we just had to go with the flow.

Three months passed and Amberlie was bearing the situation well, catching up on her sleep with small naps during the day. I didn't have the heart or energy to keep her awake; if she couldn't sleep when she wanted to she got very upset, so it wasn't worth it – I couldn't bear any more crying. She used to stay alert if we were out, so in an attempt to put her into a routine, I tried walking the streets, some days for hours, but however long we were out, I found the instant we were back indoors she would fall asleep and sleep longer than usual. Either way I couldn't win. There was no point in continually upsetting her, and through fear of bringing on any seizures, I opted for the quiet life and took any peace while I had it.

Bill and I were both shattered. I was now four months' pregnant, dog tired, and at the end of my tether. We were snapping at each other and snapping at the kids. He still of course had to go to work and there was never any time for either of us to rest. I just did not know what to do about the whole vicious circle.

One night after a dreadful day generally, I finally lost my rag. It had been my turn to do the night shift and I had decided to risk putting Amberlie, who was already fast asleep, into her bed. As soon as I turned my back she let out her usual whinge. I screamed, 'You have to bloody well sort this out, Amberlie, because I can't take it anymore! You want to shout and scream and act like a normal child …' and I stopped dead in my tracks.

Bill shot up in bed in a panic, 'Wassup? Wassamatter? Is she OK?'

'That's it!' I shouted, realising what I had said. 'Right, Amberlie Murphy – if you want to behave normally, normal is what you're going to get!' She looked at me as if I had totally gone off my trolley. 'I'm going to lie beside you so you know I'm here and then you can cry till you bloody well get over it!'

Bill groaned and slumped back down on the bed.

Amberlie continued to complain for some time then slowly the tears stopped. She kept looking at me to see if I was going to pick her up. When she realised I wasn't going to (and believe me it was hard not to … with her big beautiful eyes she knew how to look irresistible), she threw a huge temper tantrum, banging and crashing her arms and legs on the bed – she was so red in the face, you could almost see smoke coming out of her ears! After a few more tears she went to sleep. I persisted over the next few nights and from then on she would just give a small moan and a whinge when I laid her down – just to make the point – then drop off to sleep and go through most of the night. However, she had decided that there was no way she was ever going to go to bed before 1 a.m.!

To see her sleeping so soundly, looking so innocent and beautiful, I instantly forgave her all the last few months of grief and trauma. I also felt terribly guilty that I had shouted and been mean to her.

'I'm so sorry, Ambams,' I whispered, 'Mummy is just so tired.' And the tears burned my eyes.

It was as if a shadow had lifted. Amberlie's interest in everything re-ignited and she listened intently when she was spoken to, seeming to understand some of what was said. She was more aware of her surroundings and the people around her. Most noticeable was her reaction to strangers or people she didn't recognise or see very often, when she would look at me as if to say, 'Are they all right?' Is it OK for them to talk to me?'

Amberlie was making strides of progress in her play and she could pick things up better, hold things longer and shake and bang a toy to cause lots of noise; she could even lift her whole driving activity centre off the desk. The muscle tone in her trunk had come along so much that she could now right herself if she started to topple, and her head control was much better, especially when she was on her tummy on the floor, when she held it beautifully upright. The push in her arms and legs was still improving all the time but she showed considerable reluctance to put her arms onto the floor, preferring to keep them in at her chest. Playing games such as swinging her through the air and pretending to let her fall helped her most by stimulating her reflexes, and it was also great fun for her. Amberlie was also rolling from her tummy onto her back and vice versa, as well as moving slowly around the room. She managed this by moving her head in the direction she wanted to go and somehow the rest of her followed – much like a caterpillar movement! Occasionally, she managed to bring her knees underneath her to form the back end of a crawl position, but her arms were still not strong enough to support her body at the front. We hoped that she would adopt the 'commando' form of crawling to help her get around.

This had all opened up different perspectives for Amberlie and she was delighted to explore the room freely without my help as well as enjoying the floor space with Ray, Clare and their toys. If she got stuck up against the furniture and couldn't manoeuvre out she would shout to let us know.

We had bought a wobble man dressed in brightly coloured clothes, and when he was knocked he jingled. Amberlie liked him and often sat touching and stroking his coat softly, slowly drawing him closer to her so that she could cuddle him and rub her face on him. She moved on from him to find that exploring our faces was fun, especially if we mouthed her fingers when she put them over our lips. Bill and I were over the moon as she was identifying the connection between feeling, thinking and responding.

Her teeth were still giving her gyp, and at one time we had five or six teeth breaking through at once. On the bad days Amberlie slept a lot, which was her way of coping with the pain. We still had the occasional bad night and still could never get her to bed earlier than midnight/1 a.m. Still, five or six hours' sleep was better than none at all!

As things were now reasonably settled, Dr Ramsay reminded us that it was time to give the clonazepam reduction a go.

Amberlie was now eating more solid foods in her diet and as a result constipation had set in. she started by eating pureed versions of whatever I had cooked but then began to refuse these in favour of cereals, fruit and dairy produce, so I couldn't understand why she was having a problem. Dr Ramsay explained that handicapped children are often constipated because when there is slowness in the brain there is slowness in the bowel and things don't go along quite as they should. She said it was one of those things that the medical world didn't really understand because there was no scientific evidence, but medicines could also play a part. The doctor recommended that Amberlie take a daily mild laxative. I hated the thought of yet another medicine but she assured me that there really wasn't anything in Lactulose to harm her, and all it would do was oil her insides to help her to pass her stools. It did help a little but it didn't make her any the more regular, and didn't stop it hurting her when it finally happened. She only went to the loo every three days or so and those days were murder, with crying and screaming until it was over. Dr Ramsay suggested I try pureed prunes, which also didn't work ... and she hated them!

The local surgery kept reminding me that Amberlie hadn't been given her MMR (measles, mumps and rubella) vaccination. I hadn't done anything about it because she had either been ill or edgy and it seemed a real shame to bring her down again when she was OK. I dreaded her having it as Ray and Clare had reacted badly to theirs and I knew Amberlie would do the same. However, I didn't want Amberlie to have measles or mumps either. She was now 17 months old and I braved the event. As expected, she developed a temperature and was as miserable as sin. It was vital to control her temperature quickly because that could influence her fit control, although she had never reacted febrilely (from fever). The next fortnight was awful and culminated in a rotten cold with conjunctivitis.

As usual, Amberlie's routine and feeding were disrupted. She would try hard to drink her bottles with a bunged-up nose, spluttering and coughing, trying hard to get a decent drink. We tried a baby beaker but the liquid ran out too fast for her to cope with swallowing, so we just persisted with the bottle no matter how long it took.

It was time for our final baby scan at King's College. The professor pushed the wand so deep into my stomach I thought I would burst! He looked at the scanner, squeezed my hand tightly and said, 'Go home Sandra! This baby is fine … I'm not worried about him at all!'

'Wow! Thank you, thank you, thank you!' I cried.

Bill and I were so relieved and excited – now we could get on and look forward to our new baby without reservation! I had seen so much of him on the scanner – even down to the little tooth buds in his mouth – and I couldn't wait to see him for real!

Ben arrived when Amberlie was 21 months old and he proved to be quite a stimulant for her. She really didn't know quite what to make of him or his noise. She would look at him for ages but the minute he opened his mouth and cried, her face would screw up and she would go to pieces crying as well. I used to have one in each arm screaming in unison. Unfortunately Ben had an awfully loud cry and I could see why it jangled Amberlie's nerves every time, so I made sure I was ready and armed for feeding before he had the chance to moan. Luckily, he only fed once in the night and did not disturb Amberlie at all. I was conscious that this part could have shattered her nightly routine and we could have reverted to our previous night-time shenanigans.

As the weeks went by Amberlie grew used to him but would give out a few 'put out' signs such as temper tantrums or some real dirty looks. I don't think it was jealousy, rather her reaction and objection to all the new noise and hustle in the house. We were all adapting to a new inmate! She was also now well into the 'terrible twos', which could also have inspired her changeable emotions.

When Ben became a bit more interesting and started to move around, Amberlie found him totally fascinating to watch and never took her eyes off him! I never put his toys away, always leaving them at one end of the room, and in the evenings when Ben had gone to bed, Amberlie used to move herself across the floor to examine what he had played with that day. She knew which ones to look for and would giggle when she got them. It was wonderful to watch her touch and stroke them.

Clare and Ray were pleased to have a new baby brother. Clare was a real mother hen and Ray smiled and stroked Ben's head, just like he did with Amberlie. It was as if they were so precious they could only be touched gently. It was interesting to note Ray and Clare's idea of fairness – if they spoke to one of the babies, they always made sure they acknowledged the other.

To make it easy to take Ben and Amberlie out together we bought a tandem-type double pushchair and sat Amberlie in the front while Ben lay in the rear happily booting the back of her seat. She didn't mind at all – in fact she was quite amused and just as excited about going out as usual. When Bill and I were both around they were put into separate buggies.

Although it was tremendously hard work at times dealing with two babies plus Ray and Clare, it was great feeling 'normal' again. Ben washed away the awful 'unclean' feeling that I had been left with since visiting the geneticist. I had also been plagued with various minor ailments since Amberlie's birth, in the form of a persistently recurring dark green discharge necessitating strong antibiotics, plus a number of abnormal cervical smear tests that had continued through my pregnancy. When Ben was born all these things miraculously cleared up and my smear tests reverted to normal. It was all very strange. I had obviously been plagued by some sort of virus or infection in my reproductive system for a long time and couldn't dismiss the possibility or probability that it may have had something to do with whatever caused so much damage to Amberlie. I mentioned it to my doctor and he pondered the thought. All in all Ben had made me feel good again and was proving to be an absolute godsend for Amberlie, in fact for the whole family. He was making Amberlie think and do things we would not have expected and although he sometimes spurred a negative response from her, it was all stimulation – and that had to be a good thing. Ben had brought a lot of happiness back into our house.

I never really spent too much time thinking about the ins and outs of coping with another child and integrating him in a mostly chaotic world. It was easy really – he just had to accept it! He was a breath of fresh air and a very happy little boy. The only thing it brought home to us, sadly, was just how very much Amberlie was disabled and how much she had been robbed of a normal life. And that pain was horrendous. I felt so bad for Amberlie – she was so beautiful, how could it be that her brain wasn't right? Why couldn't she do all that Ben did already? He did it so naturally, without trying ... it just happened for him ... it had just happened for Ray and Clare ... It made me feel bitter and twisted and question again and again why it had happened. Why her? Why us? Why our family? Not that I would wish it on anyone else. Other people had four children and they were all OK. Some people smoked and drank throughout their pregnancies or worse. I had tried hard, made an effort to do the right things and take care of our growing baby. It wasn't fair!

I tried not to be too introverted about it because I knew it would eat me up, but when it hit, it hit hard and when I felt low I would dwell on all the philosophical questions that couldn't be answered:

Was this meant to be – was it fated?

What had we done so wrong that this had to happen?

And if we had done wrong, why should our child suffer?

What kind of God allows children to suffer? Etcetera, etcetera.

More and more I doubted my religion. I would analyse it and analyse it over and over again and each time it made less and less sense, and for every point raised, I had a good argument. I couldn't take away my belief that there was a God but I couldn't give him any credit either. It was more sensible to me that we were all a product of nature, a life form that gives birth and dies, and that problems happened when nature is interfered with, such as infections or pollution in the environment or indeed through inflicted abuse of some kind (the geneticist said Amberlie's condition could have been the result of something environmental). Something has to be responsible for Amberlie's condition. There was always a reason or cause but not always an answer. It was all down to us, the human race. The successes, the failures and the ability to live longer, and controversially better, was down to our science, our reason and our logic; a result of evolution – powerful innovative brains ... not a greater being. I certainly had to thank science for saving my Amberlie. Left to God, she would have died at four and a half months old.

But ... I liked to think there was a God, someone I could look to for hope and support and who at the last minute could maybe work a miracle and help Amberlie. I sometimes used to see Amberlie as a 'gift from God' because it provided something special, maybe a hope that she was here for a reason, a purpose other than her whole existence being possibly futile. I had been brought up to believe in God and now there were too many valid, scientific, logical reasons for doubting it all. Plus I was bloody angry with him.

I was also conscious that I might just be feeling sorry for myself and was looking for an easy and convenient someone or thing to blame. I was searching for a reason. I wanted a reason why my Amberlie was disabled, and the likelihood was that no one, not even science, was ever going to provide one, so under that premise God had to be a possible cause. What was his agenda?

I had a lot to be thankful for, I had four beautiful children and a loving caring husband, and I would much rather have Amberlie as she was than not at all. If God was the all-powerful then where was Amberlie's miracle? I wanted one for her. Maybe she already was ... my little miracle.

My mind swung this way and that, convincing myself then unconvincing myself. I had to keep my mind open. I had to preserve my sanity for everyone's sake. Once I had managed to file it all away in my brain and put it aside, I vowed never to compare Ben and Amberlie again and to cherish and nurture their individual potentials whatever they might be.

Keeping Amberlie well and free from colds seemed to be the biggest battle of all and I was very anxious about her lying on her back too much in case she developed another chest infection. She was not an unhealthy baby, her immunity was just so low, and of course, we did have two other children unavoidably bringing in germs from school.

Amberlie wouldn't go in her standing frame or sit for too long when she wasn't well, and sometimes I worried that her development would lapse because of the frequent colds, but there was no point in forcing her. If she was not well then it was perfectly understandable that she just wanted to be left to rest.

I did have a panic one morning when I changed her nappy. There protruding from her groin, was a lump about half an inch in size.

'Oh my God! Please not cancer as well … not on top of everything else!'

My philosophy with Amberlie was to immediately check out anything unusual – after all she couldn't tell me if something was bothering her. I couldn't bear the worry … it made me feel like I was living on a knife-edge. I rushed to the phone, sweating buckets, with my heart racing, and arranged for the doctor to see her straight away.

He assured me there was nothing to worry about – it was just a gland that was likely to be down to the MMR vaccination. I breathed a sigh of relief and thought, *Another grey hair on its way*!

Along with Amberlie's newly found mobility came more determination and a constant reluctance to be in her new standing frame. She so loathed being restricted in the straps and forcibly leant in all directions pushing and shoving to escape. When that didn't work her temper flared and she would go ballistic. This also happened when she was strapped into her chair. She pushed and flexed her body, thrusting the table away until she was released. If she couldn't do what she wanted then there would be hell!

When Amberlie sat on my lap she fidgeted and bounced up and down trying to get onto the floor to discover something she had spotted across the room. Freedom was what she wanted and she would not settle for anything less. Bless her! Never ever was she frustrated on the floor where she was at liberty and totally independent. I believe this was a real key factor in all the progress she made.

Mostly she steered herself towards the windows where many hours were spent gazing up at the sky and talking to the treetops swaying in the breeze. She also studied the doorway. I suspected she was working out how to get to it and escape into the hall!

I would never knock it but sometimes Amberlie's mobility did cause a few problems. Several times she managed to roll off the bed or I could be out of the room and walk in to find her no longer sleeping on the sofa but happily cooing on the floor, despite having a small bed guard in place! She had learned to manoeuvre herself so well that she always found the gap! She was quite an escapologist. I had to pile cushions and pillows all over the place to stop her from hurting herself, and she only moaned if she got herself stuck in an awkward position! Generally she seemed physically stronger and more supple as a result of all the movement she gained on the floor.

All this development obviously increased her brain activity, and this was a double-edged sword in itself. Her achievements were brilliant but following the latest reduction in her clonazepam she had become a little jumpy, and I hoped she wasn't going to suffer with more seizures as a result of her progress.

A severe dose of tonsillitis brought her down for a while. She needed a ten-day course of penicillin, and the glands on her neck stood out on either side like golf balls for ages. She bounced back well after she gave the bug to Ben!

Amberlie's teeth were still determining her moods. Four more had recently erupted; the bottom ones weren't too bad but the uppers were a real bugger and she found them unbearable. They took forever to break the gum and she cried for days before they did. The paracetamol didn't seem to help although she was having it every four hours and herbal teething powders in between. She wouldn't eat, drink, sit down lie down, or be carried, and was totally inconsolable. She tried so hard to get her fist into her mouth for relief with no success and I would pop my fingers in to give her something to bite on, but love her, she didn't know how to bite so I gently rubbed her gums, which seemed to help. Teething just overtook her life; consumed by pain, she became obsessed and I was unable to provide a distraction. She didn't understand what all this was all about and I wished I could just put a wrench in there and pull them all through for her. I often felt so inadequate not being able to help her beyond painkillers and the usually unwanted cuddles.

If she wasn't crying there was an awful, persistent, underlying moan, so monotonous and consistent in pitch that it settled long and deep into my head, to the point that I could still hear it even when she was quiet and the worst over. Sometimes those days would continue one after the other and as much as I felt sorry for her, the noise just drove me mad. I often had to walk up the garden and spend five minutes chilling out, before going back and being with her.

As time went on, I realised that when I left her crying for a while and she couldn't see me, the noise would lessen and soon stop. I used to peep in through the window to see what she was doing and she would be cooing, smiling or playing with a toy that had been left on the floor. Obviously much of the drama was directed at me and must have been some sort of attention seeking, but for what reason I am not sure, because whatever I did didn't soothe her in the least – pretty clever really … and a pretty normal toddler pastime of playing on Mum's nerves. I used to forget that she could have 'normal' attributes too!

I found out from the Lissencephaly Society that Amberlie was lucky to have teeth, as many don't or only get one or two. Having teeth helps the jaw and face to develop properly. Whilst appreciating the benefit, it really did seem so futile, for the likelihood of them ever being used was remote and it was an awful lot of grief for her to have to go through. I crossed my fingers that she wouldn't get any more.

Of course, there was never any opportunity to rest on our laurels where her seizures were concerned. All this upset around her teeth had caused some strange episodes where she laughed wholeheartedly for no reason and then silenced instantly, leaving her totally spaced out with staring eyes. This had meant another increase in her medicine. I hated what her teeth were doing to her. Amberlie just didn't seem to be able to win whatever happened. She had made so much headway lately and it was either this or illness that knocked her back every time. It was so unfair.

Now Amberlie could use both her arms equally, the physio ordered her some new tougher boned gaiters to help her improve the weight tolerance through them. If the mood was right she supported herself in the crawl position for a while, but not for long if they were removed. To be able to bear weight in her arms would encourage her falling reflex to come into play, meaning that if she felt she was going to topple when sitting on the floor, her arms would automatically reach for the floor to stop the coming fall. The hope was to have her sitting totally unaided in the not-too-distant future.

13

Now Amberlie was approaching two and a half years old, her education was the main topic of discussion at the next appointment with Dr Ramsay. The doctor explained that it was usual for children with special needs to start school at around that age, just for a few hours or a couple of days a week. Amberlie would then have her physio and portage at school, and she felt it would be good for her generally.

Having had plenty of time to ponder the content of Amberlie's future, I had long ago decided that she would not go to school and would remain with me twenty-four hours a day, seven days a week … within reason. Knowing her lifespan was to be short, I wanted to spend every possible moment with her. I also knew full well that the school could not guarantee, or even offer, one-to-one care, and not always the same person if they did. Amberlie needed a lot of watching and observing and sometimes medical care. They did not know my daughter. They did not know her moods or how to cope with her 'crying' days and wouldn't learn either in a few hours a day or twice a week. Her fits were sometimes so small and quick that someone else might not even notice there had been one. Sometimes there were successions of them, still slight but nevertheless important, and the successions were not consistent in their guise.

They did not know how to deal properly with a lissencephaly child because it was such a rare condition and varied from child to child with different degrees of severity. They did not know my lissencephaly child.

The thought of Amberlie being sat in a corner left in her own world, unable to communicate or do much while staff dealt with other more able children, was unbearable. They did not know her feeding habits that often varied according to what her day entailed. She would be expected to eat when everyone else did and go to the toilet at certain times (even though she wore nappies). I had heard stories that in some schools the children were expected to fill their nappies at certain times and if they did it in between times they were left unchanged. I doubt there was any truth in it, but whatever the case, it wasn't going to happen to my little girl. Amberlie was still very much an infant in her day-to-day care; nothing had changed in that way since she was a baby and it was unlikely to.

I remembered the doctors at Great Ormond Street had told us that her progress would probably not exceed the capabilities of a five-month-old baby, and we had come a long way in some areas … but not enough to warrant an 'education'. To some extent we had already started to go round in circles with a few of her activities, teaching her the same things over and over again without much change. I felt she was already leveling out and reaching her optimum abilities.

Anyway, what the hell could they teach her that I couldn't? I already did her physio under the guidance of her new therapist, and her portage with or without help. After all, I had been trained to do it every day to help her develop physically and mentally.

I took her out every day in the fresh air, around the shops, to the park, to all the places she loved. She was meeting all sorts of people who talked to her and played with her, and she spent time at the local playschool, where I was chairman, several times a week. She met the kids from school every day, met other children, all of whom stimulated her brain and excited her, and her siblings constantly sought her attention and amused her no end.

To me, being part of normal society was best for Amberlie. She adored music, especially heavy metal, rock and opera, and had all the lighting and sensory equipment at home that she enjoyed. Above all, she was loved to bits and we wanted her to have and experience all the things a child should and more. It was vital to provide her with every opportunity to do the things she liked. Let's face it – she was never going to do GCSE's!

Another downside of Amberlie going to school was the prospect of more germs. The last thing she needed was a room full of snotty noses breeding hybrid bugs all over the place. This would hinder her progress no end. What mattered to me was Amberlie's happiness; and health wise, I would do everything to protect her.

Dr Ramsay went onto say that Amberlie should also be 'Statemented' to assess her needs. I hadn't heard of this (and made a mental note to find out about it), but it sounded very official so I refused it and stated my case. Dr Ramsay wasn't pleased and said we would talk again another time.

I thought, *Mmmm, I'm not going to change my mind – you're on a loser Doc!* I was very agitated that the situation wasn't going to go away and I couldn't get it out of my mind. I wasn't totally sure of my grounds legally and couldn't stand the thought that I might be forced to comply. I rested on the fact that I knew parents could educate their children at home provided they could prove they could equal or better the education provided by the school. I already knew that given Amberlie's condition, I was doing more for her than any school could.

14

We had been asked to attend at the eye department at 9.00 a.m. along with what could only have been the rest of the country. We waited for over an hour before a nurse came to put some drops in Amberlie's eyes to dilate her pupils, only explaining what she was doing after I asked. She said it would work in a while and they would call us.

Two hours later in a fairly empty department, with everyone else having gone, I started to get cross. Naturally Amberlie was getting agitated and hungry and I moaned to a passing nurse that a child of Amberlie's age should not be expected to wait three hours to see a doctor. About ten minutes later we were summoned.

The doctor explained that because Amberlie could not speak he would have to use circular lenses to determine her vision instead of being able to use the latest technology. Well, this doctor fiddled and faffed about for ages, swapping them around in his box and occasionally holding one up to her eyes. By now, of course, Amberlie had had enough and was getting upset. She began to fidget and wriggle and turn her head away when he approached, and would you believe it, this blasted doctor started to get cross!

'Oh well!' he said. 'What can I do? I am just going to have to make a guess at her vision because she just won't keep still.'

I scowled. I wasn't going to allow him to make this Amberlie's fault, so I reminded him that it was now well into lunch time and that she was very young and disabled, and had been waiting in his rotten department since just before nine that morning.

'Perhaps you should have a more child-friendly schedule?' I suggested.

Refusing to look at me and shrugging his shoulders, he continued, 'She is extremely long sighted and has small eyes. This can be quite usual in children but is probably due to her disability. There is also a slight squint but no need for any operation.'

I told him the squint was not always there and was seizure related, and only when she had a bad patch was it noticeable. As usual I was ignored but I suppose to be fair, he probably didn't understand. I think a wise doctor learns from his patients though.

Ten days later Amberlie had a cute pair of glasses with pink and green frames with curly ear bits so they wouldn't fall off while she played on the floor. She was to wear them every day. To help the squint (!), they covered up one of the lenses with a plaster. She didn't mind having them on at all and they opened up a whole new perspective for her.

Amberlie had developed a hand-mouth-distance-finder technique to work out how far an object was away from her hand, but now she could see more clearly, she wasn't using it so much. She also began to study faces and enjoyed watching her reflection in a mirror, albeit very shyly because she didn't recognise herself!

I loved putting her glasses on her after her wash in the mornings because it was so amazing to see how much her face lit up and eyes widened when they were in place. It was as if someone had suddenly turned on a switch!

The glasses also made Amberlie slightly more tolerant of the standing frame, and I thought that maybe she had felt slightly unbalanced because she had been unable to see properly, and that had caused an element of fear; or maybe it was just that the view was now more interesting. It was only for five minutes or so at a time but better than not at all. I knew deep down she hated the bloody thing and I guessed it wouldn't be any different when her brand new more upright one arrived; it would strap her in even more rigidly … a nightmare festering on the horizon.

Whilst I appreciated the need for these ghastly pieces of apparatus to form hip joints properly, together with the added bonus of allowing her insides occasional proper gravitation, if she objected to being in them then I didn't pursue it. I learned to my cost that to keep her there after she protested to the point of tears meant she would cry for the rest of the day. It was just not worth the grief. The best thing to do was to take her out and try again the next day.

The hospital had recently supplied her with an easy chair. I thought it might be a good thing as she enjoyed playing in her seat for ages and ages and a more comfortable higher chair might benefit her. It was a beauty: fully upholstered in bright blue and supportive as well. It had a detachable tray for feeding and playing and it also reclined so that if Amberlie fell asleep we could lay her back.

Amberlie had been very well despite some trauma with a tooth that had erupted so slowly it had reached only half way through in three months. The only real concern had been a rather worrying phase of not drinking. I assumed that if I managed to get the fluid into her mouth she would naturally swallow it … but not Amberlie. Refusal meant refusal, and she either spat it back or grinned at me while it dribbled out of her mouth and down her neck. She ate well so I resorted to lots of jars of baby fruit and desserts with lots of mashed, fresh soft fruit, which kept her from becoming dehydrated. I kept trying the milk and eventually she decided that maybe a small amount could be consumed with each meal and she gradually returned to normal. Once we had got over that, she then decided to refuse her food! It was just one battle after another with no indication of any trigger points that could be noted and avoided in the future. Perhaps she had just discovered that she could be stubborn and determined with whatever took her fancy. I found the best way of coping was to adjust to the changes as they occurred.

It was a real worry though, because at the back of my mind I knew that the feeding problems of lissencephaly children usually started between the ages of 18 months and 3 years. I hoped that our persistence would pay off, relying on the theory that if she did it once she could do it again. Learn then relearn as such, although I was aware that swallowing difficulties were often the result of seizure damage to the brain. I didn't want Amberlie to end up tube-fed if I could avoid it.

Luck was running at its usual low and my wish for Amberlie not to get any more teeth was unsurprisingly not granted. The last four were on their way, and what a flaming size they were too! They were already moving enough to send her into phases of absence and volatility and all I hoped for was that they made an unusually speedy appearance else we'd all be suicidal! Luckily the kids were on school holidays and that meant I didn't have to disturb her to take her out in the mornings so she could sleep to her heart's content. She was not going to appreciate early rising again!

Amberlie's spectacles (called 'bins' at home) initiated some television watching. I don't know whether she made much of it but she watched the vibrant colours and responded happily to the different sounds, especially the sudden loud ones from cartoons.

Now that her arms were fully relaxed she was able to straighten them to reach down to pick up her Skwish when she dropped it. Her travels round the front room had also speeded up and she steered herself accurately by moving her head in the direction she wanted to go. She actually managed to go backwards on her tummy on one occasion to avoid getting stuck and push herself up on all fours to get past her table. I was convinced her brain was more active than the doctors thought because here was evidence that she was thinking and moving appropriately to accomplish what she desired.

Even changing her nappy inspired her interest. She would run her hands down her body to feel the nappy and once the nappy was off, she felt again, learning the difference between nappy on and nappy off. The changing expressions on her face showed that she was taking the information in and filing it.

Bill and I found that Amberlie would quite happily stand supported by us up against the sofa and I guessed that was because she felt safe and got cuddled at the same time! She much preferred it to the standing frame and it gave her little feet a chance to spread properly and stopped her toes from curling under. Amberlie's left foot was slightly stiff and didn't bend to a full ninety degrees. She had not be able to fully relax it since it was overstretched in a physio session one day and she guarded it by keeping it tense. It had taken weeks to heal and she still winced and jumped a little during her exercises.

We took the kids to a theme park one day and saw a diving show that included a play about making a film. We managed to get front seats and Amberlie watched the goings-on intently, not missing a thing. When the time came for audience participation the noise was deafening and I thought, *Oh no, this is going to upset her!* But no, she absolutely adored it. Every loud roar, or bang reduced her to giggles! Oh, we needed a camcorder!

Amberlie had developed her cooing noises into a good communication skill, and although the content remained roughly the same, the pitch of the coos changed depending on whether they were requests, complaints or appreciation.

I was persuaded by a friend to take on a homeless kitten. Amberlie quite liked Lottie so long as she didn't attack her feet, and they often snuggled up together on Amberlie's pillows for a nap. She soon let the cat know when she'd had enough or didn't want her around by reaching out and swiping her away.

Amberlie was still drinking baby formula milk as she liked the sweet taste and it gave her extra vitamins, but I felt it was time to change it to a more satisfying nutritional formula now she had grown so much. The change didn't seem to bother her and though I thought it didn't taste too good, she surprisingly accepted it without complaint. After two weeks, however, a pink eczema-type rash appeared on her tummy. She wasn't ill and nothing else had changed so it had to be the milk, so I reverted to her old brand and the rash cleared up.

The improved tone in her body muscles had made Amberlie quite ticklish, and her massages were now sprinkled with little giggles. I didn't realise that muscles had to be toned for someone to be ticklish.

Amberlie had been enjoying her physio on a weekly basis with her new therapist called Eve, who was very gentle and soothed Amberlie with her natural and calm manner. As expected, the only thing she didn't appreciate very often was her new upright standing frame, which was such a huge monster the only place we could put it was in Ray's room. I apologised to him as it took up most of his floor space but he said he didn't mind. It was less restrictive that I first thought, relying less on straps and more on supportive cushions. The wood was light and the table was a bright sunshine yellow with red pads. I hoped having the table to play with her toys on would distract from the standing. Her favourite pastime at that moment was burying her hands in lots of beads and necklaces that I had put in the bottom of a large biscuit tin. She was fascinated by them and swirled her hands round for ages making wonderful noises.

The frame unfortunately didn't prove successful for long and once the novelty had worn off we were back to normal. I tried hard to provide a cabaret distraction system to keep Amberlie in there for a while but she used to look at me as if I was boringly mad and I knew I had lost the battle. As soon as she shouted I had her out of it like greased lightening before tears and distress commenced.

During physio one day, I asked Eve what she thought about me buying Amberlie a fibre-optic light, as I remembered my mum having one years ago and thought Amberlie might be amused by it. I had seen one advertised in a catalogue for the disabled. Eve said she thought it a great idea and told me that there was a locally based charity called Equipment for Disabled Children, who bought equipment and play items for special children that would enhance their lives.

'Oh I didn't mean for anyone else to pay for it,' I said.

'Don't be silly – that's what they're there for,' Eve replied. She explained that she could apply to them on Amberlie's behalf through the physiotherapy department. I was amazed. I had never heard of them and didn't realise there was such help available. After a few weeks we heard that Amberlie could have her light and we ordered it straight away.

Amberlie loved the moving lights and had lots of fun running her fingers and waving her hands through the soft, pretty strands. Occasionally, though, she grabbed and wrenched them out of the lamp but luckily they all came out in one clump and were easy to put back! A lot of the time she would just coo and watch the colours change. This generally made for a good ten minutes in her standing frame!

From there on it inspired us to look for other lighting and electronic toys. We found a large keyboard, which sang, made animal noises, lit up and played music and Amberlie would often accidentally rest on it causing it to start up! She was greatly amused by all this and soon learned that bashing her Skwish on them made a wonderful racket too!

At the next appointment with Dr Ramsay, Amberlie's 'education' was mentioned again as she was anxious to get things sorted out because Amberlie was now over two and a half. I had made some enquiries about my rights as a parent and was not for swaying. Dr Ramsay accepted my decision to keep Amberlie at home without comment or argument.

I was amazed to say the least. I couldn't believe she had taken it so well and I had expected more of a war. Either she had thought about what I had said the last time and decided I was right, or maybe it was because Bill was with me this time. I had noticed she was different when he was there. Anyway, the doctor just asked Bill and me for our permission for her to write to the authorities to say that this was our decision and that she had done what was required of her. That was fine by us. She was very pleased with Amberlie's progress.

15

Amberlie was growing into a really bonny little girl who seemed to enjoy watching me as much as I did her. She was a real character with a flourishing zest for life when she was well. The smallest things inspired her happiness, such as my vacuuming and dusting around when she sat in her chair with her Skwish, waiting with baited breath for the Hoover to be turned on. I had to be careful though, because if she hadn't realised what I was doing, it would make her jump and she would be upset, so I would put it on and quickly turn it off so it just made a small vroom sound. Her eyes grew wide and she giggled in anticipation of the bigger noise and then she would start banging her Skwish hard on the table, trying to match the noise level!

Her chair was on wheels so it was easy to move her from room to room, and when I went upstairs she played on the beds or on the floor. She liked having her scenery changed and seemed to know whose room was whose by responding in the same unique ways she did for each of the children.

I made the most of her nap times either rushing around doing other housework or keeping the washing going. I usually had about five to six machine loads a day, with Amberlie going through 'dribble mops' ten to the dozen. She was too big for baby bibs so I used terry nappies instead and when they wore out I invested in some hand towels. If everything was done and if I was lucky enough for Ben to be asleep too, I made the most of it by having a cuppa and five minutes' peace.

It was always a very full day. Amberlie's feeding always took an hour or so at a time, then there were a couple of physio sessions that had to be scheduled in, play and development, which varied time-wise according to her mood, and, of course, the nail-biting attempt at some time in the standing frame. The kids had to be taken and picked up from school, there was shopping to be done and sometimes a hospital appointment to fit in plus anything else that cropped up … and Ben too! I was always amazed that things ran fairly smoothly most of the time. The biggest struggle of the day was Amberlie's bath. I often sweated buckets hanging over the side trying to hold her safely with one arm and wash her with the other. It was impossible to wash her lovely long hair without help so any hair-washes were scheduled for evenings when Bill was around. Clare was a good little helper and, being desperate to play the 'little mum', she liked to thoroughly organise me and brought everything I needed. She made it her job to soap Amberlie's back and relished being involved in her day-to-day care.

Amberlie's hair was gorgeous. It was almost down to her waist, strawberry blonde with a kink in it, and little hanging curly bits that softly framed her face. It always looked pretty even when she had just got out of bed! We had let it grow long because she had a cowlick at the front and it pushed her hair the wrong way, making it stand on end! It was much easier and far more presentable to have it tied back and plaited. She never minded having it washed and brushed or blow-dried – in fact she found it quite soothing.

I spoke to Eve about the difficulties of bathing Amberlie on my own, and she immediately arranged for her to have a bath chair that strapped Amberlie in and suckered to the bottom of the bath so that I had my hands free. This worked fairly well at first, although Amberlie found it cold to the touch and seemed to miss me holding her. There was also the usual problem of her hatred of straps. She soon realised, though, that it gave her freedom in the water and she was able to kick her legs to make bubbles and splashes and, naturally, lots of great noise! Amberlie was, however, very strong when she was excited and soon kept thrusting herself out of the Velcro straps, or she would lean too heavily on one side, making her bottom slip, so we had to keep an arm round her; eventually she lost the comfort and feeling of security and we went back to square one with a now slightly nervous Amberlie.

Eve said that it really was time for us to consider what help we needed to care for Amberlie now that she was coming up to three years old and getting fairly big. She explained that it could become very difficult doing basic care if we did not have the right equipment, not only for Amberlie's good but for ours as well because we had to lift her and move her around. She said it was essential that Bill and I took care of our backs because if we were not fit, then how would we be able to look after Amberlie? It was also all part of maintaining a good quality of family life.

'You have enough to cope with without the daily routine becoming a nightmare. It's important to avoid that sort of stress so that everything isn't a dirge or a trigger for depression,' she said.

Eve was a good person who talked a lot of sense, and she was becoming a good friend. She was very laid back and not at all pushy. She respected my fierce independence and explained things and gave advice in a way that I listened to without dismissing it all outright.

I was a little wary of all the equipment that Amberlie could potentially need in the house. A lot of things were huge and bulky and it had already been difficult enough finding somewhere to put the standing frame – there just wasn't enough space. I only wanted things that were absolutely necessary for Amberlie's well-being. She was already highly resistant to anything with straps and therefore it would be pointless having awful-looking, antiquated wooden contraptions littering the place that would remain unused. Our house was also our home and I didn't want it all looking like a physiotherapy clinic. Eve laughed and said that what we had at home was up to us, and that on the physio side Amberlie had all she needed, so it was just a case of considering a few things to make life easier all round. She said she realised space was an problem at home and told me about a grant being available if we wanted to build some downstairs facilities for Amberlie; she said that now was the time to get things going, rather than wait until we were already struggling. I hadn't thought about it before and Eve suggested that the area on the side of our house which had an old brick-built shed cum coal house on it would be the ideal spot for a specially adapted downstairs bedroom and shower-room. She wasn't sure whether the grant was available from social services or from the local council, but in any case it would initially have to be assessed and agreed by the hospital social services department in consultation with Dr Ramsay. She said she would make some enquiries for us to see how to get the ball rolling.

This was certainly food for thought and it all seemed to be a wonderful idea that made a lot of sense. Bill wasn't against the idea but was naturally rather worried about the financial implications, because nothing was as straight forward as it initially appeared.

Eve also felt it was time that Amberlie had a more supportive pushchair and arranged for us to attend a specialist unit at another hospital. She met us there, as we were to be interviewed by a panel and they needed a full physio report to cover the expectations of the next couple of years.

The visit proved to be quite an ordeal one way and another. We had to wait ages and ages to be seen and then we were cross-examined to the point of feeling very uncomfortable. Amberlie was then sat in a variety of chairs and measured and assessed. I asked them not to support her anymore than was necessary because otherwise she wouldn't want to go in them, and also she needed to use her muscles to retain their tone and movement. The last thing I wanted was for her new chair to ruin her outdoor adventures. Eventually we agreed on a firm, navy upholstered chair with side supports, minimal head supports and just two straps to hold her in around her middle. It sat on top of a fold-down wheel carriage but it didn't fold completely and was very cumbersome. The chair didn't fold at all and was the same height as the base so it was going to need a large car boot space.

It needed to be specially made so we were to wait some weeks for it, and then we would be called to attend another appointment to make sure it fitted properly.

Penny Gray, the hospital social worker, came to see Bill and me. She apologised for not coming to see us on a general basis sooner. Apparently we had fallen through her net because Amberlie had been treated at Great Ormond Street. Usually she would have visited us soon after diagnosis to check that everything was OK and that Amberlie was getting all she should.

I was a little disappointed with her explanation as I was aware that there were meetings in the children's unit all the time, and I couldn't believe that Amberlie had never arisen as a topic for discussion during the last three years, particularly as she had such a rare condition.

'Well, Amberlie was at your hospital first, and returned there for nearly a week after Great Ormond Street discharged her. In fact we were visited by a hospital social worker both times, as well as one at Great Ormond Street. I'm surprised there wasn't any communication,' I said. Penny smiled and dismissed the issue.

She said she hoped we had already claimed Amberlie's Disability Living Allowance and were receiving it without any problems. I confirmed this. Funnily enough it wasn't anybody in authority who told me I could get financial help for Amberlie, it had been Jo, the mum I got to know at GOSH.

'Amberlie is also receiving portage and physio?' Penny continued.

'Yes,' I said.

With the standard checklist out of the way, Penny went on to explain about the grants that were available. She said they called them 'Major Adaptation Grants' and were available because like us, many people wished to look after their children in their own home, but due to the need for equipment and lack of space, they were keen to build on to their houses to maintain a quality of life for the whole family. She explained that at that time if a child went into residential care, it often cost the state upwards of £50,000 a year to look after it, and that the government wished to encourage home care because it was seen not only to be best for the child in most circumstances but cheaper for the state. Therefore, if families did want to adapt their homes there was a grant available tol help of up to roughly £20,000 to meet some of the building and equipment costs.

It had never occurred to me to put Amberlie in residential care and I was quite shocked that it was an option for some people … the very thought horrified me. I could never do that, I would look after her no matter what – she was mine!

Penny went on to say that one of the occupational therapists (OTs) would need to visit us to assess what we would need in the way of adaptations and equipment. She also pointed out that the grant was, however, means tested and the amount available would depend on what Bill earned. My heart sank then. Whilst Bill didn't earn a huge wage, he earned enough to be part of the middle range between poor and the 25% tax bracket, and from past experience with things such as council tax, we had to pay the full amount of everything, which in the end probably kept us on the same level as someone on income support.

As there wasn't anything else for Penny to help with, she left us saying we would be hearing from the OT department shortly. She gave us a huge information pack full of numbers and addresses we might need at some stage as well as details of what was available locally for disabled children – all stuff we should have received right from the beginning, apparently.

Eve had also mentioned that I should ask Penny about an orange badge for the car. Amberlie should have had one by now as she was entitled to disabled parking. Penny left us with the details and we sent off our application. This made a huge difference to hospital visits and being out and about generally, as well as saving us a few pennies! It was a good job we had Eve around to watch out for us!

When Liz the OT came, she evaluated how we were managing and subsequently organised another bath chair for Amberlie. She also arranged for us to have a beautiful all-round bed guard so we also didn't have to worry about Amberlie being on the move in the night. Up to that point we had positioned mountains of pillow and cushions around on the open side and base of her bed and used an old baby guard as some protection. There wasn't much else we needed. I told her that Eve had her physical development in hand and we were generally managing OK. Liz said she would review it again once the adaptations had been made, and would now contact the local council to arrange a meeting with the person in charge of the grants.

A few weeks later, Liz and Dave Wells, from the council, visited us and discussed at length what could be done and where. They also wanted assurance that Bill and I had no intention of moving house at any stage in the foreseeable future. Mr Wells explained that before they got things moving they would need to do a means test to see what our grant entitlement would be, so that we could make a decision on whether or not we were able to go ahead.

It turned out that we would need to provide the first £9,300 towards the costs, which meant our entitlement was roughly 50% of the grant. It was a lot of money to us and we were a bit irritated to be told that had we been on income support, we would have the whole cost of any works paid for in full by the state.

'You're joking?' I said, launching into a speech on behalf of the workers. 'That's just typical isn't it, so bloody unfair! Why is it when you do a decent day's work in this country you get sodding penalised? Disability is not discriminatory you know, nobody chooses to be that way and anyone can have a disabled child ... prince or pauper! Why should we be less entitled to help than those on income support? After all, there is the possibility that Amberlie's condition could have been caused by something in the environment! I also thought the idea was to encourage families to take care of their disabled children in their own homes. It really makes a mockery of the incentive to work in this country ... you are better off on the state.'

Dave said, 'I know, I agree ... all that you're saying, but that's the rules.'

No amount of moaning was going to change it, but I felt I had to make my point. It was now up to Bill and me to see whether or not the whole thing was a feasible venture.

We reported back to Liz, who was disappointed but said she would look into the possibility of social services contributing to the costs to make it a bit easier for us.

Later on Penny phoned to say that she had made some enquiries and it was unlikely that social services would be able to help because the total budget for the year, which covered the entire Surrey area, was only £45,000, and most of that had already been allocated.

Liz was still surprised and told us she would make some enquiries herself and we later received an application form to complete. We had to laugh when we got a reply saying all they could do was to offer us an interest free loan of £8,000 to be repaid within three years!

'What planet are they on?' I joked to Bill.

I rang Penny and told her to forget it. Social services had so far proved in our case to be rather inept.

Bill and I thought long and hard about it and eventually decided that in the long run we didn't really have an option. Amberlie would grow big and need bigger equipment and we knew that just supporting and lifting her in and out of the bath would be an almighty problem in itself. A shower room alone would mean a comfortable chair for her that could be wheeled under the water without any stress and strain for all of us, and the extra space would be a real bonus. We just had to do it somehow. We had no savings or money we could use so the only course of action was to re-mortgage the house.

We allowed for the building works and some extra so we could buy a second-hand multi-person vehicle (MPV) to make transporting Amberlie and the rest of the family easier. Amberlie was a package deal to take out, especially with her new pushchair. Having an MPV also meant I didn't have to bend so much when lifting her in and out of the car, and of course it made more room for Ben, Ray & Clare. This had the added bonus of peace and quiet in the back because they weren't huddled together aggravating and moaning at each other.

We signed an agreement with the council in March and they estimated the works would begin in September or October that year, and would last between eight and twelve weeks. It all seemed such a long process as six months had already lapsed since the original enquiry.

Amberlie's progress had been wonderful lately, and due to lots of swinging games, her torso muscles were well toned and she was almost sitting alone. She could hold her position for three to four minutes before her balance wavered a bit, but she controlled it to a large degree and adjusted herself when she started to topple. Her arms were now able to bear her weight, her right arm being the stronger of the two. She had a tendency to rotate her left wrist backwards, which looked dreadfully uncomfortable to us but each time we corrected its position, she moved it back so it was obviously how she wanted it. Her awareness was amazing and she responded to all stimulation. She still loved to be tickled and talked to like a baby and her laughter was incredibly infectious. Her range of sounds had grown and we enjoyed lots of conversations, mimicking her tones back to her. Amberlie had taught us her language and she was delighted!

She now let us know when she was ready for bed – not that it meant she was giving in quietly! Unfortunately she had the same level of patience as our other children when she wanted something, which amounted to virtually nil! If I didn't react immediately or got the wrong message, she went straight into one of her 'wobblies' and life was murder for a while.

Health-wise she had also been great, apart from a mild chest infection in May that she coped with remarkably well, and she didn't have the usual miseries associated with being ill. I hoped that maybe she had reached a milestone and that her immunity and resistance had developed to a better level, but on completing her course of antibiotics she started refusing food and drink. Her chest seemed clear and I could hear no bubbling or wheezing.

One day Amberlie slept all day long even while we were out and when she did wake she was exceptionally drowsy. Every time a bottle was placed in her mouth she fell asleep again. Forty-eight hours later I was concerned that she might be getting dehydrated. There was no apparent change to her fit pattern, no temperature, no indications of illness, just a worsening state of drowsiness and I was getting beside myself with worry.

We were due at the eye clinic the next day for a review so I cancelled the appointment and took her to see Dr Jonathan, our GP instead. He checked her over while I stood there sobbing away, worried sick and unable to stop my tears. He said he couldn't find any evidence of infection or illness either. He also said that he had researched some of the information I had given him about lissencephaly and said, 'You are aware, Sandra, the "eating thing" could be condition associated?'

He couldn't keep the look of concern from his expression. I felt the cold grip of fear sneaking through from deep in my grey matter, jangling the nerves through my chest, arms and legs. I didn't want to acknowledge it, I was trying to stay calm and persuade myself that there was another reason.

Looking at me, he changed tack, and said he could hear a little phlegm in her throat and that he would give her some linctus to help clear it, telling me to bring her back in two days or before if things worsened. He also gave me another bottle of antibiotics just in case she did have an infection lurking somewhere. Anyway, the next day she brought up some horrible green stuff and drank a little. I still wasn't happy so I took her back to see him and he said he had spoken to Dr Thomas at the hospital for his advice, and he said if there was no improvement to bring Amberlie in to see him and they would run some tests to see if she had a silent undetected infection.

It took about a week to get Amberlie drinking again but she was still not particularly happy to eat. She would start to struggle and try to get away when she saw the spoon coming, and then if luck had it, she would resolvedly take a few mouthfuls before she spat it back. Bill and I took it in turns and persisted at the price of her ultimately becoming upset. She was very determined and I felt that Dr Jonathan had probably been right – this was the lissencephaly eating scenario beginning to come into play, and it must have been triggered by the infection.

After much persistence over many weeks, we had reached a common ground whereby Amberlie would now only eat certain completely pureed jars of fruit and cereal and wouldn't entertain any lumpy foods at all, with the exception of the occasional mashed banana and homemade apple crumble with custard. All other liquidised food was also out. She had never managed to learn to chew so I guessed any large lumps would have frightened her.

On the positive side, Amberlie had yet again made a conscious decision on what she preferred to eat and whether or not the consistency was right; and if that was what she wanted then it was better than nothing at all, and much better than a war and a struggle every feed time. At least she still had an interest and a desire there and the food seemed to satisfy her needs and she enjoyed it. I often got a huge smile during a mouthful! I had to admire her. We tried introducing other things again from time to time but Amberlie would have none of it. If there was a miscellaneous lump anywhere she soon spat it out.

I felt terribly guilty for having persisted with the other foods. I had done it before following an infection and got her back to normal – but this time it was different – it wasn't going away and I should have seen that; I should have looked past it for all the underlying reasons or maybe I just hadn't wanted to. She had to tell me somehow that she wasn't coping, and my unwitting ignorance must have frustrated her no end because the message just wasn't getting through. I was resting on my laurels, feeling safe with all the progress she had made. How could things suddenly turn amongst all the good and this element, this warning, rear its ugly head to remind me that we were all still living on a knife-edge? And Amberlie was about the age that it was expected.

If I couldn't accept the process of her condition then how could I help her through it? I had to wake myself up and be aware of the signs to look for and I had to link them up with any previous warning or clues. For her sake I couldn't afford to dismiss anything and I needed to accept there would be rough times ahead. It was just a dream to expect her to stay the same or make continued significant progress.

I was, however, relieved that Amberlie was refusing rather than gagging on the food. I hated the thought of her being tube fed – it would take away all the tastes that she loved, and having a tube in her nose all the time would irritate and drive her mad. We were lucky.

Having gone through such a bad stage Amberlie had not been in her standing frame very much ('Who cares?' said Amberlie), and I certainly did not see the point of upsetting her over that, but subsequently the tendon in her left leg had tightened.

16

Ray and Clare had gradually become more aware of how disabled Amberlie was. All the time she was small they didn't seem to notice much was wrong, and having never experienced babies other than Ben, they had no pre-formed conclusions on which to base any assessment of their sister. Now Ben's progress had highlighted how little Amberlie could do, especially now that he was on the move.

They never really spoke much about it but spent more time sitting with Amberlie, helping her to play, talking and showing her different things. She, of course, was delighted with all the attention and cooed away in response to their conversation.

Ray was not a talker unless he had something relevant to say, but he spoke to Amberlie about nothing in particular all the time, often in whispers or in a light, gentle voice. He fussed her, stroked her hair and face and fiddled with her fingers whilst sometimes deep in thought. Amberlie found him very soothing and was chuffed and comforted in his presence. If she was ill or having a bad day, Ray kept an intermittent checking regime going and each time spent a few minutes looking at her. He worried terribly.

Clare was far more practical – a little girl playing 'mum'. She loved to help change Amberlie and find her hair bands (and borrow them!), and was good at distracting her when she was grumpy. Clare excited Amberlie more because she spoke to her like a baby and tickled her, and naturally the more Amberlie laughed the more she carried on! Clare could be quite a drama queen and would often put on a song-and-dance show for her. Sometimes Amberlie found Clare a bit much as she could be overpowering and loud, and when she'd had enough she would start to rub her eyes and throw her arms down by her sides, and occasionally ignored her or looked at her as if she was barmy!

Without putting Clare off as such, we would encourage her to go do something else for while, but every now and then she wouldn't leave well alone, and it ended up with Amberlie being upset and her being told off.

Bill and I tried to make sure Ray and Clare's lives remained as normal as possible, though we couldn't shield them from everything and sometimes sustaining any normality was impossible. In reality we weren't a normal family and most of the time Amberlie determined the day's events. When and where possible, Ray and Clare did the same as other children, going to friends' houses for tea, attending birthday parties, after-school clubs and such like. Occasionally promises and events just didn't happen no matter how hard we tried, but they took their disappointments on the chin and became accustomed to change, especially when Amberlie wasn't well. These were worrying times for them too and they were only ever concerned that she would be all right.

I was very lucky to have Ray and Clare the way they were – they never fought for my attention, and occupied themselves and each other, either on the computer or with toys. Though I was very grateful they were able to do this, I also felt hideously guilty that I couldn't give them more time, just to be with them, doing things they wanted to. I always vowed that I would spend such and such a time with them later on when Bill was home, but then I was so tired and it often didn't happen and that then compounded the guilt even more.

Bill and I probably spoiled them a lot but I think 'spoiled' is a funny word. Why shouldn't we have tried to make up for all the things we couldn't do, such as going for a long walk in the woods? We couldn't do that because Amberlie needed to be in her buggy and it was impossible to push her on that terrain. Sure, we could have left Amberlie with someone else, but I was never keen on that and the kids said they didn't want to go anywhere without her – so we found other places where we could walk easily. They

146

had lots of toys, games, books, videos and clothes, and yes, it was all they wanted but it also served to keep them occupied when we had to do other things. They were such good kids anyway.

I looked forward to them coming home from school each day – they provided a welcome and amusing relief. They both came and sat squashed up tight beside Amberlie and me and told us all about their days, and they always asked Amberlie and Ben if they'd had a nice day. They liked listening to them as much as I did. Ray and Clare seemed to instinctively know if Amberlie had had a bad day and they would keep out of the way even though I hadn't shouted or taken it out on them. I think they just sensed from me that now wasn't the time to tell me anything!

We sometimes had other children round for tea and Ray and Clare always introduced their new friends to Amberlie, proudly announcing:

'Here is Amberlie – my special sister. She's got a funny brain you know – not like ours, and she can't talk.'

The other child would reply, 'Oh, hello Amberlie.' And they would then disappear!

Amberlie always looked and smiled. The children who already knew her always made a point of saying 'Hi!' to her when they arrived. The first thing they would ask was, 'Where's Amberlie?'

It was the same in the school playground – Ray and Clare often brought different children to meet Amberlie.

They weren't quite the same to Ben. His introduction to their friends was a short, cursory acknowledgement and then they scarpered quickly. He irritated them because he followed and interfered with what they did and although they patiently steered him in other directions, he was persistent. The bigger and more confident he got, the more their tolerance was tried and I was often called to remove him! Despite that, if Ben fell over, got hurt or cried, they rushed to his rescue immediately. They were a couple of big softies really.

When Clare and Ray did want something, though, it had to be 'now or yesterday!' And unfortunately those rare times often coincided with Amberlie's feeding, so they had to either wait or sort it out themselves. If I interrupted Amberlie's meals I could never get her to finish the rest when I came back.

I never noticed any unusual behavior from them in the way of trouble. They had good attitudes that we were in excess of their years because they had needed to grow up early. Their school reports were always good and Bill and I took time to help them with their homework and hear them read. I was sure that our being honest with them about Amberlie and keeping them informed from the start made the difference. To have kept them in the dark and been secretive would have been a grave mistake. Children's imaginations can be far worse than real life.

I'm not saying they were angels – they were absolute buggers at times! – but when it counted, they were good kids and I could rely on them. They were a great support to Bill and me, and as young as they were, they knew when to give a hug and a kiss to show us they understood and were there for us. They had to cope with life on a day-to-day basis, never knowing what it would bring, and they bore it and adapted well. They knew the last thing we needed when Amberlie was having a bad time was for them to play up and cause trouble … they saved it for more settled times!

17

Summer gave Amberlie the opportunity to be outside a lot and freely roll around on the lawn. She loved its coolness and was passionate about green. Much laughter was heard when the trees moved and rustled in the breeze and various expressions of wonder shone in her face when she caught sight of a bird flying overhead or a noisy light aircraft passed over, or if the kids played excitedly around her. A startled cat streaking past always roused a giggle. One evening a hot-air balloon drifted too low over the garden and Amberlie lay rigid in the grass, eyes wide, stunned by the colours and the noise the bursts of fire made trying to get it to rise again!

I often put the stereo on and let Amberlie's favourite music blare out of the window so we could dance around the garden together, which she found great fun! She loved being swung round and round and up and down to the beat, excited by all the movement and the wind blowing around her. In contrast she often dozed off in the shade of an umbrella, peaceful and calm and warm.

When the kids were at home she liked to watch them being busy around her, playing, whooshing down the slide into the paddling pool, and of course fighting! Although Amberlie loved bath time, she was never sure about 'other' water, so was never keen when we dipped her toes in the pool, even if we added warm water. We had tried hydrotherapy at the hospital, and whilst she enjoyed having her physio in the water, she ended up with a cold every time, so for the sake of a half-hour session each week, it really wasn't worth the grief so we didn't carry on with it.

We never took a holiday as such. Between Amberlie and Ben there was an enormous amount to take, and I always worried that if we stayed in a hotel and Amberlie had one of her night-time screaming episodes, it wouldn't really appeal to the other guests! It made more sense to leave holidays until they were a little older and hopefully more settled. Day trips were far easier and we had lots of them, usually to the south coast, where the kids could all find a bit of freedom. Amberlie happily sat in her chair under the parasol watching everyone and later liked to have a siesta on a blanket on the sand. We always took long walks along the promenade or through parks so she could see the world go by. She enjoyed watching the kids on the fairground rides and spending a few pennies (or pounds!) in the amusement arcades in the evening. At first we were a little concerned about being in the arcades because of the flashing lights on the machines, but luckily Amberlie's epilepsy was never photosensitive.

Feed times could be a stressful challenge when we were out. Either she didn't want to eat because she was far more interested in watching other things and eating was far down her list of priorities, or she would find it difficult to manage breathing and swallowing because the wind was blowing a little too much. We found it better to schedule her feed times for when we were near the car so that she was sheltered and properly supported in her seat. The kids were mostly very patient as it was never a quick job at the best of times, but naturally they were restless when they wanted to go off exploring, so rather than have Amberlie agitated by their moans, Bill would take them while I fed and changed her, which also preserved her dignity as she was a fairly big girl for three and a half.

We found that most people weren't interested in what was going on with Amberlie, and only one or two would watch for a little while. A lot of people came and stroked her hair or held her hand and told her how beautiful she was. She used to go very shy at strangers but always gave an endearing coy smile. For our part we liked the fact that people approached her – after all she wasn't dangerous and she was gorgeous! They often asked what was wrong with her and I was quite happy to tell them. I preferred that to people ignoring her because of their own embarrassment.

Luckily, we never had to endure any of the prejudice that some disabled people have experienced, and I guessed that was because generally attitudes have improved and people are more aware and tolerant now that disabled people are usually no longer shut away and treated as freaks. It may also have had something to do with the fact that Amberlie looked quite normal, apart from having a special pushchair and supports. Tolerance, however, is still not universal and some people I know have been treated appallingly by the ignorant and prejudiced. These things could happen to anyone ... and why should their carers be subjected to criticism and abuse too?

These people are so blind in understanding how much love and pride we have as parents and carers for our children and could never appreciate how much is given back in the way of joy, smiles and unconditional love. Amberlie taught me so much about life ... about what being a human should be, and I relished every day spent with her, no matter what it brought.

Interestingly, children's perspectives on disability abound with acceptance and tolerance ... unless their minds have already been poisoned.

On July 7th we celebrated Ben's Christening. We organized a big party in the garden with a bouncy castle and a ball pond and the kids had a whale of a time. It was Ben's first experience of a bouncy castle (and Amberlie's too!), and now that he was 18 months old he made the most of it and managed to keep going without a nap all day!

Bill took Amberlie on the bouncy castle with him and laid her on the floor. He gently pushed the ballooning around her and she bounced gently up and down so she could become more used to it. He also held her sitting up so that she could see more of the bright colours – her eyes were already as wide as ponds and she giggled and cooed. She wasn't in the least perturbed when Ben came bounding over, making her bounce harder and higher; she looked surprised at first but then laughed heartily, loving every movement, no matter how unexpected! Everyone had a super day and there were no dodgy episodes.

The September rain soon settled in, as it usually did the minute the kids went back to school. I came to loathe September. Every year it included a nightmare of one sort or another, having begun with Amberlie's diagnosis. Why September was such a yearly trauma I haven't a clue. It was just the way it was.

When we returned from a lovely day trip to the Isle of Wight – Amberlie's favourite place on earth – refusal feeding once again menaced our tranquility. I said to myself, 'Now, I mustn't panic; we've got to take this as it comes and deal with it in the best way possible.'

The days passed and each feed time took an eternity. Amberlie turned her head left, right, up, down, anyway to escape the sight of the spoon and its disgusting contents. She wriggled like mad trying to turn her whole body in the other direction, even if it meant she was dangerously near to falling onto the floor. It was a nightmare trying to hold her and feed her at the same time, and most of the food ended up anywhere and everywhere except in her mouth, and when I did manage to get a spoonful in during a breather in the struggle, she would open her mouth wide, shout, then the whole lot gushed and dribbled out. She would also lead me into a false sense of security sometimes and gaze up at me with her big beautiful 'love me' eyes, smile endearingly, then splatter the lot straight at me!

To make it easier I tried putting her in her chair to feed her, but no sooner had I strapped her in than she burst into tears and ended up in a real paddy. I couldn't win.

Then I noticed Amberlie had started to do odd things. She would push her left hand into her left eye socket really hard, while turning her right eye towards it and resting it deep in the corner. That made her really groggy and woozy and sometimes a little blue down the centre of her face. She would also lie on her back swinging her head from side to side with a sinister glaze in her eyes. I half hoped this was just a newly found game because it made her laugh and giggle and she seemed to enjoy it. I could understand that making herself dizzy could be fun – after all, lots of normal children spin around and then try to stand still, and it could have been her way of enjoying a childhood game. It was one of my optimistic evaluations ... but deep down I knew my logic was flawed. Putting the bright side away, there could only be one valid reason or answer, and that would be some different seizure activity going on.

I was always having these lonely mind debates, trying to find 'normal' reasons or excuses for phases. It was like a quest for sanctuary I suppose, an attempt to escape from the realism before I had to accept there was another problem.

Despite all the feeding problems that had prevailed of late, Amberlie astoundingly managed to gain weight! Some of our never-ending persistence had paid off! It was logical therefore to assume that the new seizure activity had been a result of her outgrowing her medicinal dosages. There were only a few days to go to the next appointment with Dr Ramsay, so I decided to weather the change until then, rather than panic – it might just be a fluke phase anyway, and hopefully no action would be necessary. The next day Amberlie became distressed as the hand-to-eye movements increased and made her cry after each bout of activity, and her face was very blue.

Something went very wrong during this 'blueing'. Amberlie's normally supple right arm hung limply, and she made no attempt to use it. She was, however, back on the planet and aware of all that was going on. The seizure spell seemed to have passed and she appeared happy.

I theorised that the seizures must have hit the spot in her brain relating to her arm and made her forget how to use it, so I spent the next two days lifting up her arm and putting her Skwish in her hand gently manoeuvring it around, encouraging her to move her whole arm and wrist – much to her amusement. It quickly recovered and Amberlie started to use it normally again. Pleased that all seemed to be back to normal, I relaxed – it then hit me that maybe she'd had a slight stroke. I panicked.

'Oh shit! Why hadn't I thought of that before? Oh no … Jesus …!'

The adrenalin was rushing through me as I dashed to ring Dr Ramsay to explain what had happened. She said there would be no way of knowing for sure, but it had possibly been caused by seizure activity, and now that Amberlie had recovered, we would not worry about it.

'I think we should increase her vigabatrin my 250 milligrams, and all being well, I'll see her as scheduled next week,' she said.

Relieved, I made a mental note to get more information so that I was more aware or what could and was likely to occur. I had to get it into my head that my logical explanations should only be a small part of analysing what Amberlie did. I had learned not to take anything for granted or to minimise it as well as not to panic … but somewhere amongst the two evils I had to find a balance of when to worry and when not to. I never thought about a stroke happening to a child before, I just assumed it was something that happened to old people. It was something I probably would never have considered had I not been in this situation.

Amberlie's phases changed all the time and there were no specific triggers that gave any clues, so there were no hard-and-fast rules to follow. I had to go with the flow, taking each occurrence as it came and analysing its merits. A lot of the time I relied on instinct and gut feelings because what sometimes seemed to be a potentially serious episode often phased out into nothing, meaning Bill and I would have panicked, charged up to the hospital and by the time the doctors had examined her and taken bloods, she would be absolutely fine! Our nerves would be shattered and Amberlie would be smiling and playing as normal! The hospital never minded. They seemed to trust that something unusual had happened and we were right to check everything out. In contrast, a small and seemingly insignificant happening was often the first sign of something building up slowly, usually into a change in seizure pattern or indeed an illness. It was hard not to feel a 'plonker' sometimes and even harder trying to make a doctor who didn't know Amberlie aware that I knew something was brewing despite all her signs appearing normal.

I wanted to look after my daughter as independently as possible and feel confident about it. I didn't want too many official people calling at the house all the time because I found all that did was put pressure on me to attend coffee mornings, events, discussions and so on. Their intentions were all very well meant and they were offering support not only to me but to the whole family, and that was nice to know and appreciated, but I wanted to call them only when I wanted or needed to. I also wanted to be fully involved and partake in any decisions made about Amberlie's treatment, and Dr Ramsay indeed allowed me to do so.

When I tried to find the information I needed about the physical brain, how it worked and the difference lissencephaly made to its functions, I kept coming up against brick walls. No one could tell me where I could obtain the books apart from Eve, the physio, who was the only one with suggestions. It seemed as though the neurological medical books would be of no use to me as a layperson. I already knew very well there was no literature on lissencephaly, and I became a little peeved because I felt I should be the judge on whether or not I could understand the books. It would have been great to spend hours questioning a neurologist but that wasn't going to happen and doctors had better things to do than to educate me.

I didn't pursue Dr Ramsay because she had a very mother-like way of letting us only know things when it was necessary, as she knew the answers hurt, and she was always very cagey about discussing things that would potentially upset us. I did not want to upset her either, and I knew that she hated me asking her questions. Of course there was a part of me that would rather not know, but in my quest to make Amberlie's life as good as possible, and to assess things better, I had to know. I would have preferred not to have *needed* to know, and would have given anything not to have been in that position in the first place but since that miracle to make Amberlie normal never happened, I couldn't run away from the questions that were there ... and not to have those answers would have driven me mad. I knew me, and I also believed that having the information prepared me emotionally in advance so that shock would not ensue and allow panic to replace sense. What use would I have been to Amberlie if I couldn't cope? Amberlie relied on me and I had to support her and be ready for whatever came her way. So I scoured endless book outlets until I found what I wanted.

There was lots of information on epilepsy and I studied the effects this has on the brain and compared the facts I had about Amberlie's brain's composition to that of a normal child. Apart from learning masses about physical and mental complexities and epilepsy generally, I had to work out the facts, differences and conclusions relating to the lissencephaly condition for myself.

It all helped me to try to put myself in Amberlie's shoes, and allowed me to think 'out of the box'. It provided a lot of answers to questions I had mulled over and over again, and as time passed I understood why Amberlie would deteriorate. It didn't make me feel any better though: often the pain was unbearable as the realisation set in, and I understood the old saying 'a little knowledge is a dangerous thing' ... but it helped me accept the situation and gave me the confidence in myself to cope.

Bill, bless him, was supportive and interested in my findings. I could see that sometimes I probably shouldn't have told him certain things because I could see it upset him, but I felt it would help him in the end as well. I often had to remind myself that not everyone wanted to know everything like I did. Different people had different ways of coping. He had always indulged me when I've become obsessive and has taken a lot on the chin in order to be a good husband and friend to me.

18

The increase in Amberlie's medicine seemed to work, the blueness subsided and the nasty edge of the activity vanished so that she had some peace. Her right eye now remained steady but some movement was still apparent in her left, albeit now in slow motion.

The feeding had not improved and instead of swallowing, Amberlie dribbled copious amounts of milk while sucking her bottle. We went through towels by the dozen in an attempt to stop the fluid constantly running down her neck. Invariably she had to have her clothes changed after each drink as the milk soaked through her jumper right down to her vest. Approaching her with food totally sent her off the planet into a tantrum and meal times became very distressing for both of us.

I worried myself sick that she wasn't eating enough and felt so unable to do anything about it. She so stubbornly did not want to know. Then, thankfully, for some unknown reason, Amberlie began to let her father feed her in the evenings. Bill and I were dumbstruck! We watched without saying anything in case we reminded her to refuse! Talk about becoming paranoid! Every evening she ate all her food and drank all her milk, seeming to enjoy it without complaint. I tried to feed her during the day but she just wouldn't have it. She allowed me to give her a bottle, but the moment she spotted a spoon I was in trouble! I had to explore other ways of getting more nourishment into her milk without putting her off so that I could get her through the day until her Dad came home. I gave her four full baby bottles of milk during the day (luckily she was now swallowing them), two taken with sugar or as flavoured milkshake, and, taking advantage of the fact that Amberlie never went to bed before midnight, Bill managed to squeeze in two meals per evening so that we were nigh on meeting her daily needs – though Amberlie's idea of daily needs were obviously quite different from ours!

I tried to work out why Amberlie had decided on this course. She must have either sensed my stress and frustration at not being able to feed her, so maybe I had put her off and she couldn't relax, or maybe she just preferred her Dad to do it . . . or was it a game? I don't know. I had to give the girl credit; she had made her decision and was sticking to it. She was thoroughly delighted when her Dad appeared through the door after work! I left them to it ... I needed the break!

Rest on our laurels ... we shall not! Our bliss was then shattered by two nights of murder! Wherever Amberlie was, in whatever position, she was bending backwards again, extending herself and going completely potty. Something was giving her terrible grief, irritating and disturbing her and not allowing her to rest at all. There was no comforting her. Whatever we did made no difference. Maybe it was the last late feed of the day causing bad indigestion, or maybe it was another change in seizures. We were worried. Then it passed like it had never happened.

At Amberlie's next appointment with Dr Ramsay we mentioned this had happened and after fully examining Amberlie she said she could see nothing to worry about. She said Amberlie's distress could possibly be caused by stomach acid, as her diet was unbalanced, being virtually fruit based with cereal.

'Since she is drowsy at times from seizure activity and lies down a lot, the stomach doesn't fully empty,' she said, and suggested giving Amberlie some Tagamet syrup to line her stomach to prevent some of the acidity. Anything was worth a go and sometimes Amberlie did pull her legs up to her tummy, so I supposed it could be the cause. I thought it worth mentioning that Amberlie used to do this exact same thing when she first had seizures. Taking note, Dr Ramsay decided to increase her Vigabatrin again to 1000 mg twice a day. She also said she had thought long and hard but could not explain what had caused the problem in Amberlie's right arm recently, and reassured us that since things had returned to normal it was not a cause for concern. She had considered doing another EEG but felt it would not prove anything, and would confirm this by taking advice from her colleagues.

I braced myself and asked if all this was looking very bad and she said that at the moment she did not feel that Amberlie was in the early stages of deterioration, and it was more likely to be a bad phase, with problems that could be solved. Bill and I heaved a huge sigh of relief but were nervously aware that the problems just kept on coming.

I pushed her to tell us what we should look out for in the first instance of possible deterioration. Reluctantly, and with a deep sigh and a long pause, she said that the first sign was usually that the child starts to gag whilst feeding. I threw in that occasionally Amberlie did seem to choke a little but not all the time and Dr Ramsay shook her head dismissively. She was more concerned about the refusal of food element of lissencephaly and that Amberlie was intermittently having these phases. She explained that we needed to watch out because if Amberlie started to constantly refuse food, especially as her diet was not good anyway, it would lead to increasingly bad nutrition which would compromise her immunity and open the door to any old bug that came along. This would then result in a decreasing resistance to chest infections, which were often fatal to severely disabled children.

Severely disabled children like Amberlie are usually very sedentary, and because they are not mobile they do not disperse mucus made from colds and infections as normal children do, so it runs down their necks where it settles on their chests, becomes infected and often results in pneumonia. Good nutrition helps immunity, and moving the child around and keeping them upright, together with a regular physiotherapy routine, helps keep their chests clear.

We found with Amberlie that it was vital to get antibiotics into her as soon as we heard noises on her chest to avoid her becoming really ill very quickly.

Despite Dr Ramsay's encouraging answer to my question about possible deterioration, my relief quickly subsided and was replaced with pain and sickening worry about all the possibilities or certainties to come. It was just a warning, but I could already see that pattern of a slippery slope and felt we were sort of teetering at the top. I resisted visions of suddenly losing my footing and having to go and face whatever waited at the bottom. And then ... could we ever manage to get back up?

'Keep control,' I mumbled to myself, 'what happens, happens ... I'll deal with it.'

Dr Ramsay went on to mention that there had been much progress on the genetic side of detecting lissencephaly and that a new probe had been discovered with a deletion on another chromosome, which apparently was genetic but not passed on. They wanted us to return to the clinic for a further test to see if this was applicable to Amberlie or us. She also wanted the eye clinic to take a look at Amberlie's left eye because it was turning inwards every now and then, just in case it was hurting her in some way and causing stress that could be affecting her seizure stability. That reminded me that Amberlie was already scheduled for a full eye examination the following Monday (groan!).

Bill and I left, both of us not saying a word and chewing over all the points raised. We both hoped that perhaps if the tummy syrup worked or if there was an eye problem that could be sorted out, maybe, just maybe Amberlie wouldn't need her drugs increased. Fingers crossed.

As always when I had a reminder of the down side of Amberlie's condition (it was different when it was just in my head – I coped with that – but when someone – a doctor – actually said it ... ouch), it led to much philosophical contemplation about the meaning of life … the meaning of Amberlie's life, and what she might think or feel about it all.

Knowing Amberlie very much had her own mind, in whatever context that might have been, I suspected that in the same way a normal, seriously ill person decides when enough is enough, Amberlie, too, had an ability to make a similar decision. To see Amberlie in one of her major tantrums that lasted for hours, when she had no control of her reactions to whatever upset her, illustrated the theory. The problem entirely engulfed her, became her one and only focus, and once in the depths of it she was unable to come out unless she fell asleep exhausted or I managed to eventually find a distraction that she would accept. At what point would it all go too far, so that she would give up, sick of it all, or drive herself into the most dreadful seizure that couldn't be stopped? What if her brain found only a reason to destroy itself, having no intelligence and only a kind of prehistoric instinct … like a life force in reverse, and making Amberlie accept without question that there was no point in her survival? For what is an aim without a reason?

Bringing myself back to earth away from the unanswerable, I kept a logical and optimistic control. I believed wholeheartedly that Amberlie had a more complex intelligence, so therefore something had to have upset her in the first place … and just because I couldn't find the cause didn't mean she had no reason.

Analysing Amberlie's ways did me no favours at all. Whilst I did find some solace in lateral thinking, I found I put myself through more turmoil trying to analyse situations than was wise; but when Amberlie cried incessantly for hours on end and there was nothing I could do to end the misery and help her, I couldn't stop myself from wondering, when all the illness and grief was put together, what on earth she saw in life that made her want to go on.

It was my job to persuade and convince her every stage of the way that it was good to live. I was fully aware that I wasn't dealing with normal human reason and could not use language as a tool – but there again, who says she didn't understand what I said to her? I knew she understood love and I hoped that love was enough of a reason to live.

Music was always one of the most successful distractions from a tantrum, but we had to find the right sort at the right time! Amberlie loved opera but never a soprano – that made things worse … it made her cringe, tense and would intensify her rage! We discovered opera quite by accident when her portage teacher brought round one of her tapes to see how Amberlie responded. The first track played was 'Carmen' and Amberlie sprang to life, giggling and making noises and kicking her legs like crazy. As the music changed from softly-softly to loud booms she paused, eyes wide in anticipation, and as the booms came she laughed loudly and excitedly, swinging her head from side to side. It was awesome!

Heavy metal was also a good option, especially if it was very loud – she would have been in her element at a headbanger's ball! With most rock music she would go from sheer misery to dancing within a couple of minutes! Sixties music and some types of relaxation sounds, such as ocean waves or whale music were good.

The fresh air was another good sidetrack; initially we'd go into the garden, and failing that, out onto the streets. At first it was an enormous battle to secure her into the pram as she fought hook, line and sinker to wrench herself free from the straps, but by the time we had got down the path there was peace!

Some days nothing worked and she would scream endlessly in the living room while I sat on the floor with my back against the wall in the hall, the tears rolling down my face as I wondered how I was going to survive it all as well.

The eye clinic confirmed there were no problems with Amberlie's left eye that they could detect, certainly nothing that would cause any pain or peculiar movements. In fact they thought her sight had improved and she no longer needed to wear the patch on her glasses! I was so chuffed for her. Even she smiled knowingly!

Amberlie was still having two to three funny episodes a day with her hand/eye routine. The Tagamet syrup hadn't made any difference either and we still had screaming days. The banging of the eyes in the corners was as bad as ever and Dr Ramsay said that as the eye department had not found any problems, it was likely that Amberlie was stuck with the movements because they were probably 'complex partial' seizures which are very difficult if not impossible to control.

Partial seizures, depending on where they occur in the brain, only affect certain parts of the body. For example, Amberlie would turn her head and raise a twitching arm whilst still awake, but at other times her leg or face would twitch. People in partial seizures are usually dreamily aware of their surroundings and/or notice strange smells, or things appearing odd to them. When the seizures are 'complex partial', then their consciousness is also affected.

I have no idea if Amberlie knew when these seizures were coming or when they were about, but she did seem more upset when in a phase of them. This could have been because a partial seizure occurring in the temporal lobe is known to cause emotional experiences of either a horrible sensation or overpowering fear. Obviously I never knew what Amberlie experienced, but they certainly disturbed her acutely. These seizures also had the potential to develop into major tonic-clonic seizures and although Amberlie had only experienced these once or twice she had been really frightened before they happened.

Amberlie, I think … well, I know, experienced virtually all types of seizures at one time or another, and it was often difficult to work out which she'd had.

One morning Amberlie started to gasp for breath. Afraid that she had a serious chest infection, I got an emergency appointment at the surgery and the doctor said it seemed more like an acute asthma attack as her ribs were sucking in the skin as she struggled to breathe. She was immediately put on a high dose of steroids, taking four straightaway to be followed by another two tablets later. I was to give her the same the next day and then wean her down slowly over another three days. A bottle of penicillin was also given in case the asthma had been caused by an underlying infection. The steroids gave her complete relief an hour later.

I then got to wondering why on earth would Amberlie suddenly develop asthma like that when there had been so sign of it before.

'What was she having different?' I said to myself. 'Her food is always the same; as far as I know she's not been stung, she's never been allergic to the cat. Medicine's the same … wait a minute – the Tagamet!'

I rushed to find the information leaflet that came with the bottle.

'… in rare circumstances may cause a shortness of breath.'

'That's it!' I said out loud. 'How did I miss the first signs that she was having difficulty breathing?' Applying rationale, it seemed obvious that short breath could easily be missed, since Amberlie never physically exerted herself to any degree where her breathing would be noticeably affected, also she had been sleeping a lot. I rang the doctor and explained what she had been taking and why and what it said in the leaflet. She said it was a possibility and to stop giving it to her but to make sure she took all the antibiotics. As the Tagamet hadn't made any difference to her anyway, she wasn't going to miss it

19

One morning, having dropped the other kids off at school, I popped into the local supermarket for a few items. Halfway around the aisles, Amberlie launched into an ear-busting paddy, screaming and thrashing about in her pram. I couldn't see anything wrong, so, fearful of an oncoming major seizure, I rushed to pay for the shopping and whizzed off down the street. I hoped the fresh air would calm her but it wasn't having its usual effect so I undid her straps and lifted her out for a cuddle. As I picked her up, I peered into her wide-open mouth and there I spotted a huge hole in one of her lower teeth.

'Oh my God!' I exclaimed, not believing what I was seeing – after all she had only just got the damn things! 'Is this what's been hurting you all along?' I asked her.

As soon as we got home I contacted my dentist who recommended I took her to the national health clinic in the town centre, as they would be better equipped to deal with Amberlie. I immediately called them and they asked me to come in that morning as Dr Aston, the consultant special needs' dental surgeon, was available to take a look at her.

Dr Garth, the in-house dentist, initially examined Amberlie. She asked me to lie in the chair with Amberlie on top of me, so that she would be in the right position and feel safe while she looked at her mouth. She had a good look in her mouth, which Amberlie didn't seem to mind at all, and found that she had a total of six holes in her new teeth! I couldn't believe it and felt so bad for her. I had always cleaned her teeth, although I'd had to do it blind, as she would never open her mouth very wide and would bite down on the brush. I did the best I could in the circumstances.

Seeing my dismay and devastation, Dr Aston said that it was not my fault. She explained that children on lots of medication have problems with their teeth and gums. 'It seems to rot them before they have even come through,' she said. 'Amberlie also has a condition called hyperplasia, which is an overgrowth of gums due to being on medication.' She explained that this also extended the duration of teething as the teeth had further to go through the gums. This explained a lot and I felt a little better, but I was very concerned about the next step.

The doctor said, 'The teeth have to come out and it will be easier to have a good look at the rest while Amberlie is under anaesthetic, so we can sort out everything to keep them fine for at least the next two years.'

I was horrified. 'But what about all the drugs she's on? Isn't it dangerous for her to go under anaesthetic?' I didn't know how on earth I was going to deal with her going under, but I knew there was no option because she would never tolerate them pulling at her mouth, and I couldn't allow Amberlie to suffer any more grief with her teeth. She never used the damn things anyway, and any pain like that could only have the effect of increasing her seizures. Maybe this had been a lot of the trouble all along. It made sense. I was just terrified of losing her.

'Yes, it is more dangerous for Amberlie to have an anaesthetic than for other children ... but I assure you that she will have the best man to do it and he is used to the needs of special children. Try not to worry, I know it's difficult.'

'Will it be at the local hospital?' I asked.

'No,' she said, 'I am a private consultant and work at a private hospital.'

'But what about payment – how do I go about that?' I asked.

'There will be no cost to you. That will all be sorted out. I will write to you with a date and what you need to do shortly.'

'How long will she be in for?' I asked, my brain already contemplating all the arrangements that would need to be made.

'Providing all goes well with the anaesthetic, she will be in for just the day, but be prepared to stay overnight.'

In the meantime, she recommended that we start giving Amberlie fluoride tablets. She explained that they would not normally recommend this but in Amberlie's case it was more important to prevent problems than worry about the appearance of her teeth. She said that fluoride would give her protection from up to 60% of cavities but at the expense of making the enamel on her teeth have white blemishes. I sighed. Something else to remind me that Amberlie was not just an ordinary little girl whose beauty would be marred – that wasn't a consideration applicable to Amberlie. I sighed again.

'We also recommend you buy Amberlie one of the electric rotationally spinning toothbrushes which are available. Most mums find these better to use with special children, as none of them are especially good at opening their mouths when you want them to.'

I got her one on the way home and Amberlie seemed to like the sensation when we tried it.

I broke the news to Bill on the phone. He sighed deeply and after a silent pause he said, 'Poor kid … all the things she has to go through.'

'Mmmm,' I replied.

Two days later Amberlie came down with a throat infection and needed a course of penicillin. She didn't want to drink and as of that moment wouldn't have a bottle anywhere near her without going off her trolley. Strangely, though, she decided she would eat! I was beginning to wonder whether I was coming or going but at least I would be able to resort to fruit, jellies and custards to keep her fluids up. She certainly had a relentless determination to do what she wanted and was perfectly capable of making decisions and letting us know them in her usual way. The lady was never for swaying.

This all meant that the bad days would continue for a while, but luckily at that point, if she woke grumpily, a trip to the shops soon sorted her out. It was wonderful to see how much she adored being out, watching the people, the traffic, the trees, chuckling at different noises and happily surprised by the breeze or wind or spots of rain. She never got drowned in the rain – I could never risk that, but I thought it was important for her to feel life and when we eventually had some snow, I let her feel the flakes settle on her skin, and because her tongue was often out she was even able to taste them! Sometimes the minute we returned home she would grumble again and often I could keep her good humour going by getting the music on quickly and giving her the Skwish so that she could enjoy them both. Even when she started to get tired she would still be giggling to herself with her eyes closed until she fell fast asleep and I would lay her down and turn the music off so she could rest. She was so endearing to watch and enjoy – she made me fall in love with her more every day.

On 29 October 1996 Amberlie went into hospital to have her teeth sorted out. We were there as required before 7.45 a.m. and waited in reception until a staff nurse called Jackie from the children's ward collected us.

As soon as we were on the ward Amberlie was weighed along with me. This was the only accurate way to weigh her because she could not stand or sit in a weigh chair unsupported. Numerous forms were completed. Soon after, Dr Shaw came and introduced himself as Amberlie's anaesthetist and asked our permission to examine her. He asked many questions about her general health and confirmed her medications. He seemed a lovely man, very gentle, friendly and reassuring.

'She'll be just fine,' he said as he gave her a shot of something to 'dry her out'. After a short while, Dr Aston arrived to tell us they were ready for Amberlie in theatre.

Bill left to get the kids off to school and make sure Auntie Pat had everything she needed for the day to look after Ben. He didn't want to go and I knew he would be dashing about like a wild thing to get back as soon as he could.

'Be careful!' I called after him.

The nurses gave us a colourful little gown for Amberlie to wear and told us to leave her nappy on. They made her comfortable on the bed and we were taken down the corridor. Amberlie looked very bemused, tightly grasping her black-and-white Skwish. I think she realised her bed did not usually move! We were led into a small room and greeted by a friendly man dressed in blue. The cot side of Amberlie's bed was taken down and I was asked to hold her hand and talk to her. Amberlie didn't seem bothered – there again, she didn't know what was coming anyway! Her eyes were fixed on the glaring bright theatre lights above her. She was always attracted to bright lights and could stare straight at them without blinking her eyes or closing them at all.

Someone once told me that people with brain abnormalities were often able to look at bright lights without any bother, because as the brain was impaired, it was short of light so its need was therefore greater. I had no idea whether this was true, but it certainly appealed to Amberlie without ever fazing her.

Dr Shaw arrived and perched himself on a stool at Amberlie's head. He started to wave a green tube infront of her nose. I felt quite bewildered, having never seen anybody anaesthetised for an operation before, and I stayed close to her, brushing her hair back from her face and whispering that it would all be all right. Amberlie, bless her, grabbed hold of a part of the tube and pulled it away. They just let her. They continued waving it around in front of her, avoiding putting anything on her face. Gradually the doctor asked his assistant to increase the gas and Amberlie's eyelids started to get heavy. As she closed her eyes the doctor replaced the tube with a little black mask and there she lay, arms and legs wide apart, totally out cold. I felt overwhelmed and was fighting hard to bite back the tears, gripping her little hand tight. I didn't want to let her go, I was very frightened for her and frightened that she wouldn't come back to me. The nurses then ushered me out to sit in a conservatory just outside the theatre. They said they needed me to stay close, as it would save time if they needed to make any decisions.

Oh my God! I thought. I closed my eyes ... 'Please, please don't do this to me ... please God, please look after her,' I begged in a whisper so no one else could hear.

I tried to think of something – anything that would take my mind away for a while. The conservatory was light, airy and gave a good view of the gardens and other buildings of the hospital. There was a coffee machine, as well as comfy blue chairs and lots of magazines to look at. An old couple sat opposite me and smiled. I smiled back ... I didn't want to talk. I sat by the windows and kept my gaze outside so that I didn't look at anyone in case it prompted a conversation.

The old couple had started to talk together and I listened to how wonderful private care was and how many X-rays the man had endured, and what they thought was wrong and when the next operation was due. Then Dr Aston appeared.

'Mrs Murphy ... we're extracting two of Amberlie's molars on the bottom because the holes are too deep. We'll fill the rest, OK?' she said with a sympathetic smile.

I nodded. My heart was thumping like a drum.

After a while, out she came again to tell me that Amberlie was now in recovery and everything was fine.

'They'll call you shortly,' she said.

Bill was back and I was glad of the company. Ten minutes passed which dragged like an eternity and I fidgeted the whole time wishing they would hurry up.

'OK, Mrs Murphy, please come this way.'

The poor little mite was awfully pale and the blood left in her mouth gurgled away as she whimpered. She obviously felt terrible and didn't know what had happened to her or what to do with herself. I took her hand and kissed her cheek. 'It's OK, it's OK sweetpea … Mummy's here …'

The doctor presented us with two of Amberlie's teeth in a little vial and said, 'We filled four others.' Seeing us looking at the vial, she said, 'Big teeth! Lots of large roots!'

Dr Shaw joined us to see how Amberlie was. I shrugged my shoulders.

'Not happy,' I said.

'She'll be OK soon – she'll settle,' he said.

We returned to the ward and I grabbed the opportunity to pick Amberlie up and give her a cuddle. I walked her around trying to soothe her. Jackie the nurse made her a warm bottle of milk and said she might like a drink, but Amberlie was having none of it – it was too sore for her to suck at a teat. Bill squirted a tiny bit in her mouth to clear some of the blood and take the dryness away and then we gave her tiny amounts of pureed baby fruit and she started to settle down. She finally took about two thirds of the jar and then started to perk up, quickly returning to her usual self. She had a drain in her foot, which was put in while in theatre in case she had a seizure that might have needed treatment. The doctors said they had also given her a painkiller suppository, which explained why her nappy had been askew.

As Amberlie had settled, Bill went home and I dressed her, which seemed to please and relax her, and she lay on the bed happily playing with her Skwish before gradually dropping off to sleep. I was relieved. I felt I could take a breather and chill out in a chair for a while.

Amberlie slept peacefully for well over an hour and woke smiley and happy. She turned onto her tummy and pushed herself up so that she could have a good look round. A bit later Dr Shaw came to check her over, and told the nurses to remove the drain from her foot. He said Amberlie was fine and Dr Aston would be along shortly to have a chat with us.

We didn't have to wait long, and Dr Aston perched herself on the bed with Amberlie. She said there was nothing I could have done to prevent the holes in her teeth: it was all due to the sugary medicines. She said it would be a good idea to ask the doctors to prescribe sugar-free medicines where possible, and to take the fluoride supplement permanently. She asked if I was happy for Amberlie to continue seeing Dr Garth, as she was the 'tops' in her job, was used to special children and much admired throughout the profession. And, apparently, also a forensic dentist! I said that was fine by me.

There was no way I would let an ordinary dentist treat Amberlie now, and I have to say that the care and treatment she had was outstanding and exemplary. The sister awarded Amberlie with a 'Certificate of Bravery' and she was then discharged.

When we got home Raymond asked if he could colour the certificate in for her – and he did, very beautifully, so we later framed it to put on the wall by her bed.

Amberlie slept most of the afternoon and had a decent meal around 5 p.m. Bless her. I so hoped this would make her little life more comfortable and pain free now. Maybe if those complex partial seizures disappeared a bit she might be able to go back down on her medicine.

20

In view of all the traumatic experiences of late and the fact that Bill had earned a decent bonus at work, we decided it might be nice to do something exciting for the kids and risk going away for a few days.

We knew that anything that involved being away from home could be potentially stressful rather than relaxing, especially if it was in another country or a fair distance away from hospitals. On the other hand, we desperately needed a change of scenery and the kids all deserved a treat.

Bill and I talked for ages about it and decided that if we organised ourselves ready for all eventualities, then maybe most of the worry could be avoided. The main risk was Amberlie getting a chest infection. There wasn't much we could do if she had a fit and generally they were fairly well controlled. The last thing we wanted to do was to end up in a strange hospital trying to explain all that was wrong with Amberlie, especially if there was a language problem. There was also the amount of stuff we would have to take to keep her comfortable, so wherever we went we would need to take the car. Having convinced each other that everything would be just fine, and we could cope with whatever happened, we grabbed the bull by the horns and booked a four-day excursion to Disneyland Paris, departing December 6th.

Just as we hit December Amberlie got a cold. I asked Dr Jonathan if we could possibly have a precautionary bottle of antibiotics to take with us to France just in case it developed into a chest infection. He asked the chemist to give it to us in powder form with instructions on how to make it up if we needed to. I was very grateful.

We kept the trip a secret so that it would surprise the kids. They were fairly bewildered to be roused from their beds at 5 a.m.

on the day! We had planted several clues around the house, such as notices saying 'Guess where you're going today!' and 'Where's the Eiffel Tower?' They had to answer one to move onto the next. They looked at us as if we were barmy. By the third notice they were fully awake and laughing. Ben stood by them bleary eyed and sucking hard on his dummy! Disney had sent us some posh Mickey Mouse labels, stickers and other bits and bobs, and these were left at the end of the trail.

They didn't twig. They stood looking at each other with looks of disbelief on their faces, then Ray shrugged his shoulders and said, 'Disney?'

Bill and I laughed and nodded. They all went berserk! Ben didn't know why – he just joined in with the noise! I have never seen them get dressed so fast!

Amberlie didn't mind being woken early and took her breakfast well. Bill had loaded the car the night before so we only needed to sort ourselves out and collect up a few bits and pieces. The kids excitedly jumped in the car and we were away. Unfortunately we made the big mistake of going to Dover via the M25, where there had been an accident and we got stuck for an eternity, eventually missing our ferry.

'So much for no stress!' I moaned. I'd suggested to Bill that I thought it a good idea to avoid the M25 and go a different route. He disagreed and said it would be quicker to go that way. Both biting our tongues, we managed not to have a war!

Surprisingly the kids stayed happy as we reassured them that we would get another ferry at some stage!

Amberlie took it all in her stride, happy to be out whatever. We finally arrived at Dover two and a half hours late and we luckily managed to get on the next ferry due in, so we only had to wait 45 minutes. Amberlie found the ferry very soothing and slept right through the channel crossing.

We eventually arrived at the Davy Crockett Ranch. The whole journey had taken eleven hours and I was amazed that the kids had behaved so well. We felt self-catering was the best option as we would be in our own cabin and less likely to disturb other people. It was lovely and comfortable and only a 15-minute car journey from the Disney Park.

It was Christmas at Disney, so all the decorations and lights were up in abundance, and Amberlie was very excited by all the brightness, colours and noise. I had never seen her so happy for so long – all day every day, even though it was often very cold, especially waiting for the rides. I had her wrapped up in layers of clothes, multiple pairs of socks and blankets, and she didn't care! She attracted the Disney characters like a magnet and they readily posed with her for photographs. She adored their colourful wide-eyed huge faces and gazed up at them in total awe and fascination. Of course Ray and Clare made the most of the attention that Amberlie attracted by grabbing lots of cuddles from their favourites; and Ben, bless him, hid behind us when he saw them coming, not liking them at all … and Robin Hood actually reduced him to tears!

Amberlie fed really well the whole time, and we saw no evidence of any nasty seizures; everything was far more relaxing than we expected and a whole lot of fun. It was wonderful to see the kids really enjoying themselves and it was so nice to escape from reality for a while and have a little magic. The only bit of stress we had was on the last day when I realised that Bill had not brought enough vigabatrin with us. I couldn't believe it.

'You bloody idiot!'

'I forgot her dosage had been increased … oh shit!' He was upset with himself.

'It's just as well it's the last day, we'd better keep our fingers crossed!' I groaned, worried sick.

Thankfully we got home without any problems, and even managed to pop into a French warehouse to load up with a few bottles of wine whilst waiting for the ferry. After shoving some medicine into Amberlie as soon as we got in the door, she fell asleep and apart from coming up for food every now and then, she slept solidly for the next 24 hours. She was exhausted, but it was worth it! She had a very 'tired' week after that with a few twitches here and there but nothing unusual.

The other kids were totally exhausted and delighted to have been to Disney. They all had new toys and clothes and we were glad we had made the decision to go.

Amberlie was coming up to four years old and had not had a decent Christmas Day since she was born, but this one turned out absolutely great! She was happy all day long, loved the lights and decorations and was enormously interested in her parcels whether they were large or small. She especially enjoyed one small present of socks that made a nice squashy-paper sound when she touched it, and it remained unopened for ages after Christmas because she liked it so much! She even managed to eat a small amount of Christmas dinner! We were so pleased for her, it made the whole family's day. We'd had a wonderful December!

I was having my usual shower one morning when I heard a strange noise. I grabbed a towel and rushed into our bedroom to find Amberlie in the midst of the most god-awful fit I'd ever seen. She was shaking all over with her eyes flickering and was foaming at the mouth. I quickly turned her on her side. I had just heard the front door slam as Bill left for work. I grabbed Amberlie in my arms, keeping her on her side so she would not swallow her tongue, and shot down the stairs yelling for Raymond to go and get his father who was waiting for the car to defrost at the end of the drive. Realising I was standing stark naked on the doorstep, I went into the front room and laid her down on the floor. The seizure went on for at least another five minutes and then subsided. Instead of going to sleep, Amberlie stared straight ahead. Her eyes were large and black like deep voids and she was totally still and silent. I was petrified. Her breathing was very, very shallow and I thought, *This is it ... she's a goner*. I picked her up.

By now everyone was up and we all just sat looking at her in my arms; no one said a word. I cuddled and talked to her, stroked her hair and played with her fingers, hoping it would spark something. About 15 minutes later she finally came back to us totally exhausted. We were relieved but shocked. Bill was now in no fit state to go to work and I got a friend to take the kids to school. Luckily there was no recurrence.

Bill accompanied Amberlie and me to see Dr Ramsay two days later and we told her what had happened. She said that she would give us some diazepam (Valium) in case it happened again. This was to be given rectally and would stop the seizure. She said Amberlie had obviously had a tonic-clonic (grand mal) which had gone on too long, and explained that if Amberlie fitted for more than five minutes, we should give her diazepam.

'If the fit has not stopped after ten minutes you should call an ambulance immediately,' she said, staring hard into our eyes. She also said that after administering diazepam, Amberlie would be very drowsy for about twenty-four hours.

'How does it work?' I asked. The doctor explained that it was obviously unwise to give Amberlie anything orally during a seizure because of the risk of choking, so an alternative was to give her something rectally.

'This is because the bloodstream runs very close to the wall of the rectum, and is very similar to the inside of our mouths. The medicine is quickly absorbed in this area and enters the bloodstream almost immediately. That is how the seizure is stopped.'

She went on to say that there was some research going on in the hope of a similar medicine that could be rubbed into the inside of the facial cheek during a seizure. The idea behind this was to alleviate the embarrassment problem connected with administering medicines rectally – to find a nicer way for everybody concerned.

'Is it not possible, then, to replace the other drugs with this?' I asked.

'No,' she said. 'Diazepam is only used in an emergency because like most other similar drugs it can be addictive. But worse is the fact that if it is used too often, the patient becomes used to it and therefore it is rendered ineffective. And we don't want to be left in that position do we?'

'No … I see.' I sighed heavily.

The following Saturday Amberlie was sitting playing when she started her familiar dry cough that usually spelt trouble in the chest department. It was late in the day and I could only get the Health Call weekend service. The doctor eventually came out at 1 a.m. and when he examined her he felt that at that moment she did not need antibiotics.

Unfortunately, I let him persuade me that she was OK rather than following my own gut instinct that told me to insist. There was no improvement the next day and as time went on Amberlie became more miserable and her feeding stopped. She had not really had a decent drink for thirty-six hours. Her temperature started to soar and her breathing worsened. I called for the doctor but again got the Health Call service. This was around 6 p.m. By 8 p.m. no one had arrived and she was deteriorating fast so I rang again and the switchboard girl paged the doctor on duty. He rang back but said he could not come at the moment because he had other emergencies to see. Try as I might I could not get him to understand that because of her condition this was an emergency. He was so condescending that in the end I was so cross I told him that I would take her straight to the hospital myself and slammed the phone down.

Bill and I took her to the hospital, where she was seen immediately, had her chest X-rayed and was taken to the children's ward. There was indeed a bad chest infection and she had a temperature of 39.5 degrees C. This prompted a nasty fit on the ward and a lot of distress for the poor little soul, who was intermittently screaming as if in the most awful pain. Luckily the fit didn't last long. We had to go through the usual search for blood from her tiny elusive veins, and the nurse took a urine sample as well. She was then put on a saline drip because she was dehydrated and was started on intravenous antibiotics.

Amberlie then settled down a bit and Bill left for home at around 2 a.m. to relieve Christine, who was looking after the kids. Amberlie then had a peaceful night.

Bill said that the Health Call doctor had phoned to see whether we had taken Amberlie to hospital. He told him we had and that she had been kept in and was very ill. I hoped that this doctor felt appropriately guilty and I resolved never to accept that Amberlie did not need antibiotics again when I damn well knew she did. The next time I saw Dr Jonathan I moaned about the Health Call service. I tried to be fair – I knew they were busy and that Amberlie was an unusual case. He smiled and apologised for them. He said that in a case like Amberlie's it was often better to prescribe antibiotics straight away because special children can deteriorate so quickly, rather than wait and see what happened.

I was always amazed at how soon the antibiotics worked and how quickly Amberlie recovered. We stayed in hospital almost three days. Once Amberlie started to drink again she was taken off her drip and put onto oral antibiotics. We were then allowed home.

A week later Amberlie seemed really peculiar – she was almost unconscious when she slept and was now noisily wheezing. I called Dr Jonathan and he came to see her.

'I don't have a clue what's that matter with her,' he said. 'I think it's best I ring the hospital because I don't feel confident in what to diagnose.'

The hospital told us to come in straight away, so I phoned Bill and told him to come home from work.

This time her X-ray didn't show any sign of infection but Amberlie was still wheezing. She had also stopped eating and drinking again so the doctors decided to keep her in for observation. They ran all the usual tests again, which were all returned negative. During the evening they decided to let us go home as Amberlie had started to drink again.

Two weeks later we need the doctor again. It was another weekend and all that was available was the bloody Health Call service. After a couple of hours a doctor arrived and left a prescription for antibiotics, with an interim sachet to take immediately to get us through the night until the chemist opened. Three hours later Amberlie was worse and her breathing was deteriorating fast. I called the doctor again and he rang for an ambulance. In casualty her chest was X-rayed but there was no sign of infection. They put her on a nebuliser and this seemed to give her some relief.

We were then taken to the children's ward, where they gave her another nebuliser treatment and the doctor instructed the nurses to start Amberlie on a course of steroids in the morning. Amberlie settled down and slept all the next day but I disappointedly had to remind them that she should have started her steroids twelve hours earlier.

I was very anxious to get Amberlie sorted out this time because it was Clare's seventh birthday the next day. I asked Dr Thomas if there was any chance that Amberlie would be discharged that day and he said that all being well it was possible. In the evening he came back to reassess her and explained that they believed Amberlie had viral associated asthma and that's why she responded to the nebulisers. She was to have a Ventolin inhaler and a 'spacer' to take home.

The spacer is a device with a facemask at one end to cover the nose and mouth of the child, and a hole at the other for an inhaler to be inserted. The inhaler is sprayed into the spacer while the facemask is held over the nose and mouth, and the child then breathes in the steroid in about 10 breaths.

Amberlie needed this because she did not know how to breathe in the steroid if the inhaler was positioned directly in her mouth.

Dr Thomas explained that when Amberlie started to develop a cold, we should start using the spacer as a precaution as this would keep her tubes open, allowing mucus to escape from the lungs, and hopefully preventing some of her chest infections. He was happy to let us go home but said should Amberlie deteriorate in the night to bring her straight back – which of course I would.

I was desperately keeping my fingers crossed for Clare's sake. She was very understanding of Amberlie's plight and wasn't worried about her birthday going pear-shaped at all. She had a perception much older than her years but she was still only very young and I wanted her to have a good day with all of us together.

When we got home I made a few calls to say that Clare's day was still on, and while Bill watched over Amberlie I dashed about organising things. Clare was very excited and she helped me make some jellies and cakes. She said, 'You know, Mum, I wouldn't have minded not having a birthday tomorrow if Amberlie wasn't well.' The tears shot into my eyes and I smiled and gave her a big hug. I told her what a good girl she was and promised her that she would have a super day. Fingers crossed, I thought. We put lots of balloons and streamers up after she went to bed. The next day her aunties and grandparents arrived together with a few of her friends and they all had a great time. As I tucked her in bed that night and kissed her cheek she said, 'Thank you, Mum – I had a lovely day, and Amberlie was OK too, wasn't she?'

The Ventolin inhaler certainly freed Amberlie's breathing but boy did it make her miserable! Three days later I could hear a rattle in her chest so I took her round to Dr Jonathan and he gave her some antibiotics. He said the hospital should have given her the antibiotics anyway, as more often than not an asthma attack caused virally will end in an infection.

Dr Jonathan was also concerned about Amberlie being labelled too readily as an asthmatic. He had researched as much as he could about lissencephaly and noted that it was common for these children to have gastro-oesophageal reflux, which happens when the muscle at the bottom of the food pipe is lax and the contents of the stomach come back up the food pipe and seep into the lungs causing damage and weakness. This often presents with consistent respiratory problems and recurrent chest infections.

Jonathan thought this might be the case with Amberlie of late and suggested he write to Dr Thomas to remind him of this aspect of lissencephaly. After a couple of weeks I received a letter from Dr Thomas saying that he was arranging for Amberlie to spend twenty-four hours in hospital while they performed a pH test to determine whether or not gastro-oesophageal reflux was a problem. No sooner had I read the letter than the registrar was on the phone asking us to bring her in on 21st April.

In the meantime Amberlie seemed to sink to an all-time low. She was constantly miserable and both Dr Jonathan and I were at a loss as to what to do. As time progressed we noticed she was having the odd shaking session, which was obviously some sort of new seizure activity, and usually happened when she woke in the mornings. After a couple of weeks the shaking was happening on alternative mornings and really set up those days for sheer misery. Amberlie was totally inconsolable and I didn't know what to do.

One day after having to abandon a physio session at the hospital because Amberlie was in a screaming frenzy, I bumped into Dr Ramsay in the corridor. She asked how Amberlie was and I explained that she was very up and down and that she was fitting on alternative mornings after waking. As luck would have it, all Dr Ramsay's appointments for that afternoon had been cancelled and she told me to bring her back later on so we could sort her out. I phoned Bill and he said he wanted to come with me so he asked for the afternoon off.

After explaining all Amberlie's new, different physical movements and all that had happened, it turned out that she was having four different types of seizures. Dr Ramsay thought it was time to introduce a different type of drug as she couldn't increase the vigabatrin further and if she did, the likelihood of it doing anything was remote. She suggested trying lamotrigine while at the same time dropping the clonazepam entirely but slowly. She warned that if Amberlie developed a rash we were to contact her immediately. I was really worried then, because as the Disney trip had been such a success, we had scheduled a week's holiday in the Isle of Wight and were leaving in two days' time. Dr Ramsay told us not to worry; it was a fairly rare reaction and that we weren't on the other side of the world.

'If she gets a rash we'll come back!' I resolved.

The next day was Amberlie's fourth birthday and the day went well. She had a good time, stayed happy and had lots of visitors and presents. Bill and I racked our brains on what to buy her and finally decided on a Star. I had seen advertisements about naming a star after someone, but had associated it with being a 'celebrity thing'. Amberlie received a beautifully framed certificate of ownership and coordinates of the Star named 'Amberlie Rose', and later on a copy of the book listing it in the British Library. The following day we left for the Isle of Wight.

The mixture of the new drug and being on holiday seemed to calm Amberlie, and apart from gritting her teeth a little, she didn't seem to have any reaction from the reduction in clonazepam. She did have a scream for an hour or so in the evenings but then slept all night.

The days were unusually sunny, but it was more than a bit cold in our chalet at night and the wind blew in constantly through the vents. We went round blocking them up as far as possible to try and keep the warmth in. The only fire was in the sitting room so it didn't do much for the bedrooms. The best option for Amberlie was to sleep swamped under duvets and blankets with her dad, as he has always been a walking central heater! The rest of us snuggled up as best we could. It still turned out to be a nice break though.

After fourteen days we were to increase the lamotrigine again and then leave everything stable until Amberlie's May appointment. The lamotrigine had stopped all the early morning seizures and Amberlie was back to her old self. She was now sitting in her chair again and enjoying playing with her toys – something she hadn't wanted to do for some weeks.

It was time for Amberlie's pH test and she was admitted to Compton Ward. A tube with a probe on the end was inserted up her nose and down into the bottom of her food pipe. It was then linked to a small computer that Amberlie would wear and take around with her for twenty-four hours to monitor the acidity. The test proved negative – hooray! I was so pleased because a positive test would have meant an operation to tighten the opening at the bottom of the pipe. Bill and I were relieved, but it obviously didn't prove anything regarding the chest problems.

I had wondered if I'd done the right thing when I dropped her Tagamet syrup despite the possible allergic reaction, in that I may have aggravated her stomach in doing so, but now I could file that one away with no regrets.

Everything seemed to point to Amberlie's misery and irritation being caused cerebrally. There was obviously nothing wrong with her stomach and everything coincided with the appearance of new seizure activity. Maybe she had cramps in her stomach, which were connected to the muscle tightening during fits. It had to be possible. Seizures made muscles tighten and surely they affected everything internally as well as externally? Theoretically, tightened stomach muscles could also push or leak acids into the wrong places, causing discomfort and/or pain. It was so important to maintain control of Amberlie's seizures.

Dr Ramsay asked whether Amberlie was still taking Lactulose to help her bowels along, and I said she was but it only helped a bit. She was still very constipated and going to the loo was another event that made her scream. She increased the dosage but Amberlie still screamed the place down when it happened. At least we knew what was causing this particular upset.

We had fought our way through yet another battle for another reprieve and it was all very exhausting. The normal times were a relief to be relished and gave us all a chance to chill out and regroup before the next trauma occurred, because it was always just around the corner. Even if Amberlie was happy for a day in amongst several miserable ones, it made it easier to cope and lightened the whole house. It was the ongoing, incessant grief that made life hell.

June brought us another murderous week with a sickness bug ravaging its way through the house. Ben started it, passed it to Ray, and then onto Amberlie. The boys were over it more or less as soon as they were sick but Amberlie unsurprisingly continued to vomit through the night, unable to settle at all. At around 6 a.m. it appeared the worst was over and she settled into one of her awful coma-type recovery sleeps. She woke at around 9 a.m. and drank two ounces of milk and drifted off again. When she next opened her eyes I quickly put her into a warm bath to make her smell desirable again and then she slept for the rest of the day. Bill tried a little food that evening but she couldn't manage it without catching her breath so we kept her on milk. Amberlie then had a peaceful night and I loathed having to wake her the next morning so that I could get the others to school. She took her medicine but had trouble swallowing it and as soon as we were back home she went back to sleep until 1.15 p.m. She then took a full bottle and later attempted a small amount of food, which she managed quite well.

Although intermittently sleepy and floppy she had perked up a little and the next day she was a little brighter but very pale.

Amberlie was also having more mental absences as a result of being ill, and these were making her spaced out but there were no physical jerks, although she jumped occasionally. Amberlie was also showing signs of wanting to go to the loo and this was naturally adding to her grief. Despite her laxative, prunes, fruit and fibre it often took Amberlie two to three days to pass a stool, so her bowels were indeed very slow workers. It wasn't at all surprising that there were a few fits about.

I suspected things were on the change again as Amberlie had shown signs of stress over the past month. She jumped a lot for no apparent reason, which left her upset and distressed. I noticed that preceding the jump she turned her head to look behind her with her eyes full of fear like someone was chasing her or going to leap out and scare her. I suspected an increase or difference in her partial seizures. A lot of the time she was in the extension position and the power of their thrust was enormously strong. I wondered if the lamotrigine needed increasing or whether there was something else lurking.

The last reduction in clonazepam had possibly instigated two odd seizures, and coincided with the appearance of a runny nose, so I knew Amberlie was coming down with something again. The runny nose seemed to dry up within a couple of days and no sooner had I dismissed it as nothing, then she developed a chest infection and another course of antibiotics was needed. After completing the course I could still hear a rattle in her chest and hoped that it wouldn't mean another surgery visit. The next day she started another sickness episode but it had the positive effect of completely clearing her chest.

Amberlie did not seem to recover so well this time. She was very, very tired and had lost some of her zest. She had to shrug off so much time and time again, that it was bound to hit hard somewhere along the line. She must have been so exhausted, but to have been so resistant for so long made me think she must have a very strong inner self and a real determination to live.

I continued to worry about the difficulty Amberlie was having every now and then with her swallowing. It was usually linked to spaced-out days and I could understand that. After all, if she was not fully conscious in any form, regardless of the fact that her eyes were open, then how would she be able to sort out everyday actions like eating, especially something like alternating swallowing with breathing? It just showed how hard her seizures hit her brain. Sometimes she had trouble swallowing anyway, even when she was OK otherwise. It had to be possible that there was now damage to this area of the brain, but I preferred to explore the possibility that she was using it as a tool to refuse her food as well as turning her head away, sealing her lips, spitting it back and wriggling like crazy to get away. Maybe I was just being optimistic again and had granted it too much credibility, and perhaps in reality it was far more serious. It had to be dreadfully frightening to try to swallow when she felt she was going to gag or choke. Maybe it only happened when her seizures were prevalent, maybe they were more prevalent than I realised or could see. Perhaps the seizures shocked her swallowing muscles into a paralysis that wore off after a while.

I know I did not see all of Amberlie's seizures – they were often a split-second event, or happened in her sleep. Amberlie was not able to let me know they were there and possibly some surprised her too. I knew the medication masked a lot of her seizures, and by 'masked' I mean that the seizures were happening inside but the medication did not allow them to surface to be seen, and as a consequence they often upset her because the drugs stopped the release of the stress they caused. To a point Amberlie needed to have some fits because that was her norm. Mostly the small blips and interruptions in Amberlie's everyday awareness didn't bother her and I guess it was like moving from one moment to another without ever realising there had been one in between. Some of the larger seizures were a result of the building up of pressure caused by the smaller ones, and the disillusioning part was that it was virtually impossible to control most of the smaller ones. It must have been so confusing for her sometimes when the nasty phases happened, to feel OK and happy and then suddenly feel lousy, upset or extremely tired, and not be able to understand why. There again perhaps she couldn't remember how she had felt prior to the seizure(s). To some extent she must have learnt to live with it like normal epileptics or those with other chronic conditions do.

Obviously a certain type of seizure affected Amberlie's swallowing reflex more than others but it was hard to pinpoint which when I was unable to witness them all. Oddly it never affected her ability to drink her milk – in fact, she took it very readily, often with enthusiasm and relief. It had to be that the consistency of the milk was right for her to swallow, because when I tried watery fluid such a fruit juice or squash, she coughed and spluttered and then refused it.

I wondered how long her drinking would be OK. Prolonged persistent refusal as well as the progressing physical inability to swallow and breathe at the same time were bound to affect her drinking eventually. It was also the signal I dreaded, the mark of a significant deterioration in her condition – evidence of brain damage caused by uncontrolled seizures.

Amberlie's 'spaced-out' times worried me endlessly. I realised how dangerously close we teetered on the edge of keeping her alert and able to develop and lead something of a life, instead of being comatose and on massively high doses of antiepileptics in order to keep the seizures under control. Spaced-out was OK though, I accepted it and could live with it – it was far more preferable to comatose, provided she was happy and not in any discomfort. I imagined it must be similar to being 'high' on drugs. Amberlie laughed a lot at these times, so some of it must have been nice and appealing to her, albeit rather sinister in origin. It was much easier to deal with a happy Amberlie.

This of course was not ideal, though it was a liveable middle of the road and preferable to the unbearable misery we all endured when Amberlie's head was strange. Those times were unbelievably hard and I felt totally powerless and inadequate to help her. I tried my hardest to understand and work out what was happening or causing it, and I knew it was either fit related, or that she was trying to go to the loo or that she was becoming ill. I sympathised, cuddled, tried distracting her, hoping to comfort her in some way, whilst waiting for signs of what the problem was. Sometimes it would go on for days and days. It was so frustrating and so exhausting, and the constant 'mental' moans, screaming and crying for hours on end, together with my inability to find the answer, drove me insane and I had to walk out of the room to get away from it. After a cry I'd go back and try again, walk her round, take her out or just sit with her on my lap hoping it would pass – telling myself it would sort itself out soon. When I couldn't stand it any longer I too would throw a tantrum, and shout and moan at her and anyone else who was there. Amberlie ignored me and continued as she was and the kids just looked at me. I knew it wasn't their fault, it was my own stress and frustration, but I'd go berserk yelling at them for doing things they usually did, for no more reason then I'd had enough of Amberlie for one day. And then I'd feel massively guilty for getting so stressed and burst into tears again.

If she started to settle I used to ask the kids to be quiet in case they started her off again. I knew I couldn't really expect them to be that quiet but if one of them screamed and set her off again I'd go mad. It was hard to come out of a vicious circle like that but I found the answer was to just give up and let it all happen. If Amberlie was going to yell then she was going to whatever and I couldn't expect the whole world to shut up because of her. I didn't want a house full of misery so I learned to get over it.

It was easier to walk away – anything to escape the agony. Strangely enough, when Amberlie had pushed me to the very limit and I finally shouted and left her totally alone to get on with it, she would stop. She had always done this. Why we had to get to this stage I don't know. Maybe it was frustration that she couldn't get her message across to me that made her persist for so long, or perhaps my disappearance made her forget what was bothering her, who knows? It could even have been Amberlie's continuing version of the terrible twos – or maybe it reached the point where we were both too exhausted to continue. I could analyse it forever and still be wrong!

The sudden silence in the house always alarmed the kids and they used to come and tell me that Amberlie had calmed down because I was never aware of it straightaway, as her screaming would still be banging about deep in my head! They'd hold my hand and tell me she was OK – they had forgiven me for yelling at them. The guilt set in hard and my face would be running with tears as I hugged and apologised to them for being such a mean mummy. They just hugged me back and happily went off to play again.

When I got back to Amberlie she would either be smiling and cooing or zonked out fast asleep. I would just slump in the chair wondering how on earth I was going to cope in the future.

There were also many individual days that started off bad and would stay that way, but it was always worth the effort of trying to change them. If I was lucky enough to get the timing right, Amberlie's music would make her boogie in her chair, nodding her head and swaying from side to side with a huge grin on her face, and banging the Skwish hard in a certain rhythm. She had a favourite song now and the effect of that was truly amazing. It was Edwyn Collins' 'A Girl Like You', and she loved it! She always stopped to listen and it could stop the worst of wobblies! The Manic Street Preachers were also a great bet and made her dance, and the louder the music was the better she liked it! The kids adored watching her and joined in the fun by dancing round the room, which pleased Amberlie no end, as she liked them to join in with her excitement.

Taking her out was still good but I don't think it helped much having Ben sat next to her in a twin buggy. He was such a noisy so and so and once he'd got a reaction from her, he just carried on making it worse. His terrible twos were pretty horrific and he never ceased to wind Amberlie up, irritating her at every opportunity. She didn't quite know what to make of him because one moment he would be amusing her and the next yelling his head off!

If Ben started shouting or went anywhere near Amberlie during her meals – even if all he wanted was to pat her on the head – she would cringe and refuse to eat or drink. He adored her but his approach was overwhelming and he was often perturbed by her reaction. He did eventually learn that if he approached Amberlie gently and chattered quietly to her in his garbled toddler way, she smiled and eagerly listened with her eyes fixed on his face. She loved that at any time, and especially if he helped her while she played. Ben rarely took her toys away, just accepting that they were hers and he always picked them up for her if she dropped them. I don't think she would have minded him borrowing and playing with them at all.

It was interesting to see how the kids showed their love for Amberlie, each having their different way and she seemed to like and enjoy them all. Clare loved to have Amberlie perched on her lap for a cuddle and Bill and I used to have to position them both well enough to support each other. Ray was still content to stroke her hair, gazing at her deeply, lost in thought. You could just about hear him whisper a few words every now and then but they were just for Amberlie and no one else! Ben was very much her playmate.

21

It was now June 1997 and I was sitting restlessly waiting for Dr Ramsay to ring me back. There had been an increase in the number of Amberlie's seizures and she had developed some peculiar stretched-out postures. If it hadn't been for the expression of concentrated terror on her face, it would have been easy to mistake them for natural but intense body stretches. These progressed into puppet-like poses with her arms raised up in a wonky, spiked manner and her body and legs following suit – just like they were attached to strings. Her face contorted in a similar way and her features almost imitated the uneven hanging of her limbs. It was very harrowing and strange and shocking to think that her brain was doing this. I dreaded to think how she felt.

Although Dr Ramsay often assured me that Amberlie wouldn't know anything about her seizures, I wondered whether this was the case all the time, and if so, why did they often upset her?

'Come on Doc, hurry up and ring!' I said looking at the phone, feeling my nerves fray by the second.

It had all started a few evenings before when Amberlie had suffered a really nasty seizure. She had eaten her dinner beautifully and calmly, then as she took the last mouthful she went very cross-eyed and rigid. The fit progressed into some jerks which were non-symmetrical, similar to the puppet ones, and alternated with an awful rigidity. Her head jerked forwards intermittently and I placed her onto her padded floor mats to give her some room, but she turned onto her tummy and bashed her head really hard onto the floor. She was obviously totally out of it because she didn't react to this at all. It was too difficult to keep her on her side with the ferocity of the jerks so I picked her up again to avoid her getting hurt. The whole thing continued for about five minutes and just as I decided it was time to give her diazepam, she paused. Bill and I sighed with relief as we thought she was coming out of it ... but the seizure was merely changing form.

Amberlie then went into what I can only describe as extreme electric shocks that curled her up with an immense force that held her rigid for a few seconds. These repeated at about two every minute and with each one she screamed out as if in pain. She seemed to come to for a few seconds between each one but her eyes would dull off again as the next shock came. Again we grabbed the diazepam, but the force started dying away and the shocks lessened to slight jumps, and then to slight jerks until they disappeared. She then looked around to see where we were and snuggled up to go to sleep.

Bill and I sat with her not saying a word. We both sighed as the trauma passed and felt empty and exhausted.

The next day brought another five of the puppet-like episodes and about the same amount of stretches. The day after that Amberlie was very jumpy and endured countless stretches and one puppet episode. She could not settle at all and spent a lot of the time shouting out in a spaced-out sort of way. I think it was her way of protesting because she absolutely loathed seizures that made her jump, and she knew they were around. By the end of the day things had changed into laughing absences.

It looked as if Amberlie had really entered a bad spell, and the only way I could interrupt her seizures was by taking her out or putting her in her chair to play. Keeping her focused helped a little although the lulls were punctuated with absences. If left alone, her seizures increased. Whether that was due to her brain being allowed to wander or whether it was drowsiness induced by the previous seizure I am not sure.

Unsurprisingly, Amberlie's swallowing had also been affected, and on one occasion her drinking was disrupted. The seizure had disorganised her momentum and left her panicky, making her suck hard and quickly on her bottle, gasp desperately for air then carry on sucking again. She was obviously thirsty and wanted her milk and was intent to get it before being interrupted by something again. Once again she became reluctant with her solid food but took some of it quite calmly.

The phone hadn't rung yet. I knew Fridays were clinic days for Dr Ramsay, and despite having bitten away every fingernail, I decided to wait until lunchtime before chasing her secretary. I didn't want to go through the entire weekend without having spoken to her.

I had cancelled Amberlie's physio session that week. There was no way she was aware enough to go through that. They would only be able to stretch her legs at the most and I could do that – although Amberlie was managing quite well on her own ... albeit unintentionally. I wasn't sorry about cancelling because I had discovered a connection between her attending physio and becoming ill. The soft mats they used were vinyl covered and Amberlie often rolled on them, ending up face down with her mouth open against them. I had seen other children do this and dribble the same as Amberlie did, and although the mats were wiped with a paper towel, there was no antibacterial used and I was convinced she was picking up germs she could well do without.

Amberlie was physically quite strong and the movements she did exercised her very well. She vigorously kicked her legs sitting in her chair, on her back and even on her tummy, and she used her whole body to roll across the floor. I tried doing what she did and I couldn't! Even her extension position, although sinister, had its benefits, as it stretched her hips and spine, helping to keep her nice and straight. The only thing she couldn't do was to stretch her calf tendons.

It was a shame her seizures were not following the same path of improvement. More seizures meant more medicines, which meant more drowsiness and/or stress, which led to more infections. She had a persistent rattle in her chest that I think was down to the additional secretions caused by the seizures, and she had become quite run down generally, highlighted by a cold sore having erupted on her bottom lip.

At last the phone rang. Dr Ramsay put Amberlie's clonazepam up a small amount and suggested we give it two weeks to work. She did not like the sound of her bad fit and was not happy with the swallowing problem, saying, 'We can't have that.'

She checked that we had some diazepam and said to give it to her after five minutes of a seizure whatever, so that the seizure wouldn't take on another lease of life.

'It will stop the fit, but be warned that Amberlie will go the most awful colour as she settles and it will seem like she is dead.'

'God!' I replied. 'Is there a risk with it then?'

'No! I just want you to be aware that it will be frightening if you do have to use it.'

I came off the phone thinking, *Please don't let me have to use it ... please let the clonazepam work.*

I never seemed to be able to offload any worry, even the lifeline of a dose of diazepam wasn't without a 'but'. I never felt any better or confident of anything anymore. Every course of action was a shot in the dark, never knowing if anything was going to work. I couldn't go back and say to Amberlie, 'Everything's going to be OK, sweetpea.' I could only promise her that I would try to make it better.

I sat for ages holding her tight, rocking her and gazing at nothing out of the window. I don't even know that I was thinking. Her little snores brought me back to earth. She looked so beautiful asleep in my arms. She didn't deserve all this. I could not understand or reconcile why a child should suffer so much.

'I hate you God, I hate you.'

22

We had just received notice that the building of 'Amberlie's Suite' was to start on 23 July and the man from the council was popping by to go over the finances.

When he arrived he looked a little cagey and I wondered what was wrong with him. He said that after working out all the costs, our contribution was to be about £15,000 - £5,000 more than we were originally quoted! I was stunned. He said he was sorry but costs had risen in the last few months. I said there was no way that we could suddenly find another £5,000 and he left saying that the work would need to be postponed.

I was so gobsmacked I wandered round the house with Amberlie in my arms, amazed at how easily and in an instant our plans had been snatched away. Once I'd got my head together a bit, I rang Bill who was shocked and very angry, and then I spoke to my brother Ray. I tried hard not to burst into tears but they came anyway and I blubbed on for ages about why everything always went wrong for us. He was absolutely livid and asked if I had kept any of the correspondence stating their original quote. I had – I always kept everything like that.

'OK,' he said, 'I'll talk to Bill.'

Soon after Bill called me back and said that he wanted the details of the letter and anything else that had been promised. He said it was bang out of order that it had taken eighteen months for the council to organise this and then for it to get to this stage and let us down about cost.

Bill phoned the council and insisted he spoke to someone in authority. Reluctantly they put him through to the director. He explained what had happened and said that their letter gave no indication of any potential increase in our contribution at any later stage. He said that we had agreed to go ahead with the project based upon the costs given, and that it was not our fault the council had taken eighteen months to organise it. Bill initially did not receive much sympathy and the council maintained their stance. Bill told them he was appalled with their service and would be lodging a formal written complaint, contacting a solicitor and going to the local newspapers with the story.

It seemed like hours while Amberlie and I waited at home wondering what was going on. Then Bill rang and said that after much arguing and wrangling he had accepted that the costs had unavoidably risen, but insisted that had the council been more efficient they would not have been so high. He had agreed that we would contribute roughly another £2,000, making a total of £12,000 towards the cost and that the council would pay the rest.

After a couple of hours the council telephoned him and wholeheartedly apologised that things had taken so long. To make up for some of the inconvenience they would also pay any difference incurred in having quality double-glazing installed in the extension instead of their own. They were also going to upgrade Amberlie's shower to a power shower and provide a proper glass screen for us to use to avoid getting wet whilst showering Amberlie. They also assured Bill that there would be no other hidden costs or any incidental amounts for us to pay and that the work would start as promised on 23 July.

My brother and Bill's mum helped us with the additional £2,000.

We could easily have accepted what they said and Amberlie would have gone without her facilities. Why are there different rights for some than for others? There would have been no argument or problem had we been on income support … the system just was not fair.

I can't say I was looking forward to the builders invading us, though. I wasn't so worried about the outside extension – the problem would be when they came inside to alter the staircase in the hall and knock the kitchen and dining room into one to give Amberlie disabled access in the house (wider passageways for a wheelchair). They were also going to build ramps and new pathways at the front and back of the house for easy access, and put a porch on the front of the house to aid storage and have somewhere to put Amberlie's bulky pushchair. It did not fold down well and up until then had remained in the back of the car in full view of all. I was concerned about that because although it was perhaps not the most desirable object for a thief, it was an expensive purpose-built chair that could potentially be sold on; but more importantly, I couldn't do without it, and a replacement would take forever to order, so its security was a priority.

One morning after the old outhouse had been demolished. Ben escaped out of the kitchen door to venture in the rubble and ended up falling onto a broken brick. I rushed to pick him up and he seemed OK but was moaning about his knee. As he lifted it to show me, the skin separated into a three-inch split and blood gushed everywhere. We rushed him up the hospital where he went berserk fighting and screaming while they put an injection into the wound and stitched him up. The doctor eventually managed to get five stitches in, but the rest of the wound had to be stuck with strips because he would not tolerate any more and the doctor and nurses were at their wits' end! Amazingly Amberlie took this all in her stride and patiently sat there waiting quite contentedly.

When we got home, the builders were in a right paddy over it and were worried that we were going to go mad at them for leaving the site open. Apparently the council had warned them that Bill was a real ogre so they needed to watch it! I laughed.

'Yeah right!' I said and called Bill out. I enjoyed telling him and explained to Mike, our builder, that Bill and the council had had a little dispute before the building started and that was why he was thought to be horrid!

Ben was only young and bound to investigate different things. It all looked very exciting out there to a little boy, and it was just as much my fault as theirs for not making sure the door was secure. It was just one of those things that happened.

Thankfully Amberlie had kept generally well for six weeks and either the increase in clonazepam had worked or the puppet seizures had disappeared as a phase. She was, however, now having a salaam seizure roughly every other day after waking in the morning, but at least they were short lived, petering out quickly. It seemed that the medication had brought back her usual type of bad seizure ... Very strange ...

At the end of the month Amberlie went into a full tonic-clonic seizure after waking, and after a full five minutes of shaking and jerking the fit changed to affect just the left side of her body. Her left arm jerked upwards across her chest and her eye winked rapidly. Afterwards she drifted off into an awful still absence with a deep unnerving blackness in her staring eyes. It knew this wasn't going to go away and it was now time to give her the diazepam. It took only seconds to give and worked almost instantly, sending Amberlie floating off into a calm sleep. I tensely waited for her to lose her colour and look awful but she didn't, and curiously she only slept for an hour and a half instead of the expected twenty-four as Dr Ramsay had said. It certainly seemed to sort something out though, because the next few days were very peaceful and uneventful ... but then her salaam fits returned every other day.

The days that started with a salaam proved to be very stressful. On top of having to get Ray and Clare up, breakfasted and ready for school and getting Ben sorted out. Amberlie having a large seizure when she woke was a nightmare. Everything happened at the same time, and as the seizure was now part of the routine every other day, I had to somehow organise life around that event. I wasn't comfortable with it – I just didn't have a choice, and I was well aware that anything unexpected would cause complete and utter chaos. It was like living on the edge, fingers crossed ... hoping that it would all work out until I'd got the kids safely to school. Then I'd feel my blood pressure drop.

One day Ray brought home a cough from school and gave it to Ben, who, being such a sharing child by nature, had started a very bad habit of swapping dummies with Amberlie. I kept telling him off but every time I went out of the room he did it again! Amberlie of course started to cough and I used the 'spacer' in an attempt to nip the problem in the bud and she seemed to cope well.

Bill had just started his summer holiday and we were looking forward to getting out and about again. As Monday morning arrived Amberlie woke with a wheeze and a rattle, and I knew she needed antibiotics, and that this was down to the dummy exchanges. She didn't seem too bad in herself and we thought going out might help her feel a bit better. The weather was lovely and sunny and warm so we decided to go to Marwell Zoo. Amberlie stayed happy but developed a slight temperature in the afternoon. We managed to give her some paracetamol just before it, unusually, spurred a small fit. Luckily we were alone in the meerkat enclosure at the time, so while we waited for Amberlie to settle the kids watched the animals, and the world was none the wiser.

Amberlie improved over the next couple of days then, disastrously, by Saturday her chest was terrible. I left it a while to see if it would pass but her breathing started to deteriorate and the Ventolin was having no effect. I rang the Health Call service (God I hated having to use them), and they said it would be hours before anyone could call because they were inundated. They suggested we go to their headquarters, about half an hour away, where there would be a doctor in house waiting for us. We didn't hesitate because we knew that unless Amberlie had treatment soon we would be back in hospital in no time. The doctor agreed that her chest was awful and that she had so much muck on it that it would only be a couple of hours before she was in dire straits. He gave her several sachets of two strong antibiotics and said I would need them if we couldn't find a chemist open to complete the prescription. He said that if one medicine did not work, the other one would, but we could not afford to waste time waiting to see which one did the trick.

Naturally there were also lots of fits about and Amberlie had already had a salaam that day on top of several others that week. The antibiotics were very effective and the additional fits disappeared along with her infection, leaving Amberlie back in her usual alternate-day routine. I was glad it was time to visit Dr Ramsay again.

The doctor was not happy. We told her about all the puppet seizures, the salaams that had established themselves, and the horrible dark absences Amberlie was having, and said that she was now spending a lot of time spaced-out.

The doctor thought long and hard and was most concerned about the salaams. She thought the 'puppets' were also a type of salaam and it was imperative to try to bring them all under control as quickly as possible. She said she would like us to bring Amberlie into hospital every day for two weeks so that they could administer a course of steroids, as she felt this was the only way they could try to control the salaams. She explained that Amberlie would normally be admitted to do this but she would be at such high risk of catching an infection in the hospital, especially being put on steroids, which would make her more susceptible than normal. Dr Ramsay explained that on the good side they would wash out her system and give her usual antiepileptics a new lease of life to continue their job.

'Jesus wept,' I said, feeling everything sink to the floor again. I knew we had to try to sort out her seizures but the thought of her immunity being compromised again was just devastating, and more so since we had only just got her over a bad chest infection. Almost in tears I told her that Amberlie had just been through a hellish infection and had only narrowly escaped hospital, plus we were approaching September, which traditionally was Amberlie's worst time of year – she never failed to be ill in September. I went on to explain that she had already been admitted to hospital three times for her chest, and there were also the illnesses we had managed to control at home. I really felt we were caught between the devil and the deep blue sea. Dr Ramsay understood what I was saying. She said, 'It is important to try to control these salaam fits as they do funny things to the brain and are very dangerous. You don't have to make the decision straight away, but will need to very soon. I also want Amberlie to have an EEG, and I need to talk to another neurologist to get their opinion. In the meantime, I think the best thing to do is to raise her lamotrigine, a little twice a day.'

So what were we to do? I didn't want to choose any way to be perfectly honest. It was a dead cert Amberlie would get an infection whatever. Either we risk her life with the fits or we risk her life with the infections.

'You know God … you have no idea of what you do, and if you do then your fucking ethics are totally wrong!' I yelled to the sky.

Bill and I decided the fits were probably the lesser risk.

By the end of the week Dr Ramsay was on the phone saying that she'd had another idea. She would like to try Amberlie on a drug that was used years ago before modern antiepileptics came onto the scene, to control infantile spasms or salaams. She explained that Mogadon was given at night and very occasionally in the morning, and that it would cause drowsiness but that Amberlie would get used to it. She felt this would be a better idea than steroids. She said we would need to pick it up from the hospital and she would have it ready for us on Tuesday morning.

Bill and I both breathed a sigh of relief. What would we do without Dr Ramsay?

On the Wednesday Amberlie had her EEG. I dreaded it, but she sat through it really well. I think the Mogadon from the night before had sedated her and made her more tolerant. It was the usual procedure of endless electrodes stuck to her head (I wished there was a better way) and she sat there for a good hour while they took their readings. As usual the machine was making a huge racket as it graphed the enormous amount of electricity in her head. I didn't want to look at the graphs – they had been explained to me before and I knew they showed a nightmare. Amberlie naturally moaned a little when they finished as they took the electrodes off her head and tugged and pulled at her hair. Bless her, she looked like Tina Turner with her hair all sticking out stiff with gel and paste, and when we got home I gave her a bath and got rid of it all. She enjoyed that, finding it relaxing and soothing, and after a bottle and some food she slept for ages.

I was always ultra careful when I washed Amberlie's hair. I had to make sure it was absolutely dry afterwards, and that she was as warm as toast in case she caught a chill. Before she was bathed at any time we made sure that the bathroom radiator was fully on and that the rest of the house was as warm and draught-free as possible. I usually ended up sweating buckets but she was nice and comfortable. In the summer it was less of an issue but I never took any silly risks.

Amberlie was fit-free for a couple of days but then had a nasty salaam when she woke up one morning. I was not convinced about the Mogadon – it seemed to have only taken the edge off things, but I guessed we needed to give it time and it was certainly worth the try. I began to feel that if Amberlie was going to have a major seizure there wouldn't be much anyone or anything could do to derail it. I feared the fits were becoming very powerful.

I was not wholly optimistic about her drinking either – we now seemed to be entering the realm of classic lissencephaly symptoms. Mostly she allowed the bottle in her mouth, but sometimes it activated a rather strange, smiley laughing fit or absence where she cooed, oohed and laughed, letting the milk dribble out of the side of her mouth. She made no attempt at all to swallow it. If she decided she didn't want it in her mouth, she turned her head away and arched her back in an effort to turn her whole body around and escape. She would accept food at a push. I thought maybe the milk was now too fluid in consistency and needed thickening so I tried Complan but it made no difference. Dr Ramsay recommended a tasteless thickener that could be bought at the chemist. That helped slightly.

On the days when she was determined not to drink at all and would in no way suck a bottle, we had to resort to using a 5-ml medicine syringe to get milk into her so she didn't dehydrate. Even then, if she was calm she would not swallow the milk and it was only when she started to moan that she would actually swallow. I didn't want to give into the fact that she might need to be tube fed, but I did not want to put milk into her mouth that she was frightened of choking on. How soul destroying and futile was that for both of us? The last thing I wanted was to make this a nightmare for her and put her off drinking altogether, so I telephoned the registrar on the children's ward to talk it over. He thought it might be better to introduce the tube at bad times so that we got over the worst before trying Amberlie without it again. I didn't know what to do for the best. I was very worried in case Amberlie forgot how to drink even in such a short time, because then it would become a permanent thing with no turning back. Amberlie needed reminding all the time of what she could do, in the same way that we maintained her ability to play with different toys – except her Skwish of course – that needed no reminder! Amberlie mostly returned to normal after a bad phase anyway. I really, really did not want to introduce a tube until I knew for certain that this was no phase and that her condition had deteriorated irretrievably. At the same time I was acutely aware that things had deteriorated significantly to be at this stage and I was conscious that I had to do what was right for Amberlie, even though I was fighting my own acceptance.

The salaam fits had probably started their destruction of vital brain cells due to them being starved of oxygen (atrophy), and were probably the reason why her drinking had diminished; either that or her chest was still giving her grief. We were struggling to maintain control of her seizures and as a consequence there were now other problems, which, if unchecked, would result in a no-win, no-return situation. I felt that somehow Amberlie would sort it out. She would come through. I had to give it a few more days.

Amberlie's absences weren't just little flickers anymore. Some days I looked into Amberlie's eyes and saw nothing but an eerie, unearthly blackness. It was like a void of nothing, a dark impenetrable curtain hiding the horrors inside her head, and every time I felt a deep disturbing fear seep into my bones. When I spoke to her she would turn her head towards me but I don't think she could always see me. It hurt so much when she was like this … like she wasn't in her body … almost an alien. And it underlined just how serious her condition was. It was hard then to keep up my optimism and I fought desperately to keep myself under control. Dr Ramsay said:

'There's nothing we can do about them – they cannot be controlled. The situation is very bad. I'm not giving up on her … we mustn't give up … she's not on her way out yet and I have more things to try!'

I was grateful for the support and her optimism. Dr Ramsay was very good in a crisis. I certainly had no intention of giving up on Amberlie and would do anything and everything to keep her going. I wasn't daft though … I knew we were at the beginning of the worst and if Dr Ramsay said the situation was very bad, then it was bad, she wouldn't have said it otherwise – she was our great protector from bad news. I knew she was trying to keep us all going.

23

It was now September again and my usual paranoia about that time of year was setting in fast. I was begging not to have another bad autumn and tried hard to head off the lurking depression but knew I was already sunk. Why does it always rain the week the kids go back to school?

Amberlie had started the last two mornings with a seizure. The first one was only short but it knocked her out nonetheless. She remained very jumpy up until she had another small one in the afternoon before zonking out for about five hours solid. When she woke she refused to drink but happily ate some food. Her drinking was still very unpredictable and was slowly diminishing again.

On the second day, Amberlie managed a whole fifteen minutes awake before the seizure took over and shattered my optimism for a fit-free day. While she slept I rang Dr Ramsay for advice about her drinking and she asked me to bring her in so she could check her hydration. Anyhow, miracle upon miracle and after sleeping for only thirty minutes – which was usually a signal for a bad day – Amberlie woke up bright and cheerful and the little madam drank a whole 8-ounce bottle without hesitating, closely followed by a whole jar of banana yoghurt! She even took her medicine without too much trouble.

Giving her her medicine was usually a fraught twice-a-day practice. Amberlie's tablets had to be crushed and mixed with fluid to enable her to take them and of course she saw this as another type of drink, and did her utmost to avoid swallowing it. It didn't taste too bad – I'd tasted it so I could sympathise with her. The last thing I wanted was to upset her, so for a change I thought I would put it in half a spoonful of her yoghurt instead and she barely noticed it! *Great!* I thought. *This is the way to give it from now on.*

Amberlie watched my face, smiling and cooing as we had a long talk about drinking and keeping her body nice and watered, and not letting it dry out so that she would stay out of hospital. Her eyes were wide and bright with her lips pursed, as she seemed to be trying to imitate my expression while listening to every word. I took this to be her full agreement, gave her a big hug and got her dressed. When Amberlie was happy and responsive like that she made me feel so good. She gave out such a powerful energy, which made the whole house fill with love and happiness. She inspired so much love and devotion in one smile that it was like being in a state of permanent ecstasy that I never wanted to go away. She was like a huge shining light on the world and I wished it could be like that all the time.

Dr Ramsay was quite happy with Amberlie's general condition and after weighing her she stunned me by telling me that she had actually gained weight – from 14.2 kg to 14.8 kg (OK … so it was only 0.6 kg but, hey, I was chuffed!) – all the worry and effort had been worth it! Mind-blowing child!

We then discussed Amberlie's drinking and Dr Ramsay felt it was a refusal problem rather than an inability to swallow, so logically it must be a behavioural pattern of some sort. She explained that handicapped children are often psychologically similar to normal children so we should not assume her behavior would be different, and hinted that maybe I was reading too much into it.

I could understand that to a point, but we were still battling with an element of logic that could not be related to or entirely understood? Or maybe 'childhood psychology' is only basic instinct and not influenced at all by environment or ability?

Why would Amberlie have chosen not to drink? She must have got thirsty. The only times I had ever known my other children not to drink was when there was an element of pain, discomfort or sickness which overruled their desire. If Amberlie did have some normal traits, and I am sure she did, then it should follow a similar pattern to the others. This meant there had to be a cause. Surely it wasn't bloody-mindedness or an attention-seeking device? Why would she cause herself discomfort? I didn't have a clue what Amberlie's psychology was on this – if it was a psychological game – and I'm damned sure Dr Ramsay didn't either. Amberlie had been recently put onto a new medicine, and maybe that made her feel nauseous. It did say it might on the patient information leaflet. Being on lots of different medications could made her tummy feel odd – they all had potential side effects. But we couldn't prove that unless we took her medicines away one by one, and I certainly wasn't about to do that. There was also the possibility that the recent virus and antibiotics she'd had were still hanging about in her system. Things took time to go especially when she only passed a stool twice a week … if we were lucky. Why did she often suck and dribble her milk rather than swallow it? And why did she look worried and get panicky when the bottle came towards her? No, there was definitely more to this than refusal.

I was without a doubt worried about Amberlie's feeding. As a mother it was my natural instinct to feed my children and if I couldn't do that or was stopped from doing it, then it preyed on my mind. Missing a drink once or twice was fine … but consistently was another thing. It was easy to intimate that I may have been rather sensitive about it – but the doctor wasn't living with it every day. It meant so much and alleviated so much stress when Amberlie fed properly.

Talking about Amberlie's toileting moved Dr Ramsay onto seizures. She said that just the physical movement involved in passing a stool could cause a seizure. She said it was one of those things that the medical world could not scientifically prove, like the misery of teething, but in her years of experience she had found that there appeared to be a link with the bowel and the brain, and that seizures were frequently a consequence. It was linked to the vagus nerve that runs in many directions from the head to the stomach, and was also known, particularly in old people, to have the effect of making them pass out while going to the loo.

Despite doing all we could to soften Amberlie's stools nothing seemed to work particularly well. The trouble was obviously down to the combination of her medicines and Dr Ramsay's theory of the link between slow brain and slow bowel. Her diet of fruit and cereals, though not ideal, should really have helped, and I don't remember Amberlie having any problems going to the loo before she needed medication. The fact that she was sedentary must have also played a part, as well as her drinking being erratic some days.

I tried to return to the drinking but Dr Ramsay had decided she'd solved that one and wanted to stay with seizures. She remembered that she had not had Amberlie's recent EEG results and rang for them there and then. She was delighted to report that naturally the readings were horrendous but showed no degeneration of the brain that would show up on EEG.

'This is good news!' she beamed.

'That's great!' Bill and I said in unison.

But this still hadn't accounted for the 'first thing in the morning' scenario. Dr Ramsay explained that having a seizure shortly after waking was fairly normal for epileptics because as the brain wakes, the electricity starts flying around in response to stimulation. Ultimately the brain cannot cope so a seizure occurs.

Dr Ramsay told us to go on as we were for the time being and to give the drugs a little more time to work. She said she would contact another neurologist to see if they could offer any other advice, as she was still looking to eventually reduce the amount of medication Amberlie was taking.

I groaned. This was the one problem I was permanently neurotic about.

'We must reduce her medicines! Ideally she should be on two at the most!' she explained.

I loathed the thought of reducing Amberlie's drugs and I told her so. Of course I wanted to give her fewer drugs, but every time we messed about with her medicines, something happened and we were back on a downward spiral. It was fraught with risk and stress and I was terrified of releasing seizures that we couldn't control again. I felt as if Dr Ramsay was possessed by the idea. I realised that doctors have codes to follow and 'ideal' levels to maintain but where Amberlie was concerned it was quality of life, and I felt at the end of the day it was more important for Amberlie to be fit free and awake no matter how many antiepileptics it took to achieve it. I knew the risks with the drugs and I understood we had to watch for the point of toxicity but if too many seizures were allowed through, Amberlie would have no life at all … and what was the point of that? Dr Ramsay made no comment and I felt I had been ignored. The doctor asked me to keep her informed with a phone call in a week's time.

On the way home I asked Bill if he thought the EEG proved Dr Ramsay's theory of Amberlie's drinking being behavioural. He said it seemed to.

'"No signs of deterioration that would show up on an EEG" … I wonder what that means?' I said. There was silence. 'I do think I have valid points though,' I said bluntly. Bill nodded in agreement.

Amberlie went down for a nap as soon as we arrived home and then she ate and drank normally all day.

'How's that for sod's law!' I said to Bill. 'I guess she must be feeling better today.'

We were happy for her – it always gave us a boost when she was in good form. It was great to see her later sitting in her chair smiling and playing with her toys; she looked much brighter than she had done for ages. She looked so beautiful with the evening light burnishing the reds in her strawberry blonde hair, and her porcelain skin had a gorgeous rosy glow to it. I hoped we were in for a good phase. It would be nice to relax into the mundane routine of life for a while.

Things were relatively stable over the next few weeks, with Amberlie having a salaam fit roughly every other day, and occasionally there were spells lasting 2-3 days without any episodes at all. The worst seizures coincided with her bowel movements.

We always knew when it was due to happen as she followed a specific routine: about 12-18 hours prior to the event Amberlie would have a nasty salaam that started slowly with twitches, particularly in one leg that would go into a frog-like pose, with loud heavy breathing. There would be some very gentle (so subtle an unaccustomed eye would miss them) bows of her head in an irregular pattern, followed by lots of absences. This all culminated in her going smack-bang-wallop into a severe and nasty shouting salaam which knocked her out cold every time. She would remain tense, miserable and twitchy in stages until she managed a stool. I dreaded it every time, feeling so bad for her. She couldn't even go to the loo without it being a huge trauma. Oddly, and luckily, her feeding remained unaffected and she generally took what food was offered amongst a few moans and wriggles.

Wednesdays were portage days and June came to play with Amberlie. June was a lovely lady and very easy to talk to, and both Amberlie and I looked forward to her visits. Naturally it was pot luck whether or not Amberlie would be receptive or interested on that particular day, but June was very good in going with the flow and was quite happy to try again another day if necessary. We never attempted portage if Amberlie had had a bad seizure or was unwell.

Amberlie had not really learned anything new for ages and between us June and I looked for other interesting ways to stimulate some development. It did seem as if Amberlie had peaked and I was sad that she had reached one of the predicted plateaux of her condition.

Lissencephaly children are expected to reach a plateau in development at some stage, that stage depending on the individual and the amount of seizure activity. They gain little or no further ability from that point so it becomes important to stimulate them and remind them of what they already have to keep their brains alert, and keep them from the impression that they should shut down.

Amberlie was already short of usable brain and it was imperative to preserve what she had so she could keep her tiny amount of independence. It was also important to try to keep her attention and concentration as far as possible rather than let her spend hours day-dreaming, which seemed to coincide with more seizure activity, though it was hard to work out whether the day-dreams resulted from the activity or the other way round. Keeping her focused seemed to waylay a lot of them.

I didn't really expect Amberlie to change or do very much. Once I had been told my child would be able to do very little, my expectations were shattered. It still went through me like a knife because there was always a part of me that hoped she would be the different one and surprise everyone. I was grateful for whatever ability she had and occasionally something clicked, teaching me a lesson in never giving up hope. One of the most amazing things I remember was how she suddenly started to respond to people she recognised. When they spoke to her, instead of looking away shyly, she tried so hard to talk back using her noises coupled with excited leg kicking. There were definite and different pitches in her sounds and she talked in sentences of an 'Amberlie' kind. I was so proud of her I could hardly contain my own excitement.

There were times when she would sit so poised and controlled in her chair that I would almost forget there was anything wrong. She would be totally engrossed in her game, with her coordination spot on, and showing lots of interest in new or different toys placed on her table – particularly if they were Ben's.

I loved to just sit and watch her when she was like this. Naturally I thought she was the most beautiful child ever. She had huge blue fish-shaped eyes and her lashes were so long they often bent against her glasses! Her nose was cute and tiny and her full lips were rosy red. She had a small chin and high cheekbones, and the most unblemished, glowing, English rose-tinted skin I had ever seen. She always put me in mind of a Victorian porcelain doll. She was gorgeous. I was delighted that she had been blessed with such beauty because with a brain abnormality like hers, she could have looked bloody awful, and her drugs could have ruined her skin and hair.

Amberlie's hair had grown so long that she wore it high in a ponytail plait most of the time to keep it out of her mouth and eyes, and to prevent it getting caught under her when she was on the floor. When it was brushed out it came down to her hips in cascades of waves, making her look like a little mermaid. It was fine and springy and her fringe kinked anyhow!

Amberlie was also getting very tall and stringy but kept the appearance of a baby in structure and movement. Her muscle tone was great and some of her physical ability was so Houdini-like, she had to be the most double-jointed, elastic-muscled person I had ever known; she got into some of the most amazing positions without showing any signs of discomfort, although some were obviously pre-empted by seizure activity, and made me cringe.

Amberlie's eyes expressed a lot of how she felt, shining brightly on settled, happy days when she took in the scenery, watched faces or watched television. Sparkly things caught her attention, little fairy lights, glints of rainbow colours from crystals hanging in the window, something floating by, and she responded to it all with a shake and a bang of her Skwish, a giggle or a laugh, or with 'Amberlie' sounds. If she drifted into an absence her light would go out, and her eyes became two dark tunnels of mystery as her huge dilated pupils overtook the beautiful blue, leaving a deep, alarming, lifeless, and clandestine blackness. Her brain always turned her head towards the window as it searched for light … but she still looked at nothing, still and quiet. It was sometimes possible to distract her by touching her or waving something in front of her face, but often it didn't work and it was apparent there was nobody in … a temporary step off the world.

The kids used to come and tell me if this happened when I wasn't in the room, as they had noticed her Skwish had stopped banging and her contented noises had been replaced by silence. Clare used to sit and hold her hand, Ray would watch and Ben would do his best to distract her into life by standing in front of her with his eyes wide and bright, chattering away, with his dummy wobbling all over the place and his head moving from side to side to make her look at him.

I was amazed at how well Amberlie coped with the building works, considering the noise, dirt, dust and sheer inconvenience of it all. The builders had estimated the job would be finished in two and a half months but I could see there was no way that estimation was anywhere near accurate. The foundations had taken longer to put in than expected due to some trees being too near the property. The builders were used to constructing disabled facilities and did their best to make things as easy as possible, cleaning up and leaving things tidy and keeping us regularly informed of progress and schedules.

Two of our friends, Christine and Sharon, visited one evening to ask whether we would give our permission for them to hold a fundraising event to help furnish and equip Amberlie's new suite.

'Stunned, I said, 'Oh no, that's OK – we'll manage to sort something out later!'

They both looked at me and Christine said, 'No, Sandra – we know you have used all you have to build this for Amberlie, and as your friends and neighbours, and because we all love Amberlie, we want to help her get all the things she needs now to make her life good.'

I was stunned. The tears welled up in my eyes and I didn't know what to say. It was so kind and generous of both of them to think of us and I was chuffed to bits that my Amberlie was cared for so much outside the family. I was also a bit embarrassed. I thanked them over and over again and when I told Bill, he couldn't believe it.

Christine and Sharon asked us to put together a letter explaining Amberlie's condition and a list of the things we would like to buy for Amberlie so that they had some information to give businesses and shops.

Amberlie's new room would only take a single bed, so the main thing we needed was a sofa bed so that someone would be able to sleep with her because of her seizures, and that could be folded up so that she could have plenty of space to play on the floor. Other things we thought of were a soft comfortable carpet, new curtains, shower-room accessories and fixtures, plus some multi-sensory stimulants like a bubble lamp and fibre optics, mobiles and textures to feel, as well as musical toys.

Chris and Sharon launched instantly into action and booked 'Amberlie's Fun Day' for 25 October in the local school's playground. The girls trawled the shops and local businesses asking for raffle donations and organised a car boot sale, stalls and bouncy castle (courtesy of our builders). Christine's husband Dave had gorgeous long hair and organised a sponsored head shave to lose it all, and Bill volunteered himself as a target for wet sponges!

Sharon contacted our local radio station and managed to get a spot on an evening show that advertised local events. She said I would have to go along with them so they made sure they got all their facts straight! That was all well and good but I ended up on it as well, and my nerve having totally absconded, I felt my answers poured out in one huge burble, making me wonder if I had made any sense at all! What an experience! Bill taped it as he listened with the kids at home, who were so excited to have heard Mum on the radio!

The Fun Day finally arrived and we were all nervous and excited at the same time. The girls had a special sweatshirt printed for Amberlie with her name on to wear for her day. The weather held out and things got going well. The family turned out for the occasion and lots of people attended, including our builders! It was all quite awesome but Amberlie loved all the attention and even had her face painted, which delighted her no end! Ben did nothing but scream and everyone took it in turns trying unsuccessfully to placate him. Luckily Amberlie was far too distracted to let him bother her and was much more interested in all the other children surrounding her, chattering away and asking her lots of questions! There wasn't a seizure in sight and she was in fine fettle. Poor Dave was now bald and Bill was battered and wet! Everyone was really happy (especially as Ben had now gone to sleep!), and all in all they raised £1200!

Later on we learned that the local Lions Club had raised another £675 and the church had collection £100! We were completely overwhelmed by the generosity shown towards Amberlie.

With the money raised at her Fun Day, Amberlie got everything on the wish list and more! As she loved music so much we bought her a juke box that lit up red and orange and gave her something to look at as well as listen to. She also had her own towels, two mirrors and a host of toys and bits and pieces to colour and enrich her world. We were and always will be eternally grateful to everyone who helped make Amberlie's life more special that day.

Having finished the outside work, the builders moved into the house to knock down the dividing wall between the kitchen and dining room and take out the back wall to prepare to put in the patio doors to the garden.

The dust was horrendous and I was paranoid about it getting anywhere near Amberlie's chest. Everywhere was dirty and dusty, and with only a tarpaulin covering the hole in the rear wall, it was very draughty too. It was a bit better once the doors were installed and relieved the nocturnal worry of someone getting in while we were all asleep. I strategically placed the ironing board each night so if anyone did venture in there would be an almighty crash to wake us up!

We confined ourselves to the living room for three weeks, with the kettle, toaster and other sustenance at hand. We lived on numerous take-aways and I caught up with washing and ironing in the evenings when Bill could look after the kids. It wasn't pleasant.

The kids found it very hard not being able to be free around the house, especially when the builders changed the layout of our staircase to create disabled access along the hallway, and they missed not being able to go in the garden when they pleased.

It was hard work not being able to change Amberlie's scenery too well while indoors, and keeping her stimulated and stable in between making endless cups of tea for the builders. I knew we only had another two or three weeks before it was all completed but it had taken five months in total and I was sick and tired of it. I probably didn't help matters by buying a puppy.

Bill had promised me one for my Christmas and birthday present. My Yorkshire Terrier had died just before Ben was born and I missed having a dog in the house.

The kids had set their hearts on a pug after seeing one at a dog show. The litters were few and far between and we had to wait for one to happen. The Kennel Club told me of a litter in Wales. I wasn't hopeful, as the puppies were already 12 weeks old and had probably all been sold, but I telephoned and the lady said she had one male left. There was now the dilemma of what to do and Bill decided we might as well take a look. My friend Christine volunteered to look after the kids while Bill, Amberlie and I went off on a day trip to the Rhondda Valley. We returned with a dear little chap called Ming.

The kids were delighted with Ming, who provided something for them to love and play with amongst all the restrictions in the house.

'You must be mad!' everyone said. 'Haven't you got enough on your plate?'

'We have to live life, you know, and animals are good in a house and good for stress, and you never know he might even help Ambams!' I would reply.

Amberlie seemed to like him and didn't mind a little playful chewing. We had to teach him straight away that she was special and not to be jumped all over. He had to get used to leaving her alone. After a few pulls away and some stern 'nos' he got the message. Amberlie often dozed off on the floor and Ming found her to be an ideal warm spot for a nap as well. He snuggled right up close to her – their pact sealed. I wasn't going to keep her off the floor where she love to be – that wouldn't have been fair to her. Ming often checked her in passing and when he did she looked dead straight into his eyes, hers widening in amazement, undeterred by his flat, wrinkled face and black mask! There was never any fear from either of them. Amberlie was puzzled by his play and often looked at him as if he were barmy! She enjoyed watching the others play with him, sharing their excitement.

Ming wasn't any worse than another child! The cat was the only one not sure. Lottie spent the first three months of Ming's residence three feet above ground, walking on tables, cupboards, radiators, watching his every move and avoiding confrontation. He, on the other hand, was fascinated by her and would stand on his hind legs sniffing and yapping, begging her to come down. When they eventually met, it was all quite civilised, although Lottie was paralysed rigid with her hair on end!

On 17 December the builders left and we were glad to have our home back. 'Amberlie's Suite' was wonderful and we were thrilled to bits. The state of the place was another thing and there was so much to do to get it straight before Christmas, which was only eight days away. I launched into a panic!

Auntie Pat came to help get us into a reasonable state of normality and I went berserk painting the living room and kitchen, working into the early hours to get it done. What with organising the extra shopping too, I didn't think we would make it!

It was really important to get the tree up as fast as possible because the kids had seen all their friends' trees lit and wanted to know when we would do ours, and it was also one of the things Amberlie really loved – that and the fairy lights. When those were lit her little face shone and the wonder in her eyes was simply magical. It was like a pause in reality, a moment to forget all the stress and to stop for a while to ponder special things. I loved to watch all the children's faces when the lights went on – their enchanted expressions were spellbinding. Ben was now old enough to appreciate things like decorations and he sat in awe with his dummy moving up and down as he sucked away! We could now all get excited about the time of year.

I was absolutely exhausted. I had set myself a silly quest but couldn't bear the thought of Christmas in a mess. I was so tired I felt I was about to have a nervous breakdown and swore I would never have any building work done again.

Amberlie was in the throes of a bad ear infection, which I think must have been caused by all the brick dust lying around. I did my best to Hoover it away but it just seemed to keep on coming. Her poor ear flared up on three consecutive occasions, each time discharging itself and causing her terrible pain. On top of that a cold and throat infection followed, with the last of it tailing into Christmas. She had needed numerous bottles of antibiotics and she was also totally exhausted. One by one we all caught the virus except Ray. I think we all had got so run down with all the stress and upheaval of the building works. We all got through Christmas Day OK but Bill was bad from Boxing Day. I waited until after the New Year.

I had never felt so ill in all my life. What started as a sore throat developed into full-blown flu and I could not get out of bed. Bill took time off work to take care of us all. I couldn't swallow at all and the pain that ran all over my body was so bad and incessant that in the middle of the night I thought I was doing to die. I couldn't rouse Bill to call the doctor. I was so desperate and so hot. I managed to slowly drag myself out of bed, with the pain searing through my every move and the room spinning round and round. I held on tight to the chest of drawers and made it to the banisters at the top of the stairs. I didn't have a clue how I was going to make it down to the phone and the stairs looked as though they were moving towards me then moving away again. My knees sagged and shook with every step as my legs strained to hold my weight but I eventually made it to the bottom and grabbed the phone before I slid down the wall to the floor.

'Thank God for memory phones,' I said as I struggled to focus on the small screen. I pressed the button. I gave my name and address and they said someone would be with me during the next couple of hours. 'Jesus!' I said to myself. I crawled into the living room, leant against a chair and waited in the dark. After an hour I hauled myself back to the bottom of the stairs so I wouldn't be too far away from the door when the bell rang. Eventually the doctor came. She gave me some antibiotics there and then and said that I had tonsillitis in one of its severest forms. I was covered in peculiar red spots. She left. I collapsed on the sofa until daylight when I faced the stairs again in an effort to return to bed. Bill had slept through the night and was surprised when I shoved the prescription in his hand when he woke.

About a week later I was able to do some little things around the house but the red spots had evolved into huge red eczema-type patches and I looked a real mess! I had to put up with my bad eczema for about a year and still have the remnants on my arms today. The doctor said it was not unusual with bad tonsillitis and was probably heightened by stress. I found out later that it could also have been an allergy to the masses of brick dust that had been in the house.

Luckily Amberlie had been steady seizure-wise and had spent the days quietly sleeping and recovering. She was now growing stronger day by day but had lost some weight and was looking a bit skinny.

Life was indeed a lot easier now we had Amberlie's shower room. Social services had delivered a plush padded shower chair on wheels and we could strap her in safely and comfortably and wash her all over without a struggle. Amberlie loved the shower and giggled away as the water fell on her. It seemed to soothe her enormously when we washed her hair and she held her head back in sheer bliss when I combed the conditioner through.

We bought her a little bright cerise pink towelling robe with a hood to wrap her in afterwards to keep her snug and warm.

At the next appointment Dr Ramsay noted Amberlie's weight loss and referred us to the dietician to see if we could build Amberlie up more.

The dietician said that what Amberlie ate, though unexciting from our point of view, was in fact absolutely fine and she was getting all she needed apart from fat. She advised us to load Amberlie's diet with high fat foods such as cream, chocolate, oils, sauces and anything we would ourselves avoid calorie-wise. She also told us to get the doctor to prescribe 'Caloreen', which was a calorie supplement that could be added to drinks and desserts without altering the taste. The most important thing though was to give her what she wanted to eat so that she ate! We also started her on some different vitamins and minerals.

I was really pleased to be told that Amberlie's diet was generally good because I had felt a little worried that she wasn't getting all she should. As her mother I felt it best to give her what she would eat rather than force the issue for I certainly could not reason with or advise Amberlie as to what was and was not a balanced diet! To have persisted would have been far more traumatic and futile, and could have potentially led her to refuse altogether. She didn't have much in life, so the least I could do was to give her what she liked.

After about three weeks Amberlie was looking better and her diet seemed to be doing some good. Her cheeks were filling out and she had more colour. She was having regular banana and strawberry milkshakes and seemed to like fatty puddings provided they were not chocolate! She hated chocolate – it always made her shudder and she'd spit it straight out. I also dropped her formula milk because normal full milk proved better nourishment. I had kept her on it because of the extra vitamins and minerals it contained but now she was having them from other sources, it wasn't necessary anymore.

It was always dangerous to relax into thinking, 'Hey, we're getting somewhere!' One step forward – three steps back! The optimism that kept us going through each and every storm, the belief, the dream that maybe, just maybe, it could all actually get better, was dispersed like an exploding balloon. Now it was more sinister, more demanding and more head-banging than ever. There was a tummy bug in the house.

No one had any symptomatic signs of illness and there didn't seem to be much discomfort either but it was causing diarrhoea.

Amberlie did not escape as she usually did with tummy upsets and she had been to the loo every day for ten days. Not diarrhoea, but still very soft for her. Her seizures surfaced again and were as violent and exhausting as I had ever seen. She had a permanent wandering expression on her face and was certainly not on the planet. I couldn't be sure whether it was the bug or the change in her diet that had aggravated her stomach. It was possible that a change to her intake would cause a change in her chemical make-up, and how her body dealt with it. If the chemicals had changed then the balance of medicines in her blood would alter, potentially provoking a change in her seizure activity, in much the same way that a period of excitement could alter the chemistry to cause a seizure. Having a stomach upset would speed up Amberlie's body to process everything far quicker than she was used to, also potentially upsetting the medicinal balance in her blood. It was a conundrum. In the end, and as it coincided with the other children's stomach upsets, I decided to see how things panned out and hoped that her seizures would settle down again quickly.

One morning Amberlie woke without her usual seizure, although she did push her face hard into her pillow three times as if she was going to fit, but then it passed. It was later than usual and she seemed to be very tired and drowsy and her whole body was floppy. Her eyes, filled by her pupils, were as black as night. There was nothing in them, no life, no sparkle, and it was very eerie. Amberlie's skin was also bluish in colour, around her eyes and down the centre of her face. She must have been having bad seizures under the surface. She didn't want to go back to sleep, so I washed, dressed and fed her.

That afternoon she fell asleep on my lap during a drink when I suddenly felt a vibration running through her like an earthquake. It lasted for several minutes and I could not see it at all. It was similar to the sensation of resting on a nerve. It didn't disturb her at all but lately all her sleeps were rather coma-like and no matter how much noise anyone made, even if the kids were screaming, there was not a murmur. If I hadn't been holding her, I would never have known it had happened … and that worried me.

I called Dr Ramsay and she suggested splitting Amberlie's nighttime nitrazepam (Mogadon) dose to help at night and half in the morning in an attempt to pre-empt the morning seizure; as she was quite often awake for fifteen minutes or so before it emerged, and that then might improve the day for Amberlie and make her less drowsy. Anything was worth a try. Dr Ramsay just said, 'Mmmm ...' when I told her about the vibration.

The doctors always allowed a two-week period for antiepileptics to become established in the bloodstream and now that Amberlie's tummy had settled, I hoped things would improve. After three weeks, Amberlie was still having her waking seizure but on some mornings she woke already in the midst of the fit. Things were changing once more. I called Dr Ramsay again and suggested putting her medicine back to nights only but at a slightly higher dose. She was happy to revert to nights only, but not to increase it, explaining that as she had recently put up one of her other drugs, we were bordering on the verge of toxicity, and also she did not want to increase her drowsiness.

The pros and cons had to be weighted up seriously, especially as Amberlie was so sleepy. Whilst I understood the medicines contributed to her drowsiness, I was more convinced it was mainly down to the amount of seizures she had. Amberlie was pretty tolerant of all her medication and none of them, with the exception of phenobarbitone (which she had taken for three months as a baby), had made her drowsy for any length of time. Considering all the possible side effects of her medications, such as drowsiness, hallucinations, sickness, hyperactivity, liver and kidney problems and even sudden death, I thought Amberlie bore them amazingly well. I put the nitrazepam back to its original level at night and gave up on the morning attempt. The best I could do in the meantime was to rely on the diazepam if things got bad.

Dr Ramsay said the sleepy part was bad whatever, and Bill and I could see that – Amberlie was not with us much at all, though she did perk up from time to time for short periods, but soon tired herself out again.

Amberlie continued to feed well although erratically, and mostly her feeding had surprisingly remained unaffected. There were still times, though, when she obviously didn't want food or drink, and would not swallow anything even if it was already in her mouth.

Giving Amberlie her medicines twice a day had always been a nightmare – she didn't like or want it whichever way it was given – and now that she was drowsy, and some of it was in liquid form, it was even worse. She had sussed out that I put it in her food and happily spat back the evil spoonful. When she wouldn't swallow, I had to hold her nose with one hand, catch the dribbled medicine in a small vial with the other, and shove it all back in as best I could until she eventually swallowed it. She was amazingly stubborn but I don't think I ever lost enough of the doses to destabilise her. I hated having to do this every time, but she really needed her medication.

24

It was now February and Amberlie's seizures were continuing to be a major problem. Her physical development was a huge factor in the appearance of more seizures. She was growing into a little lady – she was nearly five years old and about a metre in height, and this alone would have produced more electrical activity and given her brain more to cope with, and thus more salaam seizures were surfacing. These seizures had never been easy to control for any length of time because of their origin, and as far as Amberlie was concerned, things were becoming far more complicated now that she was already taking most of the effective drugs.

Amberlie had recently recovered well from another nasty chest infection and had managed to put on some weight, so Dr Ramsay felt that she might now be able to tolerate an increase in the lamotrigine. The last time it had been increased it made her stressed and I didn't feel very comfortable about it even though I knew we had to try something. So up it went. Within a day Amberlie was throwing up and was as miserable as sin. I knew it was down to the lamotrigine but I also knew it was no good going straight back to Dr Ramsay, as she would have said I hadn't given it a chance.

'Maybe it is a bug,' I said to Bill.

'Yeah right,' he said, knowing that I was fumbling around for another reason.

'I'll have to give it a couple of days ... perhaps it's just the shock of the initial increase?' I pleaded for some agreement. I could see in Bill's face that he knew I was kidding myself.

It was Friday and I was very twitchy, knowing that if Amberlie worsened I would never be able to get any reasonable response from anyone at the weekend unless I took her to hospital. There hadn't been any improvement so far and she had started to be sick again. She was permanently bent over backwards and her consistent inconsolable crying and stress was penetrating the depths of our sanity. It wasn't fair on her and I'd had enough. This wasn't life – it was hell. On the other hand, her seizures had lessened dramatically and she had not needed diazepam for days … but at what cost?

On Sunday I decided enough was enough and, feeling that I had given the increase a fair shot, I reduced the lamotrigine. I knew it would take a few days to sort out but there was no choice. The next day Amberlie had a seizure – whether it was down to the reduction or all the stress I do not know.

Monday and Tuesday were murder and Bill came home at lunchtime on Tuesday to give me a break. That night Amberlie was very restless and unable to keep still. She developed a high temperature and was burning to the touch. I stripped her clothes off and gave her some paracetamol, but not in time to spare her a nasty seizure and a dose of diazepam. I now knew for sure that this was all down to the lamotrigine – all these symptoms together were as listed on the side-effects sheet.

By the morning Amberlie had settled down and was happy and calm. I took her round to see Dr Jonathan so he could check her over and he couldn't find anything wrong. I explained what I had done with the lamotrigine and he agreed that it was a strong possibility that it had made her ill and was known to cause flu-like symptoms. He felt that to be on the safe side it was wise to give her some antibiotics in case there was an infection brewing. Amberlie, though exhausted, had a fairly cheerful day apart from one seizure in the afternoon.

That night Raymond got up with a sore throat. He said it was deep down and felt like a lump when he tried to swallow. Dr Jonathan had checked Amberlie's throat, but if the soreness had been low down, he would have been unable to see anything. I was glad I had the antibiotics – Amberlie didn't need anything else to add to her suffering.

Amberlie continued to brighten very slowly and her heating and drinking improved a little. She certainly was more settled but jumping a lot (a bit like little frights), though they didn't seem to bother her at all, and she actually came out of them smiling! There were indications of salaams, but they were not materialising, although they were having a significantly tiring effect on her. She also managed to go to the toilet three times in one day after not going for several! I really didn't know what was going on in her little system – perhaps it was down to the antibiotics. I pondered whether it was all a culmination of her new diet, the rectal diazepam, the antibiotics, the possible bug and the lamotrigine. I really didn't have a clue. Too much had happened to upset her system. The poor little mite never got a break.

Amberlie was caught up in an eternal vicious circle that went from one thing to another. We managed to sort out one thing to be hit by another within hours or days. If she wasn't ill then she was in trouble with her seizures, either having too many or reacting badly to her medicines. She was an awful shade of pale and her feeding was slow although better than it had been, and sometimes she couldn't be bothered to swallow again and I put that down to her exhaustion. It was so difficult to work her out and do the right thing. The seizures did not appear to be too serious on the surface but I knew the medication masked a lot of what was going on beneath and sometimes the less serious ones knocked her out the most. Either way, whatever was going on in her little head was having a gigantic effect on her now and I guessed that over time, the damage done would be irreparable. She must have felt awful and wondered why I, her mother, the person who was supposed to make everything right, was so bloody useless to help her. I was useless … because I couldn't make her better and I couldn't promise her that I could either … and I hated myself for it. All I could do was cuddle her and wait for any signs that would point to a way forward. I couldn't bear the fact that I just had to sit there and watch it happen. Piece by piece this damned lissencephaly was taking away my baby and there was nothing I could do about it. I wasn't giving up hope though – no way. Together with Dr Ramsay, we had to keep searching for the right balance so that Amberlie was as comfortable and happy as possible.

I was very wary of facing Dr Ramsay at the next appointment, as I had taken the medicine away without consulting her first, but I knew what I did was right for Amberlie and I was just going to have to take the flak. I felt like a naughty schoolgirl nervously waiting for a punishment from the headmistress. Amberlie and I waited outside her office and I sweated buckets as my heart thumped. I kept saying to myself, 'For goodness' sake, Sandra, calm down. What can she do apart from tell you off? Get over it!'

Dr Ramsay put her head round the door saying 'Come on Amberlie … How are you?'

'Aw gawd … here goes!' I mumbled to Amberlie.

As soon as I got in the door I blabbed it straight out.

Dr Ramsay looked at me with a horrified expression and said, 'Oh poor little Amberlie … You did absolutely right – it can be a very dangerous drug that one.'

I stood there in stunned silence and felt relief hit me like a downpour of rain. I nearly cried. She said that I should not take all this on my own all the time, and if Amberlie was consistently unwell or doing odd things, she was just on the end of the telephone no matter when or what time of day.

'You can call me anytime at home. It's not a problem,' she said.

'Thank you, I will next time,' I replied, relieved and wishing I were more able to ask for help. In my need to retain control and never give the impression that I couldn't cope, I forgot that I could have full, understanding support if I asked. I was used to being independent as mum and dad had both died before I got married. I always felt I should be the one to take care of and decide what was best for my children, and I knew Dr Ramsay worked a

hugely busy week so I was reluctant
She obviously realised I had worried my
and I thought that perhaps I should now try
not on day-to-day issues but certainly when
happened.

The doctor asked me to take Amberlie to th
they could take a urine test and give her a full exami
thought that whilst it did seem that the high temperature
related to the lamotrigine, it would be a good idea to check to
there were any deep-rooted, underlying infections lurki
anywhere that normal antibiotics wouldn't cure. It was also
important to find out whether or not we could use the lamotrigine
again because it was an effective antiepileptic; despite the toxic
effects, it had stopped her seizures.

We waited a good couple of hours to be seen by the doctors
and then we were allowed home. They never called us with any
results so I knew they had not found anything. It was the drug. It
was a crying shame, because now we had to look for alternatives to
control Amberlie's salaams.

Dr Ramsay told Bill and me that there was another drug to
consider but it would mean Amberlie would be on five different
antiepileptics and she wondered what sort of effect that would have
on her vital organs and her body in general. I wanted to try it of
course, but not at the expense of making her ill again, so I said I
would prefer it to replace a drug rather than add to the Molotov
cocktail she already took. It seemed sensible to me to get rid of the
lamotrigine altogether, but the doctor felt it was working on the
level it was on. She was keen to get rid of another one instead.

The only way to find out if a drug was effective was to take
it away, gradually over a period of time, and if Amberlie remained
seizure free it denoted either that she was on too much of the drug
or that she was not missing it, so that part was deemed ineffective.
If a reduction was made and Amberlie's seizures increased then the
idea was to reinstate what was taken away to resume control.

) before putting the drugs
ff reaction to them being
because there were never
ething we couldn't stop
evably stressful, hoping
r seizures. I hated it but
— to keep my Amberlie
e different. Introducing
f hope and expectation
er out. If it failed, the

medicines were made when
is used to drive me insane. I
understand why, if things were good, there was a need to start messing about with her drugs. We had never yet succeeded in reducing a medicine without causing more or new seizures. I kept making the point that perhaps we would maintain her stability if we stopped trying to reduce them.

It was professional practice that after a certain period of time certain drugs rendered themselves ineffective because the patient would be used to them or, indeed, unnecessarily addicted to them. It was therefore a good idea to try to remove them (one at a time) from their system. The theory made a lot of sense and of course successfully removing a useless drug could make room for another effective drug as well as keeping a lid on toxicity. It was also possible that sometimes drugs, either singly or when mixed with others, could work in reverse and cause more seizures; and lots of drugs made it very difficult to assess and measure the effectiveness of any one of them or of the combination. It was all a gamble, and took for granted the fact that the drug to be removed was not working in combination with any other. In my opinion, this was a very valid possibility because until her clonazepam was reduced (directly after the vigabatrin proved itself a wonder drug), Amberlie had had a very stable existence. Of course between now and then other factors, such as growth, contributed to the amount of seizures she was experiencing. Hindsight is a wonderful thing.

We couldn't have asked for a doctor with more experience in such a specialised field, and Dr Ramsay was just as frustrated with the drug situation as we were. She racked her brain and consulted other neurologists to try to come up with an answer to control Amberlie's seizures. She of course had to keep within the boundaries of her professionalism and medical ethics and was already pushing it with the amount of medicines Amberlie was taking. She too was a mother and could understand where I was coming form in that I felt 'quality of life' had to be the priority. In turn I sympathised with her: it must have been extremely hard for her to balance the job with emotions when she got to know her patients so well over so many years. It was obvious she had a soft spot for Amberlie, and occasionally she would be a little brusque with me in an attempt to keep a little distance. Sometimes the combination of her maintaining medical correctness and my insistence on quality of life caused a few polite differences over Amberlie's medication. I understood her concern about the amount of drugs Amberlie was taking – all of them had potential side effects and the risks were multiplied by mixing them. In a better world she would only have needed a couple to have complete control (in a better world she would not have needed them at all), but where would Amberlie be without them? ... Dead is the answer.

Our quest had to be to find the right chemistry to achieve a decent quality of life. We had to give Amberlie comfort, safety, happiness, enjoyment, and hopefully consciousness every precious day. Life owed that to her.

Amberlie's hospital appointments provided a good chance to catch up with Dr Ramsay, who liked to know what Amberlie had been up to and how we all were as a family. She made sure we had everything we needed and nagged us every time to take more holidays! Sometimes the outcome of these appointments depended on how Amberlie appeared in that all-important half an hour.

Amberlie might have been having lots of seizures for days on end but during her appointment she would often find a window where she was calm, happy and alert. It was then very difficult to get across to the doctor how bad things had been without me appearing to be totally paranoid! It was very frustrating to walk out of the hospital and watch Amberlie's seizures resurface and continue for the rest of the day. If the situation persisted, I would then have to call the doctor when perhaps something could have been done sooner. On the other hand, Amberlie might have been poorly, drowsy and pale for the appointment but have been great for a while beforehand. This would then worry Dr Ramsay and I would have to get across the fact that this was not unusual and Amberlie was very much up and down. It wasn't the doctor's fault – the system gave us half an hour, and all it provided was a snapshot of how Amberlie was.

The nice thing about Amberlie's good times was that they gave us all hope and showed Dr Ramsay just what a delight my little girl was. The doctor loved to see her roll on her office floor and/or play with a toy – it made her day.

Getting any answers from Dr Ramsay was still like getting blood from a stone. I knew I probably wasn't fair to her on occasions as some of my questions were unanswerable because she just did not know. The doctor wasn't about to give me any educated guesses because if she said something and it turned out wrong, we might be upset and it would then make her vulnerable professionally. I respected that.

I felt that it was then too easy to assume that Amberlie would follow an expected path, the standard prognosis, and be a certain way; and consequently some things were too readily put under universal headings, such as behavior being linked to 'emotional stress' or an occurrence too easily filed away as a 'normal' childhood thing. The essence of what made Amberlie

Amberlie – her individuality, and what made her different from other lissencephaly children – was then lost.

Naturally Amberlie had lots of similarities to other children – needing the security of routine, throwing 'terrible two' tantrums – but there were shady areas too, unusual things which I had not seen with any of my other children. They might still have been 'normal', but I doubted it. I, of course, was too sensitive, bordering on the over-imaginative, and maybe a little less worrying would have been good for me – and yes, perhaps the doctor had a point – but I was conscious of not looking for things that weren't there and I often ignored things that in hindsight I probably shouldn't have. I too had a brain that was searching for answers, a breakthrough; I had learned masses, analysed, and applied everything, and now I often disagreed with theories and decisions. Sometimes I said so and sometimes I didn't. I tended to follow my instincts and ventured off the beaten track in an attempt to make life good for Amberlie.

Why should things always follow a predicted path? We were talking 'Amberlie', a little miracle, managing to survive against all the odds. If I had not spent twenty-four hours a day, seven days a week with my precious bundle, I would not have been able to work her out to the extent I did. I knew my girl, and I could see reason and logic in things she did. I spent hours watching, observing, linking patterns ... and they made sense, but I had to think 'out of the box' or laterally, and the information was often given to me in 'jigsaw' pieces. Amberlie knew I knew her. She often looked at me to tell the kids something if they weren't responding to her noises or wriggles, and I often went wrong in my attempts to go right because I had misinterpreted the clues. I could almost see Amberlie shake her head and she would let me know again. I was truly amazed at how clever she was in working out how to communicate. Whatever was missing from Amberlie's intelligence did not remove the fact that her brain was working to its full potential, and Amberlie used every scrap of it.

It was hard to explain, give example or indeed prove this to Dr Ramsay but I felt it was vital not to ignore it, and in some way it must surely affect the prognosis?

I once said to Dr Ramsay, 'I would like to spend a day in Amberlie's head so I can know for sure how she feels and what her life is like.'

The doctor turned to me, her face shocked, and, with her eyes stretched wide, she said, 'No you wouldn't. It would be an unimaginable nightmare.'

And the pain seared again.

One morning the postman delivered a letter from the Make-a-Wish Foundation, a charity that makes dreams come true for life-limited children. I had not heard of them before and they were asking me to fill in a form giving them Amberlie's details and names and ages of everyone in our family.

'How do they know about you?' I said to Amberlie, who was watching me open the mail. Bewildered, I put it to one side as we had an appointment with Dr Ramsay at 9.30 a.m.

When I got there she said, 'What are you going to do … swim with the dolphins?'

'Huh?' I answered.

Dr Ramsay looked at me, grinning. 'Don't you know?'

I shook my head wondering what on earth she was on about.

'Make-a-Wish have written to me asking all about Amberlie,' she said.

'Riiight,' I said slowly, still confused. 'I did have a letter this morning about something.' She must have thought I wasn't all there.

'What would Amberlie like to do, do you think?' she asked.

'I dunno, dunno …' I just wasn't taking it in.

'Oh, do let me know!' Dr Ramsay said excitedly.

We left it there and continued with the appointment.

When I got home I picked up the form. There was no information at all. It was just an application form. I rang Bill and asked him if he knew anything about it and he was just as surprised as me. That afternoon Amberlie and I walked with Christine to collect the children from school and I mentioned it to her. She grinned from ear to ear.

'You know something, don't you?' I urged.

Christine said, 'When we did all the fundraising last year, we asked Raymond what his greatest wish for Amberlie would be. We asked him if would like to make that wish come true for her by writing a letter to some people who might be able to help. He said he would, so we got him to write the letter when he came to play one afternoon and told him to keep it a secret. We then sent it off.'

'Strewth .. huh ... wow!' I couldn't believe it.

'I kept a copy of the letter so that I could show you,' Chris said. 'It'll break your heart when you read it, and make sure you fill in those forms or you'll break Raymond's.'

I was amazed that Ray was able to keep a secret like that without telling anyone. He was only 10 years old. My kids never ceased to amaze me!

This is what he wrote:

Dear Wishing Well Foundation,

I have a sister called Amberlie who is infected with lissencephaly and is disabled. If I had one wish, it would be to make Amberlie better but I know nobody can make that happen. If I could have two wishes, the second one would be to go to Disneyland in Paris. Last time when my family went there for a weekend we had a happy time especially Amberlie. She liked the best the lights, sounds and the trees. Amberlie has lots of fits which make her twitch and do head-downs. She crys when she has fits because she is frightened. When we were at Disneyland, she didn't have one fit whatsoever probably because she was enjoying herself.

237

So when Amberlie is happy, my family is happy. Please make my wish come true.

From

Raymond Murphy

I couldn't stop the tears. Christine's arms were around me and she was crying too. Poor little chap, I thought. You understand so much, don't you? I wished things had been different. I wished Amberlie had been normal. I wished that the kids didn't have to feel such pain. I wished they didn't have to learn so much about life so young. God, it hurt. I couldn't protect them from all this, they had to face it every day just like Bill and me, and they had accepted it all without question – they loved Amberlie so much. I had to fill in the form for their sakes. All my children deserved the chance to have some fun.

You're a very special person, Chris … and I don't know where to begin to thank you enough.'

'We just wanted to make sure Amberlie has everything she can, and you all deserve this. Just go and have fun … that's all we want,' she replied.

A short while later we had a phone call to say that three ladies would be visiting us from 'Make-a-Wish' so they could meet us all. They were very glamorous, beautifully dressed ladies with lovely, laughing and gentle dispositions. They knew just how to talk to the children and brought each of them a wrapped present, which were excitedly opened straight away! They spent a good hour listening to the kids talk about their lives with Amberlie. It was very interesting to listen to them. They recalled umpteen traumas and emergencies, but most of all what Amberlie did when she was happy. They described her playing and laughing and her love of really loud music! They put her favourite CD on to show them how Amberlie danced, and Amberlie happily obliged!

Later, when it was time to talk to Bill and me, the ladies said that the thing that came across most was how proud the children all were of Amberlie. I felt really honoured that they were mine.

A couple of months later they called us to say that their committee had agreed that we should all go to Disneyland for a four-day holiday and listed all the things we were booked to do while we were there. They carefully arranged things that Amberlie would like most, and avoided things that would possibly startle or frighten her. They also gave Amberlie her own pocket money to spend however she wanted!

We were really chuffed – what an amazing thing to happen!

Dr Ramsay decided that it might be wise to let Amberlie settle for a bit after the trauma of the lamotrigine before starting on another drug change. Her salaam seizures went back to their early-morning routine and varied in severity from gentle lurches to shouting, crying, and violent episodes which lasted from 5 to 25 minutes without a break, and required diazepam to stop them. The only consolation was that apart from phases of little absences she was virtually fit free for the rest of the day. Dr Ramsay and I had a long chat about it and agreed that the situation was reasonable for Amberlie, and it was best to leave well alone.

However, things never stayed the same for long for Amberlie, and the situation soon escalated and more seizures appeared. Each morning salaam was now a severe and serious one, and they were very unpredictable, with new elements surfacing all the time. There was lots of facial and limb twitching, raising of arms, chimpanzee-type expressions, lots of stiffening and slight shaking, and other peculiar physical reactions not normal to Amberlie. During the day she often threw her arms out to the sides as if she was flying but instantly returned to normal, and sometimes she would raise her arms up straight in the air with her hands limp and bow her head, also immediately returning to normal. Salaams had also started to appear in the evenings but as yet were just typical movements and not severe.

The nights were fairly quiet times, providing Amberlie wasn't ill, and she slept pretty restfully. She often woke after 4-5 hours, but with a cuddle and some gentle persuasion could be put back to bed again until morning. Sometimes it was wind that woke her and after rubbing her back she would burp and go back to sleep. I daresay any fits that occurred in her sleep could also have woken her, but there was no evidence that they were anything more serious than jumps. She very rarely ever moved in bed during the night. We always put her to bed on her side but she preferred to lie on her back with her legs hanging out of the bed, and that was usually the only movement she made to get herself comfortable. A seizure would always occur, be it minor or major, if she was disturbed or during the natural waking-up period. Her brain must have found it very difficult to cope with the sudden stimulation as her eyes opened and information flooded in.

The times between Amberlie's seizures were often happy and peaceful, and an interlude in which to relax a bit and enjoy a stable, uneventful routine. It was also nice to get a reasonable amount of sleep at night, although I often felt more tired for having slept rather than just carrying on as usual.

One night I woke to odd noises and discovered Amberlie in the middle of a tonic-clonic seizure (a severe shaking fit). I didn't know how long she had been in it so I felt the best thing was to give her diazepam straight away. Tonic-clonic seizures only usually appeared with Amberlie if there was a feverish temperature brewing and she was about to become ill, so I grabbed the thermometer and checked her. Everything was normal. The diazepam worked within a couple of minutes and Amberlie settled back to sleep. She woke at her usual time and had her usual salaam. I hoped she might have got away with that one as she had already had diazepam in the night. That episode proved to be the signal that things were about to deteriorate again.

It was a gorgeous sunny day on Amberlie's fifth birthday and we spent most of it in the garden, much to her delight! Relatives and friends visited all afternoon to join us for her tea party. There were a few seizures about but Amberlie bore them well, having several short and sweet naps to see them off. She seemed to enjoy her day but as usual didn't appreciate being cuddled and passed round to people she didn't see very often. We always knew when it was time to go to her rescue, as she would stare straight at Bill or me with a worried expression on her face. Bill was always ready to grab her. He loved to have her all to himself and would sit with her for hours. The feeling was mutual and whatever day Amberlie was able to spend on her dad's lap was a good day for her! She adored him and constantly made eyes at him, looking away shyly for short moments while he talked to her. She was in seventh heaven, flirting and smiling away the time, and he was far more interesting than food or drink, so she ate all her food totally distracted by him!

Disneyland Paris

Our trip finally came round and the kids were beside themselves with excitement. We were to travel on the Eurostar train straight through to Disneyland Paris and stay at the Sequoia Lodge Hotel. We had hesitated about travelling by train because Amberlie was a package deal all by herself and we had so much to carry. Make-a-Wish had wanted Bill to go without the car so that he could have a rest from driving, which was a nice well-meant idea but Bill didn't mind driving and, as we had anticipated, the journey proved rather tough for all of us.

We had arranged a taxi to take us to the station. We struggled getting Amberlie in and out of her pram and dismantling it into its two sections ready to board the train. It was quite a challenge doing it at the best of times and getting that, the kids and the luggage on the train before it pulled out of the station was pretty stressful. The pram did not fold down well and we found it best to keep Amberlie strapped in the chair part, plonking it onto a seat next to her dad, where he could hold onto it. Ben was only three, and was awestruck with the train and also needed lots of help. Ray and Clare had their own rucksacks on their backs and we all grappled with the rest of the bags. Then there were escalators and corridors and loads of people. We had to pick up our tickets and booking documentation from a special stand at Waterloo, which was also a bit of a palaver because it wasn't properly signposted. Amongst all the hustle and bustle we finally sat in the departure lounge where Disney had provided a barber shop quartet to entertain their waiting passengers. It was a welcome lighthearted touch, and fuelled the kids' excitement for the journey.

Amberlie took it all in her stride, as she usually did while out, and we sat her by the window on the train so she could watch the world pass by. The other kids were overcome with excitement and were enjoying the novelty of it all. Bill and I were glad to finally be on the train so we could relax for a while.

We were meant to have two adjoining rooms at the hotel but unfortunately Bill and Ray were sited down the corridor. As Amberlie only drank milk, we had specially asked that the hotel leave some in the fridge in our room ready for us when we arrived but the message hadn't got through; the receptionists couldn't help and the restaurants and shops were closed. We had to get some from somewhere so we decided to try the other hotels. It had just started to pour with rain and poor Bill walked miles around all the other hotels on the Disney site, eventually managing to find the last pint of milk in one of the foyers. We finally sorted Amberlie out, but it was now getting late and the other kids needed food. There was only one restaurant left open and we spent an age queuing to get a table. I was glad when the day was over.

Generally Amberlie kept quite well during the visit but there were lots of fits about and she slept a good deal of the time. She attracted the Disney characters like a magnet and even when she had Goofy and Mickey Mouse talking to her, she drifted off to sleep. They were very good and sat beside her holding her hand or gently stroking her head while she slept. Lots of children came up to see them and they put their fingers to their mouths to tell them, 'Sshhh … Amberlie's sleeping.' Ray, Clare and Ben naturally took great advantage of all the attention Amberlie got by getting lots of autographs, photos and cuddles, as well as enjoying the benefit of the 'no-queue' pass to the rides!

We went for afternoon tea with the Toy Story and Amberlie managed to stay awake for that. She adored Buzz Lightyear, who was huge, flashed with green, and towered over her. She gazed up at him with her mouth open and her eyes wide in wonderment. She liked it best when we were outside in the park where she had so much to look at.

Her feeding proved to be a problem each day while we were out and she really didn't want to be bothered with it at all. That was fine for her but did nothing to help our stress levels. We were afraid she was going to get ill and I really didn't want to be in France under those circumstances, even though Dr Jonathan had given me some antibiotics to make up if I needed them. At least she ate her meals properly back at the hotel and that eased our minds somewhat.

Amberlie spent all her pocket money on new clothes and a cuddly toy version of each of the Seven Dwarfs. The others all wanted a cuddly toy too and, of course, they had to have the biggest ones! We ended up having to buy another holdall just to take home all their souvenirs! The journey home was as bad as the one going but everyone remained in good spirits.

The kids had a whale of a time and were still chattering excitedly about where they'd been as they got into their beds. It was a wonderful wish to have granted and I'm sure that had Amberlie been able to, she would have thanked Raymond and Make-a-wish a thousand times over. It would have been lovely to know what she made of it all. We sat down the next day and wrote a thank-you card to Make-a-Wish for giving us all and especially Amberlie such a special and magical holiday.

As expected, Amberlie downloaded into a big sleep which, allowing for feed times, lasted for about forty-eight hours. Delighted but exhausted, Bill and I still wished we had taken the car!

25

Amberlie's arms were raised high above her bowed head and her chin pressed hard against her chest. There was an expression of intense concentration on her red face and she looked as if she was going to explode. When the seizure passed it left her eyes, nose and chin black and blue. These were new episodes that came in clusters, and went on for whole days, and I couldn't predict when they would happen.

These seizures had differing stages, each stage linked by a small pause. I hazarded a guess that they were all types of single salaams. It seemed as though they were individual fits mapping a course, and when they came up against a wall they were unable to pass, they paused, and searched for another way out, each one then presenting itself in a slightly different format.

Going out was no longer a stress-free experience, as I knew that Amberlie was likely to have a seizure, but I had to go out. The kids needed collecting from school and shopping had to be done, and it certainly wasn't fair to Amberlie to have kept her indoors away from her beautiful trees, which made her giggle and coo when they swayed. I felt so bad for her that these bloody things were robbing her of the few things she adored. The exciting outdoors used to distract her away from seizures and now it had lost that power; each time I set foot out of the door my insides knotted up with stress, worrying whether or not we would make it there and back without her having a big one.

Thankfully most of the episodes consisted of small jumps and stretches, with some odd facial expressions that generally people seemed to be unaware of. The nastier more noticeable ones made her stretch her arms out straight sideways as if she was playing 'aeroplanes', making her lean over the side of the pushchair with a fixed stare, dribbling profusely. Since Amberlie had come off her dummy, she had taken to sucking her tongue instead, and quite often during one of these intense fits she would bite it quite savagely and blood would ooze from her mouth. She was totally unaware of the pain and her teeth would remain in her tongue until the fit passed. When she came to she must have been very, very sore but only sometimes did she cry.

I used to stop walking to hold her hand and wipe away the dribbles until she settled. If the fits were just jumps and jerks I found it better to continue walking because the motion seemed to hasten the end of the seizure as Amberlie tried to focus her brain. Ben also managed to distract her sometimes as he played next to her. He was very patient and also often held her hand until the blips went away. Once the seizure was over Amberlie usually dozed off to recover and we mostly made it home without any repetition. My main worry was that one day, at some stage, Amberlie would go into a major tonic-clonic seizure in the street and I wasn't quite sure how I would handle that – apart from running home as fast as possible. I realised I needed to keep a tube of diazepam with me all the time in case that ever happened. It was also time to get a mobile phone in case I needed an ambulance or had to arrange for a friend to collect the children at short notice.

Other people were pretty good though, and most were used to seeing us out and about so we weren't an unusual event. If they did think anything strange they didn't mention it, stare awkwardly or even rush away – accepting Amberlie's 'normal' as normal.

I doubt whether they actually associated Amberlie's behavior with fits. Most people only associate major jerking and shaking with epilepsy, and because it may have never touched their lives, they are none the wiser. I used to leave it that way. There was no point in explaining – it was too complicated – and apart from a few people who regularly asked after Amberlie's health, everyone went about their daily business as usual. I knew, though, that if Amberlie and I were in real trouble, any one of them would have helped.

Occasionally a new face would show some degree of curiosity and there were a few who totally ignored us – I guessed it was because they felt uncomfortable.

I explained the new pattern to Dr Ramsay and she saw Amberlie straight away. She wanted to try a new antiepileptic called Topamax which had only just had its licence granted in the UK for paediatric use. As we had agreed earlier she would need to take one of Amberlie's other medicines away because of the toxicity risks, and between us we decided that the lamotrigine had to go. We worked out a schedule to decrease the dosages and I was to ring Dr Ramsay every few days to check in, in case the seizures escalated during the change. Oh, did I loathe it – taking out a drug when Amberlie was already in dire straits was like facing my worst nightmare, but what else could we do?

As usual I indirectly asked about the prognosis, knowing that a straight question would yield no answers. Dr Ramsay explained some more about the way fits build up and exit and said that she wished she had something good to tell us. She also mentioned (in an attempt to provide a shred of optimism) that lissencephaly children usually die of pneumonia but that of course did not rule out other causes. I said I had recently heard that a child had died of liver failure, and she said she thought that would have been down to an already existing problem or drug toxicity or both, which was what I expected her to say. I knew that the kind of cocktail Amberlie was surviving on could produce a similar result.

I took the news on the chin and sighed heavily while I chewed the inside of my mouth, aiming to hurt myself enough to keep the tears behind my eyes. It was an odd kind of feeling when I was taking bad news on board, like a pressure suddenly pushing and filling my chest and lungs, making me breathe heavily. Sharp pains stung in my heart and throat but at the same time I was numb. Everything would start to spin around in my head and I would face none of it … so it was pushed away to deal with later or maybe never. That didn't mean I had not accept it – I already knew it, but it was different when Dr Ramsay confirmed it. I just had to manage it and not let it get to me. Now wasn't the time to have a trauma and I was determined not to give anyone the idea that there was any possibility I couldn't cope. All that mattered was that we sorted Amberlie out as best we could. I didn't have time to feel sorry for myself, and Amberlie certainly didn't need a crumbling mother.

So off we went to the pharmacy silently despairing, but hopeful of a miracle. The pharmacy did not have the drug and the pharmacist said it would be in on Monday. It was now Friday. On Monday they rang to say that the drug was not available in the small quantities that Amberlie had been prescribed and that sachets were only available in the United States. There was an added complication that the company who made it were only licensed to supply 25 children in the UK and there was a waiting list. I was devastated. There was no guarantee that Amberlie would get this drug at all – not that it was guaranteed to work anyway, but that wasn't the point. I immediately rang Dr Ramsay and she said the pharmacy had already spoken to her, and she was going to fight hell for leather to get it for Amberlie. Three weeks later we heard that Amberlie had made it onto the priority list and we now had to wait for it to come from America … but they didn't know when that would be. I suggested that I went to America to pick it up and they said it wasn't as simple as that. There wasn't anything I could do to hurry it up. It was so frustrating and I started to panic a bit when Dr Ramsay suggested we start the drug reduction while we waited. It was hard to face taking something away without putting anything in. She said it might help if the drug was now working in reverse. I felt so useless that I couldn't help my baby, and I was desperately frightened for her and for us all. The constant worry and unpredictability of it all left me existing on a knife-edge.

Nothing improved as the lamotrigine went down. Amberlie was having some settled periods during the daytime and there were even a few good days when Amberlie was her old self, but Jesus Christ … a bad day was a bad day and the salaams came one after the other, tormenting and exhausting her. As usual the biggest salaams appeared first thing in the morning and now last thing at night, and were obviously triggered by the change in her awareness as she either awoke or prepared to sleep.

On one occasion Amberlie had been agitated all morning, and although I finally managed to get her to sleep early in the afternoon, she was constantly interrupted by fits. She kept opening and rolling her eyes several times then closing them again. Eventually, after making sure she had settled, I went to make a cup of tea. I returned to find her facing towards me with what looked like two black eyes. She was asleep but her breathing was very shallow and her skin unnervingly pale. I thought the worst and rang Bill to come home and called Christine to come and look at Amberlie's colour just in case it was the light. I needed someone else's opinion – with so much going on day after day I had begun to question myself as to whether I imagined half of it and whether I was losing my sanity. Christine was shocked. I wasn't sure what to do.

'I think I'm going to have to take her to hospital,' I said, but another part of me said, 'Wait.'

Chris said, 'It's getting near three. I'll collect the kids from school for you, you just do whatever you need to and I'll look after them.' I nodded. I sat beside Amberlie and as Bill walked through the door forty-five minutes later, Amberlie's colour started to come back, more on her left side than on her right, where there were still black areas and red bruise-type marks on her brow. She gradually came to but was very drowsy. I told Dr Ramsay I was stopping the drug reduction.

The next three weeks presented more bad times than good and the fits became more frequent. The poor little soul was whacked out. The seizures were also causing some clear phlegm to linger in the back of her throat, but Dr Ramsay explained this was expected as a result of some of Amberlie's seizure types. She said she thought it was now a good idea to get the community paediatric nurses to deliver a suction machine to us in case the phlegm caused a blockage in Amberlie's breathing. She said this would also be helpful when Amberlie had a cold.

It was a horrible looking old thing and I hated the thought of having to use it. The nurse taught me how to use it and how to clean it afterwards. As soon as she left I cleaned it thoroughly and sterilised all the bits. I used it a couple of times after seizure episodes and it was loud and gruesome in its suck and it made Amberlie jump. She hated it being put to the back of her mouth and top of her throat and there was a fine line between it doing its job and making her gag. Things were bad enough without having to put her through that. I hoped the fits would soon change so that we wouldn't have to keep using it.

It wasn't long before we had another cold in the house and Amberlie succumbed within three days. Her breathing was dire as she soared into another chest infection. She kept vomiting this time and I think that was due to a combination of fit phlegm and mucus lying on her chest from the infection, but at least she was shifting it. I remembered the bottle of antibiotics left in the cupboard, which I had taken to Disneyland and not used. I mixed it up and started her on that but she was still being sick, so I couldn't tell how much of the medicine she kept. I took her along to see Dr Jonathan and he gave me another bottle just to be on the safe side. Amberlie recovered fairly well, with just a few rattles remaining on her chest.

There was no let up in the fits though. They had found a new lease of life and I lost count of the amount Amberlie had some days. It had been necessary to use the diazepam more and more as the duration of the salaam seizures got longer and longer, intensifying their torture. She shouted as her body stretched to its furthest point, held her breath, lost her colour, thrust her head down hard and jerked her arms and legs with a savage ferocity.

They were cruel and merciless and I wouldn't let her suffer them. I gave her the diazepam immediately after five minutes – it was the only thing that stopped them.

Dr Ramsay always insisted that these fits were far worse for us than for Amberlie because she wouldn't know anything about them. But Amberlie was miserable and I felt it was all too easy for the doctor to pass it off … who knew what Amberlie felt? I think at the very least that Amberlie must have ached after such stretching and had headaches when she came round. And certainly her tongue must have hurt badly after she had bitten it. The poor little soul must have wondered what on earth was happening to her.

Waiting for the new drug was proving a real trial and I was getting agitated and fed up with it. I was terrified Amberlie would end up in 'status' again if the fits weren't controlled soon, and then we might never get her back. I couldn't understand why there was always so much bloody red tape with these things, particularly when the request had been made urgently by a medical professional.

As ever, the kids were taking the changes in Amberlie in their stride but the salaams had shocked them with their savageness and the way they contorted her body. There was now an edge of panic in their voices when they saw her go into one or heard her shout in that particular way to signal she was off again. Clare knew the routine and would dash out of the room to fetch the diazepam without being prompted. She knew how to prepare and administer it, which I allowed her to do once or twice. She was always my little helper at these times and would lie beside Amberlie until she was calm again – and once Amberlie was asleep, she would carry on with what she was doing beforehand. I felt as young as Clare was, it did no harm for her to know what needed to be done in an emergency. She also knew that if the fit had not stopped after ten minutes, Amberlie could have another diazepam, and after that if it then showed no signs of stopping, it was time to call for an ambulance.

Ray was not good at practical emergency things. He loathed what the seizures did to Amberlie, and his face was etched with pain and concern each time. He loved her and stroked her hair, held her hand or just sat by her ... but to give her diazepam – especially rectally was beyond him. I guess if he had to he would have done, but he much preferred someone else to sort it. Ben just watched or carried on with what he was doing, he was so used to it. It was all part of the daily routine in this house.

Amberlie's free time was rapidly being filled by smaller seizures, which now ruthlessly assaulted her. Often they were no more than a type of shrug or an outstretched arm but they knocked her senseless. They nearly always made her cry and she seemed very frightened of them; and because they were like a flash attack, they were not enough to send her to sleep to recover, leaving her drowsy and vacant instead. Amberlie would sit staring out of the window, at her new ball or at nothing. I tried to distract her by talking to her or playing with her toys, and she might have thrown a flickering glance at me occasionally but not enough to break her gaze. Sometimes snuggling her on my lap and giving her a bottle of milk settled her and sent her to sleep. She would let me know if I'd done the right thing by looking straight at me and uttering a little 'ooh' followed by a beautiful smile before sucking on her bottle. Often I sat there until she woke up, frightened to move in case I pre-empted another seizure. Ben never worried about me sitting with Amberlie and usually stayed close; he seemed to enjoy the fact that I was sitting down for a while. He often brought me a book to look at with him or sat and held my hand while drifting off for a nap himself. It was also a chance for me to grab a rest ... the housework could wait.

The seizures also affected Amberlie's feeding, lengthening the procedure and making it more difficult to get her to eat anything at all. I couldn't work out why she did not want her food, unless she just wasn't hungry, because she was still drinking well. I assumed that the fits were not causing a swallowing problem, as it seemed a logical conclusion that both would be affected. There again, I supposed the solid food may have given her more difficulty because of its consistency, and maybe fluid was easier to manage.

As the Whitsun Bank Holiday weekend approached Amberlie began to show signs of becoming poorly. No surprise there – it always happened during a Bank Holiday; I have no idea why. That was the way it was.

Amberlie was constantly whiny and tearful and I edgily waited for the first signs of an infection. On the Saturday morning she woke straight into her usual salaam and went back to sleep after the diazepam. She woke again later to have another small salaam and immediately fell back to sleep. I stayed with her, keeping close watch, and she eventually woke long enough to drink a bottle of milk before there was yet another salaam, and that too sent her to sleep. This pattern continued all day and as I kept a close eye on her I noticed that she was also having an unusual amount of small seizures while she slept.

That evening she developed a slight temperature, but it came down after I gave her some paracetamol. Her hands and feet were icy cold and I couldn't warm them up so I decided to ring the out-of-hours doctors for some advice. I explained that she had been having lots of seizures and something was obviously bothering her but nothing definite had surfaced. They apologised that they were unable to give me any sound advice for Amberlie, and suggested I took her to hospital.

I really didn't want to do that just yet. So many times we had been to the hospital and things had turned out to be something and nothing. It was such a palaver to arrange childcare for the children, and I just felt that if the paracetamol was controlling the temperature, then it might just be a case of waiting for the illness to take its course. We turned on all the heating and I lay next to her and covered us both with two duvets and blankets on top in the hope I could warm her up. It was a case of wait and see.

Amberlie's fits were always worse nowadays when she was going to be ill and I knew the fits in themselves would not cause a temperature. At least I had the diazepam to keep the serious ones somewhat in check.

Sunday was the same but there was no sign of a temperature and her colour was awful. On Monday she seemed a little brighter so we thought we would take her to the park for some fresh air, and she stayed awake the whole time, having only a few startled jumps. When we returned she went into a peaceful sleep and we hoped she was on the mend.

About 11 p.m. that night Amberlie's temperature shot up to 39.6°C and she was boiling hot apart from her hands and feet, which were icy cold. Her chest was bubbling and wheezy and her breathing was laboured. I thought she had meningitis. I called the out-of-hours doctors immediately and they came straight away. In the meantime the temperature had brought on a nasty fit and she had needed diazepam. This time the paracetamol had no effect on the temperature and the doctor examined her for rashes and said that her chest was in a very bad way. He gave her some antibiotics immediately, and left us another dose to give her in the night so she was covered until the chemist opened in the morning. He said if her breathing worsened to call an ambulance but was hopeful that the antibiotics would kick in quickly. He also told us to keep her on four-hourly paracetamol for the next couple of days. As the night went on Amberlie's temperature gradually came down and had disappeared by the morning. She spent the day sleeping and fitting.

I rang Dr Ramsay first thing and explained the weekend. She said that the increased number of seizures would have been down to the infection cooking and hopefully they should subside now.

We had recently taken away Amberlie's morning dose of clonazepam and in view of the increase in her small seizure activity, I asked Dr Ramsay if it could be reinstated. I noticed

Amberlie was also going into body stretches (which she did when stressed) since it had disappeared, and thought it might all be somewhat related. She agreed to give it a try.

By the next day the fits had subsided quite a lot and Amberlie's jumps were few and far between. She was still very poorly and upset though and needed lots of love and cuddles.

Amberlie's drinking resumed well but she only managed to eat a little pureed fruit. The doctor had given her a different antibiotic, which had worked well and not left her miserable. I found that some antibiotics made Amberlie very unhappy for a while after she had completed the course and I guessed some mixed with her other medicines better than others.

I was glad I had not rushed her to hospital – it wouldn't have made any difference in the long run. Using the GP services for infections often meant Amberlie had antibiotics sooner that if I had taken her to hospital. Had her breathing deteriorated, however, I would not have hesitated.

It was always a huge relief to see Amberlie improve again. It was bad enough coping with the trauma of all the seizures, let alone her being generally poorly as well. Bill and I despaired at what she had to suffer and every new problem seemed much worse than the one before. Her seizures were so much more serious and less tamed and we wished that the new drug would hurry up and come through soon – and that it would be the answer – otherwise I dreaded to think what lay ahead, especially if the seizures continued as mercilessly as they had done lately. I was very worried about the damage the seizures might do to her brain in the meantime. Amberlie was left to fate as our friend science had left her in the lurch for the time being … and science was the only reason she had survived to date.

Three very long months passed before we finally received a call from the hospital to say Amberlie's new drug had arrived. Relieved and excited, I bundled her into the car and dashed off to collect it straight away. I gave her the first capsule in her food at 7 p.m. that night.

Things had gone from bad to worse in the last couple of weeks and now after her usual morning salaam Amberlie continued to jerk intermittently all day, and the more jerky and jumpy she was, the more edgy she was. We had every hope that the Topamax would now improve her life.

It was around 10 p.m. and we were washing and showering Amberlie. We often did this later in the evening, as it was easier for Bill and me to tackle it together once the kids were all in bed. It was a massive organisational quest and we always fully prepared everything beforehand. Her pyjamas were laid out, the towels warmed, the door and windows shut and the hairdryer plugged in – all designed to keep her as warm as possible to avoid any chills. Showering was always speedy although washing and conditioning Amberlie's beautiful long locks was not. Bill kept the warm water running on her to keep off the cold and she usually enjoyed it, soothed by her grooming.

I had just got the conditioner on her hair and was starting to comb it through when she suddenly shot forward with her arms raised up hard and stiff with her hands hanging limply on the ends. Her face was bright red and she looked about to burst … her mouth was tightly shut and she was holding her breath. A minute passed and Amberlie started to relax, lowering her arms and her colour slowly returning to normal. Anxiously I rushed to finish washing her hair and get her dressed in case she wanted to go to sleep. From experience I knew that if she didn't sleep when she wanted to it would provoke more seizures. Suddenly another came, followed by another and another.

'Shit!' I cried. 'I can't go fast enough!'

Bill held onto her while I did the best I could to get her showered off.

They were all different. There didn't seem to be any defined pattern and some of the fits caused an electrical-type twitching in her face, and Bill could feel them radiate through her body until they petered out. As they repeated they started to gradually take the form of her usual salaam seizures. Luckily by the time I had laid her on the bed to dress her, the fits were subsiding, leaving her totally exhausted. Bill and I sweated buckets as we scrambled to get her pyjamas on and dry her hair as fast and gently as possible. We couldn't risk leaving it wet or damp for it was a dead cert that if she wasn't completely warm and dry she would come down with another chest infection. Oddly she didn't go to sleep – in fact, she became more aware and her eyes shone brightly as she looked around. She endured another hour's worth of jerks … but they didn't bother her at all.

It was very late and Amberlie had not dozed off as expected, so we took her up to bed where she laid staring straight up at the ceiling. I sat beside her with her touch-lamp on low and watched, hoping she would nod off. Three long hours passed and she had hardly moved at all. I kept waving my hands over her eyes, which were huge and black, but apart from the odd blink, there was no reaction – nothing at all. I wasn't sure about this or whether to do anything about it but neither was I overly worried. I assumed it was all to do with the earlier seizures. The Topamax needed time to work so I didn't expect a miracle. To a certain extent I had become immune to panic. Things were so dire at times but generally everything to date had being either down to brewing illnesses or phases of seizures, which (with a little help from antibiotics and/or diazepam) Amberlie seemed to get over. The only way I could try to understand all that happened to her was to go with the flow and observe and act when it was necessary. Realistically, the hospital or doctors cold or would do no more that that during a seizure phase – they would observe and act only when it was obvious things were totally out of control. Amberlie was expected to have seizures – it was normal for her – and certainly her GP would be out of his depth, something he freely admitted on several occasions. I had to wait and see.

Anyway, just as if someone had turned a light off, Amberlie finally went to sleep. She did not stir until about 11 a.m. the next day, when she woke up in an instant and lay there for a while. Bill had just warmed a bottle for her when off she went into massive seizure, following a similar pattern as the night before, but it now included severe salaams. She was very upset. I gave her diazepam straight away and she went back to sleep as the tremors ebbed away.

'This is new,' I said to Bill, 'There's something not right … especially with all that staring last night.'

'Do you think it might be the Topamax?' Bill asked.

'I hope not,' I replied.

It was unbearable to think it might not do the trick.

It wasn't a good idea to leave Amberlie alone, so between us Bill and I took it in turns to sit with her but there was no sign of her waking. At 4 p.m. we decided to wake her gently as she had had nothing to drink since the night before. We tried for forty-five minutes. We picked her up, nudged her, talked to her, walked her round, stroked her face, sat her on our laps, but she didn't wake up. He breathing was steady and there were no suspicious bubbles or rattles in her chest so we put her back to bed again. Five minutes later she woke suddenly almost as if someone had switched a light on. Again she went into a massive fit. I had never had to give Amberlie diazepam twice in twelve hours so I was unsure and a bit reluctant. I hesitated, hoping (always hoping) that the fit would stop, but fifteen minutes later there didn't seem to be any break in sight. I needed guidance so I rushed downstairs and rang the out-of-hours doctors (it was a Saturday) and was immediately put through to a doctor. I explained everything and was told to give her another diazepam, and if that didn't work, take her to hospital.

After an affirmative nod to Bill while I was talking to the doctor, he gave Amberlie the diazepam and she settled quickly. The relief was incredible but my insides were tied up in knots right up to my throat.

While I had the doctor on the phone, I asked him whether it was possible that the Topamax had caused the episode. He said he knew nothing about Topamax (deep in my heart I knew he wouldn't) and that anything was possible. He advised that as Amberlie had only had one dose it was wise not to give her any more until we had spoken to her consultant. I had already decided Amberlie wasn't going to have any more for the time being.

Amberlie settled into a decent sleep but still jerked a lot for the rest of the day. She brightened up in the evening, playing and rolling around the floor happily as she usually did when she was well. Was it because by now the initial dose of Topamax had left her system?

It was too much of a coincidence that she had three unusual huge fits on top of one another, and she had certainly never stared at the ceiling for three hours solid! Bill and I had already decided with Dr Ramsay that in view of the drug-dependency issues that already bugged us and the risks involved in drug changes, we would give the Topamax three weeks to work, which was plenty of time for it to establish in Amberlie's system, and if there was no improvement in her seizures then we would start a reduction course to get rid of it before Amberlie became addicted. Any adverse reactions during the introductory period meant it would have to stop immediately, and I felt now was the time.

Whichever way we turned we didn't win. We had to try … with the risk of making things worse hanging over us all the time. I never wanted to ever be in a situation where I looked back with regret, wishing Bill and I had done something else. I needed to be able to say wholeheartedly and without reservation that I tried everything there was to give Amberlie the best care, treatment and a good life. 'If only' was not going to haunt me for the rest of my days.

The next day Amberlie woke as usual, had her fit, had diazepam, slept and woke again. As I looked at her and said, 'Hello sweetpea', she did not appear to be the same child … there was something wrong … something different.

I telephoned Dr Ramsay and she saw us immediately. She said we did the right thing in stopping the drug and was particularly concerned about the staring episode. She said that a similar thing had happened to two older children who had tried Topamax.

Nobody knew how any one person would react to any given drug. Some worked better than others, some not at all. It depended on the individual – that was the risk. Amberlie's cocktail was worryingly dangerous. Whatever we did, whether we tried new drugs or whether we left not so well alone, her little brain could only stand so much and now I was sure the uncontrolled seizures were damaging her big time. Knowing there was now a problem with the Topamax, and knowing that Dr Ramsay was fast running out of answers, I could see nothing but blackness ahead. We wanted Amberlie. We wanted her alive, but not just alive … we wanted a decent quality of life for her. Now what were we to do?

Dr Ramsay said she would contact a colleague at St George's Hospital to see if they had any suggestions and would also contact the drug company to verify any possible interactions with Amberlie's other medicines. She made another appointment to see us in four weeks' time, saying that if we needed her at all in the meantime we should not hesitate to call.

But we had achieved nothing … not a damn thing, and we were on our own again to face at least another four weeks marooned on our family island. I knew the doctor was doing her best, but despite the fact that I could call her anytime, I knew I would only call if things were critical – after all, what could anyone do anyway? I felt like a worn-out punch bag, and couldn't start to imagine how it was for my poor little girl. I was like an empty shell, to the point of disengaging myself from the whole thing. It was the only way I could cope. I couldn't let me feelings take over and I pictured little shelves in my mind that I filed my emotions on for another time. One day at a time was enough … and I wouldn't even contemplate the next twenty-four hours. The hope of Dr Ramsay coming up with an answer kept me going.

From then on, and following months of salaam seizures, the dominant fit pattern was now 'tree' fits. It was all very strange and strange that the Topamax episode had changed things with just one tablet – perhaps it had just been one tablet too many on top of her 'cocktail'. The damage was done.

Amberlie continued to be dodgy about her food and her drinking was occasionally a little more 'coughy', but on the bright side we were still having some good feeding days. Occasionally the tree fits impacted on her swallowing directly after the fit, and for about an hour afterwards, then returned to the current normal. These seizures must have stunned the 'swallowing' part of the brain. They always left her droopy, drowsy and totally exhausted even though they might only have lasted a minute or so. After a run of these she generally went to sleep, unless they progressed into either a backward or forward salaam, when she grew stressed and agitated, stretching herself into extension (hung over backwards), and moaned and cried for ages.

I couldn't help but be irritated that we were no closer to solving the drug problem. Dr Ramsay seemed in no rush to introduce anything else, still remaining worried about the amount of drugs Amberlie was taking. I think she was exploring the possibility that it was the mixture of drugs that was making Amberlie so bad and was waiting to see if we were in a blip phase or whether, if we hung it out long enough, Amberlie's growth might even things out. I understood the philosophy – but how long does an experiment go on for? And how much time could we afford to lose?

Amberlie became more and more aware of when her seizures were coming, and looked fearfully behind her as if she was being chased by something. She got fidgety and disturbed, and rubbed her irritated nose hard with the back of her hand – something she had always done when there were fits about. Her palms became sweaty and she breathed like she'd been running fast. As each day passed the 'tree' fits slowly grew in intensity and Amberlie stared more … sinking deep into her own world. We weren't playing much together anymore and there wasn't always much response to my voice, although most times she would turn her head towards me but not always her eyes, and when she did, there was no sparkle in them. I spent a lot of the day sitting by her and if I had to go out of the room she came with me so she was never ever left on her own. I had lots of time to think too much then and lots times when I couldn't keep those tears shelved anymore.

We then received a copy of a letter Dr Ramsay had written to the drug company who made Topamax. It included a comment that she thought Amberlie was going downhill. Bill, after seeing that in black and white, took it very hard.

'We know this anyway,' I said, 'I know it's different when it's in writing but you can see it for yourself … we've talked about it. She had deteriorated … it's slow but it's there.' It did hurt and I knew he was fighting back the pain but we had to come to terms with it.

'I know … but it's different when someone else says it. It all becomes hard and real and it takes the hope away,' he said.

'Yeah … I know,' I sighed.

I had to turn away from him as I felt the tears welling. I was determined not to let it get the better of me. If I crumbled, I wouldn't cope, and I knew I couldn't cope with his pain as well. I wanted to support him, we had always supported each other, but he had to get on with it too … the same as I had to. It hurt me to see him upset but there was no way either of us could fold under the pressure … it was just not an option.

Amberlie's staring was worrying me incessantly and I knew that it concerned Dr Ramsay. Its unrelenting persistence was now really distressing so I called her. She said that she was indeed very worried and was going to arrange for Amberlie to have an emergency EEG. She said that the staring could mean all sorts of things as well as be the result of constant seizures. Frustratingly, she would not elaborate further, wanting to know what the EEG said first.

The neurophysiology department rang a few minutes after I put the phone down and arranged to see Amberlie on Monday at 11 a.m. (it was now Friday). It was sod's law that we then had a fairly settled weekend. Amberlie was brighter, there was less staring, and crucially, I think, she was not having so many damned fits. Amberlie was not her 'normal' self ... just better than of late.

The weather was great and we thought we would make the most of her brightness and treat her to a day out at the beach. This made her day! She was excited and happy during the drive down and very active on the beach, kicking and waving her arms and legs, even swaying her body in her chair. There were some seizures about but only intermittent and not too strong, and she fully recovered between them. It was great to see her enjoying herself and great for Ray, Clare and Ben too. Anything that made her happy was always worth the effort! It made the whole family relax. After feeding Amberlie, we ended the day with a fish and chip supper. I used to feel bad that we ate a takeaway and she didn't. I hated the fact she couldn't do as we did. Amberlie never seemed bothered about it ... but I suppose food was never high on her agenda at the best of times anyway! Whenever we bought ice creams she used to taste a little on a spoon but would refuse it after a while – I think she didn't like the coldness.

Monday morning arrived and Amberlie woke in a bad seizure, starting with the tree fits then progressing into salaams. She had to have diazepam and of course would not eat or drink anything before going to the hospital, which did nothing for my stress level – at least if she had eaten it was one thing less to worry about if she became agitated.

Amberlie had a little nap in the car and by the time we were seated in the waiting room she was quite calm and placid. The harpsichord music they played in the background was awful and was enough to neurologically upset anyone!

Eventually a technician called Jason collected us and wired Amberlie up. He was very good and chatted away, telling us what he was doing and why. He was open to questions but very cagey about any information concerning the actual EEG reading. He said it was not his job to interpret the graph and was unable to comment. He was obviously able to read it though and although I probably wouldn't like his answer, I did want to know whether compared with Amberlie's last EEG, there was any deterioration; otherwise I would have to wait until the next appointment with Dr Ramsay to know anything – so I persisted. After I explained that I was already fully aware of the gross abnormality and Amberlie's prognosis, and saying that if she were his child he would want to know, he finally admitted that there did seem to be some deterioration but that he was not to be quoted. He seemed surprised that I did not dissolve into tears. Perhaps that was what he was worried about. I was not shocked, I didn't like it … but it was as I expected.

'You have quite an unquenchable thirst for knowledge, don't you?' Jason said.

I smiled and replied, 'I find it easier to cope when I know what's going on. I don't need or want to be protected from all this. I just find it mega irritating that I have to fight to know things all the time.'

'Well, you have cleverly questioned me in every possible way to get an answer and I admire that. I'm sorry that I can't tell you any more – it's a neurologist's job to speak to parents and I could lose mine over it,' he said.

'I understand, but it's just so frustrating when I know you know and you have the time to talk to me, whereas a neurologist doesn't. I know I was a bit ruthless and I apologise for that. You have helped and explained a lot about the ins and outs of EEGs though, and that makes notes for the files too! Thank you.'

'No problem,' he said. 'I just hope Dr Ramsay can help.'

'Yeah,' I sighed. 'So do I.'

There was no point in asking to see a neurologist. As for Dr Ramsay, I knew she just wanted to safeguard us, but she did sift the information. It was understandable that she was reluctant to commit herself professionally, and the last thing she wanted was a major eruption from an upset parent. It wouldn't solve anything if the whole doctor-patient relationship ended up destroyed. From my point of view, I wanted reasonable explanations and prognoses so I could prepare somewhat for the future. I wanted the choice to know. I wasn't going to hold a gun to anyone's head, even if they misjudged the situation and made a mistake … although I suppose I could never know for sure how I would react if I were upset enough. I always had hope, and each tiny shred of anything positive that came along, I hung onto for dear life; and because of that I was worried that I might be given too much to hang on to, and then be totally devastated when it fizzled into nothing – like a shooting star. I knew it was a complex and very changeable situation and I had to deal with things on a daily basis whatever came to light, but having no information to reason with made me feel alone and hindered my understanding of Amberlie's plight.

Naturally some parents prefer to plod on in the dark and if that's how they manage to cope then I respect that – each to their own. I appreciate that sometimes being a doctor must be hell, especially in paediatrics and no one wants to be the bearer of bad news, but if a question is asked then let it be answered. It must improve the working relationship.

After the EEG we went home and I set about washing all the horrible sticky stuff out of Amberlie's hair. That afternoon Dr Ramsay called to say that there had been some change on the EEG but not as much as she had expected. She seemed very relieved and told us to forget the Topamax for the time being and she would see us again in August with a view to reducing the vigabatrin! She thought the Topamax could have triggered the bad run of fits and that she may have been silly to put it in with the vigabatrin because it was a similar drug.

The thing that worried me was the suggestion to start reducing the vigabatrin – Amberlie's saviour – her life giver.

'She must be off her trolley!' I moaned to Bill. 'Jesus Christ! It doesn't make sense … Oh yes it does – she wants to eventually replace the vigabatrin with the Topamax! Shit! What is Amberlie supposed to do in the meantime while she fannies about and with no vigabatrin?' I couldn't bear it. I couldn't bear the thought of Amberlie being left to fate. 'Fuck it!' I screamed.

'Why didn't you talk to her about it while she was on the phone?' Bill asked.

'I dunno … I was gobsmacked, dumbfounded … bloody amazed! I couldn't think!' I was beside myself.

At the next appointment Dr Ramsay reiterated that the EEG had shown a more settled picture than she had expected. Having had time to ponder it all, I said that I felt that perhaps the EEG had not captured the full picture as Amberlie had needed diazepam before the appointment and this would have settled the activity in her brain, and she had gone through the whole reading with only one staring episode. It had been an hour of calmness. To take one hour out of a full 24-hour day did not to me show a real or decent diagnostic picture. Especially not one to go making huge rash decisions on about drug reductions.

Amberlie was a very sick little girl, as Dr Ramsay realised, but she never saw Amberlie every day as we did. To us Amberlie was not the same little girl. She was rarely aware and happy and compared with three months ago was often not responsive to stimulation of any kind. I knew there was more deterioration. Maybe it was more significant because on top of the original gross abnormality in Amberlie's brain, any deterioration, no matter how slight, would have dire and terrible consequences. So if there had only been a small change on the graph (despite the diazepam), I believed it was big enough to have an enormous effect on Amberlie.

I could see where the doctor was coming from with regard to reducing the vigabatrin, in that if Amberlie was taking two similar drugs then it would obviously have been too much, so one needed to be withdrawn. Never had it occurred to me that Dr Ramsay would ever consider taking away the vigabatrin altogether and I couldn't stand the thought of it going. It made sense that perhaps it needed replacing because Amberlie had taken it for so long and maybe the Topamax would work given the right circumstances. The thing that bothered me was it being taken away with no other drug being put in at the same time; as it had to go before trying the Topamax again. It was a horrifying and major risk … and would it be worth it? What if the non-compensating reduction caused major fits that could not be controlled and Amberlie went back into status? What if the Topamax caused the same thing to happen again and Amberlie couldn't take it? There were so many ifs, buts and maybes and I was panicking as I tried to sort it all out in my mind. The one overriding factor of it all though was that I was not ever, ever going to let my baby suffer. There was no choice. If we didn't try then we might regret it, but then we might regret it anyway. Dr Ramsay told me to talk it over with Bill and let her know what we decided.

Bill and I so wanted to keep Amberlie for as long as possible, but we didn't want to make her life worse. For Amberlie's sake it had to be the quality and not the quantity of life that we needed to fight for. What was the point of being out cold, fitting, and not able to feed properly? Was that classed as 'life'? Surely making her aware, happy and enjoying things with the smaller number of seizures for a shorter time was the better option? *Somehow Amberlie will let me know what to do*, I thought.

Amberlie was dreadfully floppy and losing her muscle tone. Her staring eyes were big and black. She didn't want to be fed at all during the day, but luckily she still drank. When her dad came home he was able to feed her. I accepted her preference, I just wanted her to eat, but even he was finding it slower and more difficult than it used to be. It often took 1-2 hours to feed her, sometimes longer.

On the days when Amberlie needed to open her bowels the seizures were a darn sight worse – extremely violent and harsh, and she was dreadfully upset for hours on end. The grief started from the minute her stool began to move down through her bowel and could go on moving slowly for three days at a time until the event happened, and more often than not she was in the midst of the most godawful seizure as the stool passed – and it made no difference whether it was hard or soft. The seizures usually continued for a few hours afterwards until her body re-established its norm. It was terrifying and I can only say that I was extremely grateful that she only needed to go to the loo twice a week because no doubt if she had gone daily, she would have been fighting for her life.

Amberlie was sleeping more than ever, but often the fits did not let her rest completely. When she did sleep properly it was more 'coma' like, and thankfully she slept fairly well at night despite some tiny, sinister interludes, which left her arms and legs in odd positions. If she made the slightest noise or moved sharply, I woke in an instant, and I had also finely tuned myself to noticing the slightest alteration in her breathing. On top of that I got up at least three times a night to check her anyway. Occasionally she whimpered, which meant a big one was on its way and she would need diazepam.

Bill and I had to sleep sometimes, so we took it in turns. I had learned to turn myself off like a switch, knowing that if anything happened in the night I would wake. Even with Bill on guard, I still woke. I never really slept restfully at all.

26

Amberlie had had physio the day before, something she would have much rather gone without. She was very floppy and heavy and only wanted to hang backwards all the time.

The day had started as always, launching straight into a seizure that had violently isolated itself in her face. Her breathing was laboured and her eyes alternated between fixing and flickering. She was very blue from below her eyes up to the centre of her forehead. Amberlie had slept for about an hour after the diazepam, her sleep interlaced with various small fits. When she woke she did not want to sit in her chair or anywhere else – in fact, she didn't know what she wanted to do, and having exhausted every possible comfort idea, neither did I.

Some of Amberlie's fits were hardly noticeable. To the layperson they would have appeared as nothing more than squints or winces, but having watched Amberlie's every move for the past five years, I knew they were not just normal spontaneous facial expressions. Although seemingly minor, these seizures were not nice at all and because they often came in long clusters instead of singular events, they did awful things to Amberlie on the inside – stressing and disturbing her relentlessly. At those times it didn't matter whether the fit was violent or minor, each one was severe.

After a while I began to notice how some types of fit would specifically affect her and be able to predict what her reaction and behaviour would be, but that would change if one of the seizures suddenly changed its form. When they did change it was never for the best, and each time I thought there was no way they could get any worse … but they did. They seemed to have an evil crushing malevolence designed to cause as much distress and suffering to Amberlie as possible. If they couldn't do it one way, then they would find another. It was as if there were two brains in

Amberlie's head – one determined to survive and the other determined to kill her.

I should have known not to bother with her physio, but I thought taking her out and doing something else might distract her. I wanted her to be kept in the best physical shape as well.

Summer arrived and we explained to the kids that we probably wouldn't be able to go for as many days out in the holidays as we usually did, and we would just have to see how things worked out. They accepted it without comment. It didn't take an idiot to see how poorly Amberlie was.

Days out became so stressful that if they hadn't been such a treat for Ray, Clare and Ben, and if it hadn't been for the enjoyment Amberlie got between seizures, Bill and I wouldn't have bothered. We were already exhausted and day trips were hard work even though a change of scenery was nice. We also felt it risky taking Amberlie too far away from the hospital now. But it was always worth giving Amberlie every opportunity to have a bit of fun. To see her beautiful smile and her eyes gleaming with excitement was worth travelling to the other side of the world for – even if it was only for five minutes.

Feeding Amberlie when we were out was much more difficult than at home. She either refused to eat and drink entirely or would only drink or only eat, and what she did have wasn't enough to keep a gnat alive. We always fed her sheltered in the car in case the wind distracted her breathing and swallowing routine, and once she choked it usually put her off entirely. She was also much better supported and positioned to eat in her car seat - not that it persuaded her to eat any more than she deemed necessary.

We did manage to get two days out at the beach. One day was exceptionally windy and we had lots of trouble walking in a straight line along the prom, but Amberlie loved it and giggled away all the time!

The other time was a different matter. Even before Bill had turned the engine off, Amberlie went into a nasty seizure and needed diazepam. Bill took the other kids off to the fair and we caught up with them later.

The car was a life-saver in many ways and we could spare Amberlie's dignity by being able to lie her down and administer her medicine without public interest. It was also ideal for her to drop off for a nap along the back seat afterwards. Sometimes, if the other kids were restless and Amberlie hadn't bitten her tongue, it was easier to put her straight into her pushchair after giving her diazepam, lying her back so she could sleep it off while we walked.

That day, Amberlie wasn't at all happy when she woke. Her nose bothered her and she rubbed hard at it with the back of her hand, she was crying and whimpering and extremely restless. She did not want to sit on the beach – the wind bothered her, the children's noise upset her, everything was wrong. She would not eat and she would not drink. We left for home early. Just as we reached the outskirts of town she had a fit and as her head shot forward, she bit hard into her tongue and the blood gushed from her mouth.

Dr Ramsay also became very worried as we (she always referred to Amberlie as 'we') seemed to be spiralling downwards at a rate of knots. She wanted to try another drug – either phenytoin or gabapentin – in an attempt to halt the pace. I instantly ruled out the phenytoin as that was one of the drugs tried right at the beginning when she was originally diagnosed and it had proved useless. I had seen gabapentin in my epilepsy books and noted it was a mild add-on drug that sometimes boosted drugs already in the system. We agreed to try that.

It appeared to work at first and Amberlie was more relaxed, and although the seizures were still there their edge had disappeared and were not quite so violent or upsetting for her (indeed for all of us). We hoped we were on the right track again.

The medical world researches new drugs to see what the side effects are from long-term use. Vigabatrin had now been around for over five years and some research information had come to Dr Ramsay's attention. She explained to us that the main finding had been that it damages the retina of the eye and causes tunnel vision. Consequently some anxiety had set in amongst doctors and the general idea was to get everyone off it as fast as possible, although it would still have to be used on young children with infantile spasms (salaams or West's syndrome) because nothing else worked so well.

Naturally Dr Ramsay wanted to start reducing Amberlie's dosage straight away. I appreciated that she might be on a higher dose than she probably needed but I was still not ready to have it totally taken away. Amberlie had been taking it for over five years now and I therefore assumed that any damage to her eyes would have already been done. Amberlie had needed glasses early on in her life and I felt that in reality what difference would having tunnel vision really make to her now? For normal epileptics, tunnel vision would obviously be detrimental to their lives. Amberlie was spending the majority of her time in seizures anyway and our prime concern had to be keeping those at bay before anything else, because if they were not under control she was not going to survive.

After much debate, and in view of the fact that Amberlie was on what Dr Ramsay felt to be too high a dosage, and that the gabapentin was having some effect, Dr Ramsay reduced her vigabatrin, gradually increasing the gabapentin at the same time. The doctor went for a hard hit at first, reducing it by 1000 mg per day, amazingly, and with much relief, without any apparent immediate reaction from Amberlie. I have to say it felt good to be able to reduce her drugs somewhat.

Very quickly, however, we found that within days the gabapentin became totally ineffective. Amberlie was in trouble again and we were back on the downward slope. As usual Dr Ramsay did not want to rush into doing anything else, feeling that it might just be a phase!

I was sick and tired of the anxiety about the amount of drugs Amberlie was taking. I was forever being cajoled into reducing medicines and trying something else, which of course I did, because the only thing that mattered to me was that Amberlie was alive and well. But there were never any answers when things went wrong and we were left to bloody well wait and see again. I felt myself bordering close to a nervous breakdown. I couldn't grasp the logic of not doing anything to compensate when Amberlie wasn't improving either.

Of course I realised that it was a good thing to have Amberlie on the smallest amount of drugs possible and nothing was done without our consultation or input, and at the end of the day I didn't have to follow anyone's advice or directives. We were all – doctors included – locked into a vicious circle where we were all trying to do our best with no escape, and Amberlie was deteriorating. What were we to do to maintain her quality of life? We knew she wasn't going to live forever so why should it matter how many drugs she took as long as she was well and leading a reasonably happy life? Side effects like tunnel vision were irrelevant in a child like Amberlie.

I also knew that the delay in action was due to Dr Ramsay's theory that the seizures were being caused by the amount of drugs in Amberlie's system, because there was a possibility of a reverse effect; she therefore stalled to assess whether this was the case. I understood where she was coming from, and the associated medical ethics, and that it took a while for drugs to leave the system and for the others to adjust themselves, but surely all the time that nothing was being done about Amberlie's seizures, irreversible damage was being done to her little brain and this in itself would increase the seizure activity anyway.

The literature I had on lissencephaly stated that children's seizures were not expected to improve because of (a) having abnormal brains, and (b) the consequent and persistent damage caused by the seizures. If the right drug could not be found to control them or stop them at any time during their lifespan, then all was very bleak indeed. In my view it was not the time to test bloody theories.

I was having terrible trouble dealing with my guilt and I couldn't forgive myself for allowing the changes in her medicines to take place when it usually meant we could never put things right again and I felt I was breaking all my promises to Amberlie. The seizures were always waiting for an opportunity to slip through the slightest gap because her brain thought it was the normal thing to do. Dr Ramsay was doing her best, she was trying as hard as she could, nothing was simple and nothing was without risk. I desperately wanted her to come up with a miracle, something that would save my daughter.

The tree fits intensified again in quantity and severity and on some days Amberlie was having rectal diazepam four times a day to get rid of the worst of them.

One Friday night she was very upset and agitated, having done nothing but fit all day. I thought it likely that she was coming down with another bug so during the day I gave her two doses of baby Nurofen, something which had recently come on to the market and that might have an edge on paracetamol for a change. I had asked Dr Ramsay what she thought and she said it should be fine. Amberlie had been having rather a lot of paracetamol lately, as I was sure the seizures were giving her awful headaches, and it did seem to settle her. I thought she might as well have a third and final dose before bed to help her sleep. Within fifteen minutes her breathing had gone to pot. Amberlie was pulling her stomach in under her ribs in an effort to breathe and was wheezing heavily. Her face went blue and there was foam oozing from her mouth.

'Hospital job!' I shouted, and Bill rushed to call Christine to come and look after the kids while I bundled Amberlie into the car. We sped off down the road and dashed into A&E. (Why on earth we were never stopped for speeding when we went to the hospital I'll never know!) Amberlie was rushed through the doors and put straight onto oxygen.

The doctors asked us about the events leading up to this and as they did so Amberlie started to improve. They said they thought the episode had been a combination of fit and Nurofen. They realised Amberlie might have viral-related asthma when poorly and explained that Nurofen can aggravate asthma conditions. They advised us not to give it to her again.

I felt awful. I was trying to help her by trying a new pain relief. I thought it would help. The last thing I wanted to do was make her ill.

The doctors were very nice and said I wasn't to blame myself as these things happened and Amberlie was OK now. I still felt bad. They transferred us up to the children's ward so they could keep any eye on her for while. After a reasonable night and day, the consultant said that now they knew for certain that Amberlie suffered with viral-related asthma it would be a good idea for us to use our spacer four-hourly for a couple of days, and whenever we heard the slightest rattle or wheeze in her chest we should start to use it four-to-six-hourly to keep her airways wide and open. This would help us to deal with the worst of it at home and hopefully avoid an infection that needed hospital attention. He said if Amberlie needed it more than four-hourly, we would have to bring her in. He then discharged her.

Two weeks later there was still no change in the seizure pattern and still nothing different happening drug-wise. It was now September, traditionally bad for Amberlie, and I was restless.

On the following Sunday Amberlie had seizures for nearly the whole day. At 5.30 p.m. she went from one seizure to another with small stopping pauses in between. There were tree fits, jumps, mini salaams – all sorts. Each time I thought the seizures were stopping so I delayed giving her the diazepam until I saw that it was all repeating. The diazepam had no effect and I started to panic. I left it a further ten minutes and gave her another dose … that didn't work either. Fifteen minutes passed and I rang for an ambulance.

The ambulance arrived within four minutes and the men did not know what to do as we had already given Amberlie diazepam and that was what they would have done. All they could do was put her on oxygen and get her to hospital fast. Amberlie continued to jump and twitch all the way and was totally floppy, staring constantly with fixed black eyes. I don't think she noticed anything at all.

Once we were in A&E the doctors were at a loss as to what to do so they bleeped for the paediatric consultants. Amberlie then seemed to come to for a while. The secretions in her throat were very thick and she was having enormous difficulty in shifting anything to be able to breathe easily. I rolled her over and patted and rubbed her back in an attempt to help and she did manage one or two coughs but nothing much came out. She was immediately transferred to Compton and put in the high dependence unit. The seizures had now resumed.

The doctors and nurses were dashing about all over the place organising things, calling people and setting things up. In amongst this we had a thousand and one things explained to us by various people. I tried to concentrate on every word and who was saying what while I watched everything they did to Amberlie. Bill and I were both strangely calm and I sat heavily on my hands with my fingers crossed beneath me. I glanced at him every now and then. It was like being in a crowded bubble, cocooned inside the closed curtains around the bed with all the manic activity occurring in the night-light. They put a drip in her wrist in case they needed to give her intravenous diazepam and they gave her this awful paraldehyde solution rectally down a brown tube – apparently an old fashioned and very dated method of trying to control seizures. It stank indescribably and was a smell never to be forgotten. I felt so helpless and sorry for my poor little girl. Amberlie's seizures began to dwindle until they stopped. We breathed a huge but reserved sigh of relief and the nurses visibly relaxed. I noticed then how quiet the rest of the ward was. All listening, I supposed, to the emergency at hand. I knew deep in my heart that the fits would start again, and they did two hours later.

The ward sister explained that they had used the last of the paraldehyde in the hospital and she was desperately trying to find another hospital that had some so they could courier it in. Nobody had any. They hadn't heard of it or used it in years. Jesus wept. The consultant phoned Dr Ramsay at home for advice and she told them to give Amberlie a whack of steroids to try to regain control. She said it was likely that the episode was caused by a brewing chest infection, so the doctors could give her some antibiotics as well.

Amberlie was already on some antibiotics as I had taken her to the doctor's a few days earlier with a suspected chest infection. In hindsight, I think the rattles and noises I heard on her chest had initially been due to the secretions from too many seizures rather than a virus or bacterial infection, but as the secretions had settled there, they had now indeed become infected.

Amberlie had a chest X-ray and was diagnosed with pneumonia. She was kept on oxygen and suction as and when she needed it. The next morning the hospital arranged for her to have physio three times a day to see if they could clear her chest. They also inserted a feeding tube up her nose and into her stomach so that she could be fed. Amberlie hated it and at every opportunity pulled the darn thing out. What with that, the suction and everything else she was a very, very unhappy baby … and my heart bled for her.

Dr Ramsay visited Amberlie and explained more about the steroids, withdrawing the gabapentin immediately because it was obviously useless. Amberlie was started off on 30 mg prednisolone per day and Dr Ramsay said they would know within three days if it would work. In the meantime we were to record all her seizures and give her diazepam when she needed it.

Dr Ramsay had never seen Amberlie this ill and was startled and upset to find her so. She was most disturbed to find Amberlie's chest sounded so bad and was muttering a lot to herself (normal for her). She then blurted out, 'I am very, very worried this is the way that most of my children die – what resuscitation would you want for Amberlie?' – without taking a breath and with only a flashed glance at us.

I stood looking at her with my mouth open trying to register what she'd said. She looked away from me and focused on Amberlie. I had to run this through my head, yet I couldn't find a way to let it in. the silence was awkward. My automatic pilot kicked in and I asked her if she meant because of her chest or the fits?

'Her chest,' she said. 'Pneumonia. My children all seem to die of bad chests.'

Then stupidly I assumed that she was asking in a round-about way whether we would like to have oxygen at home for Amberlie ready for when this happened again. She looked at me hard. I then realised she meant when we reached the end of the road. When it was dire. When there was no hope. I felt like a prat. She needed to know whether we wanted to put Amberlie on a ventilator or for her to just have basic resuscitation. Dr Ramsay told us to think about it, saying they needed to have a note of our decision on file. She was as white as a sheet and I noticed how hard she was trying not to let the tears fall from her drowning eyes. She then disappeared.

I stood rigid. I was barely breathing. The water quickly flooded my eyes and I couldn't see anything. I couldn't stop my bottom lip from jumping and the pain soared through my body as I began to shake all over. My throat constricted, I couldn't breathe and I couldn't feel my legs. I dropped beside the bed holding onto the rails like I would never let go.

'No ... Jesus, no.'

The nurses rushed to me and between them and Bill they pulled me up and the next thing I knew I was on a soft chair in the parents' room with a cup of tea under my nose.

The tears were just spilling down my face and dozens of tissues were stuffed into my hands. They wanted to know if there was anything they could do.

'Tell me about resuscitation,' I said. 'I want to know.'

Anna and Lucy explained that basic resuscitation meant they would give Amberlie lots of oxygen and attempt to suck out any mucus that was lying in her airway to help her breathe. They would do their best to keep her airway clear. Sometimes there can be too much and they can't clear it, and consequently they would be unable to save her.

At that point, if we wanted, they could then put Amberlie on a ventilator, which would provide air to her lungs and breathe for her. They explained that it was not a nice thing for anyone to be put on a ventilator, but that it was our decision. They went on to say that in the event Amberlie was on a ventilator, they would at some stage attempt to take her off it to see whether she would be able to breathe on her own. That would also be horrid for her. If she did not respond then Bill and I would have to make a decision. This could go on but at the end of the day we would need to make the inevitable and final decision to turn the machine off.

My tears dried up and I understood. I told them that Bill and I had discussed this a long time ago and we had agreed that if her seizures became uncontrollable and she had no hope of a viable quality of life then it would only be fair to Amberlie to let her go.

'I'm so sorry I've caused such a drama. Everything is fine in theory but when you actually have to face it, it's something else and still a huge shock,' I said.

'Oh no, don't be silly! You have nothing to apologise for. We are just so sorry that you are in this situation,' Lucy sympathised.

'Do they die peacefully?' I asked.

'Yes they do,' said the nurse. 'Children die in a slightly different way than adults. They generally stop breathing and then their heart stops a little later - much like they are just asleep. We would make sure she was as comfortable as possible.'

'It seems to me,' I continued, 'that putting her on a ventilator would just delay the inevitable. A part of me would always hold out that last shred of hope that she would recover and be able to breathe herself, so there is that temptation to ventilate, but I wouldn't want to keep making the same awful decision time and time again when there is no hope at all, and it's not right to keep making Amberlie suffer, it wouldn't be right to do that to her.'

The nurses listened and nodded. One of them had been holding my hand the whole time. It felt like they really understood.

'This only applies if Amberlie is in hospital at the time though, doesn't it?' I asked.

'Yes,' said Anna, 'if Amberlie is ill for a long time and you wish to have her at home she will be under the care of the community paediatric nurses. If this is the case and things are getting very bad, there is a different procedure, which they will explain to you when and if needed. That would all be under Dr Ramsay's control.'

'Thank you.' I said.

I didn't need all that explained. My mum and dad both died at home from cancer and I knew that 'making them comfortable' meant morphine.

We were now being prepared. At some stage, not too far away, we would have to face the worst.

I needed to get back to Amberlie.

Within twenty minutes of taking the steroids Amberlie started to relax a little and the jerks, although there, had definitely lost their edge. Over the next three days the seizures slowed right down and decreased from seventy odd a day to six or seven minor ones. It was a pretty amazing result and an immense relief to us all.

As the week progressed Amberlie's seizures remained under control, and her chest now sounded clear.

Several times I had mentioned to the nurses that Amberlie's drip had been in her arm rather a long time and had not been used for ages. Each time I was told someone would come and sort it out. I noticed that there was some skin flaking away underneath the bandage and as I peeped under it there was a bit of a smell. I unraveled it and the needle just fell out onto the bed. Her whole hand was covered by a fungal infection and was very smelly. I was really cross. Her hand had not been allowed to breathe for a week. I immediately called for a nurse and a real rumpus ensued between the staff as they all blamed each other.

A doctor examined Amberlie immediately and prescribed an anti-fungal cream, saying that the drip should have been flushed regularly and if I wanted to, I could make a formal complaint. They were all extremely apologetic and acknowledged that I had constantly been reminding them about it. I didn't want to take it further, it was a mistake and they were always super to Amberlie and helped and supported us no end. I just felt it was another injustice to Amberlie, who really didn't need any more grief.

The consultant popped in to see us to say that they were allowing Amberlie home later and that because she had suffered such an awful bout of pneumonia it would be a good idea for us to have a nebuliser at home. He said this would help a lot when she started to get ill and would ease her breathing and might even mean that we would be able to manage Amberlie at home with antibiotics from our GP. I was all for that. He explained when we should use it and how often. He gave us two different medicines to use in it, one that we should always use as a first resort and the other when necessary. He also explained when we would need to get Amberlie to hospital fast. The community paediatric nurses would deliver the machine within the next couple of days and would take us through the procedure and show us how to use it.

Amberlie was very peculiar to say the least. She wasn't happy and was constantly rolling her head from side to side like she was possessed. Her eyes were all over the place.

I think that was down to stress from the amount of drugs she had been given over the last week, but was mostly due to the antibiotic, which she had taken once before and had left her totally off the wall. I spoke to Dr Ramsay about it and she felt there might also have been an emotional component to it, as Amberlie had been so ill.

Anyway, the plan was to continue the high dose of steroids for a few more days then drop them down by half for a further four weeks. Dr Ramsay hoped that we would slowly be able to reduce them down over a six-month period, and hopefully at the same time give her usual drugs a real boost.

'At least that is what they recommend in clinical trials,' she said. 'But I really don't think we will be able to get Amberlie off the last little bit. Having said that, we should aim for a "break" point just to see whether or not she can do without them in total.' We agreed.

I had got myself very well versed on the drugs used for treating epilepsy and I mentioned that Amberlie had never tried sodium valproate (Epilim). Dr Ramsay was stunned.

'Has she not had that?' she exclaimed. 'I thought you had told me she had tried it, but it hadn't worked?'

'No. If that had been the case I wouldn't have just suggested it!' I replied.

I liked her a lot and was often amused by her eccentricities but sometimes she was the most frustrating woman on earth!

'Well?' I asked.

'Mmm, mmm, I will look into that for next time,' she said.

Amberlie was seeing Dr Ramsay fortnightly now that she was taking steroids so that her blood pressure was monitored and her urine checked for sugar.

At the next appointment Dr Ramsay started Amberlie on sodium valproate and reduced the lamotrigine because they notoriously clashed with one another. This meant the sodium valproate had to be introduced very slowly to stop any adverse effects. She said that if a rash or anything peculiar happened, then Amberlie would be unable to have it. Dr Ramsay was now more hopeful that we could now lose the lamotrigine entirely and be able to get Amberlie off the steroids. She aimed to get Amberlie off the steroids by the end of six months because they might be needed again in another emergency.

'Amberlie will build up a tolerance to them after a while and this would mean they would not be so effective, and we can't have that,' she said.

Amberlie had been very settled seizure-wise and I was delighted by the change and full of hope again. However, as soon as the reductions started and the sodium valproate was introduced a few fits appeared and I told Dr Ramsay that I thought the initial amount of it was not compensating for the amount of the other medicines being lost, and things were beginning to wobble again. Dr Ramsay thought I had a point and banged down the lamotrigine by a huge amount and at the same time increased the sodium valproate to a more substantial level. Then things began to shape up more favourably.

We got Amberlie down to a tiny amount of lamotrigine, with one or two fits around. We tried to go below this but found it made her very volatile so we knew we were teetering on the borderline. We increased it again to see if the fits stopped, but as usual it seemed to have already opened a door, so we increased it again by another 5 mg and held it there. We also had several attempts to decrease the steroids but could not get them below 10 mg without adverse effects. Once again it was the cocktail of drugs that worked and not one particular drug that made the difference.

There were too many different types of seizure activities going on inside Amberlie's head and different drugs dealt with different types of activity – hence the need for the cocktail, large or small. As far as I was concerned, whatever kept her happy and did the job was fine.

During our general conversation I said to Dr Ramsay that I thought Amberlie's seizures were now getting too big for the drugs. She looked at me. I knew her silence meant I was right. She said that she was again very worried on a professional level that Amberlie was having such an awful mixture of medicines. She explained that Amberlie really should only be on two drugs – three at a push, and the current changeover meant that initially she was taking more than ever, but at least we were constructively working towards getting rid of some of them. But I knew in her heart she felt the same as I did about keeping Amberlie's seizures under control.

Christmas came upon us and I'd got the precautionary bottle of antibiotics from the doctor so I felt a little safer over the holiday, knowing that I could probably avoid a hospital stay if I was well prepared for an infection. Amberlie was as miserable as sin on Christmas Day and no amount of showing her pretty lights or new toys distracted her.

I felt so sorry for Ray, Clare and Ben. They loved everything to do with Christmas and had been so excited waiting for Santa's visit; it was supposed to be a happy time. To Amberlie it was just another day. They were of course used to days like that and ignored most of the screaming in the background, and anyway they had plenty to occupy their time. Every now and again they would check to see how Amberlie was and desperately wanted to help her open her presents. We knew that would be unlikely because when she finally stopped crying she would zonk out and sleep for hours. We told them they would be able to help her tomorrow when she would be in a better mood ... fingers crossed!

Bill and I took it in turns to either sit with Amberlie or carry her around. We made sure dinner was set up as usual and that everyone, including Amberlie, was around the table. We pulled crackers, laughed and joked with the kids and between us Bill and I managed to eat dinner, cold as usual, while swapping Amberlie from knee to knee or walking up and down and around the table in an attempt to hold her, calm her and amuse her for five minutes.

I never allowed myself to have too much to drink just in case something dire happened. On the few occasions when I was so exhausted that I had to sleep, I still managed to get up when I heard her. I knew that getting drunk would make the difference and I might not hear her and couldn't bear to think of her having a bad seizure with no one there. I never fooled myself that Amberlie got through the night without some seizures, but so long as they were small, in her sleep and didn't upset her then so be it. Although I knew Bill was there, he slept more heavily than me and I always felt I should be there for her. Bill always offered to stay up and watch her, and he often did, and was a treasure when she threw a night 'paddy', taking her downstairs and putting her music on while she bashed the hell out of her Skwish. But I just couldn't let go ... so we would both be up. He just used to glare at me and tell me off, 'What are you doing down here? We are fine ... go away.' I used to go back to bed and lie there listening instead. Most times I'd make a cup of tea and by the time I was sleepy again it was time to get up!

Luckily Amberlie was much more sociable and relaxed on Boxing Day and loved the kids helping her open her presents. From there on the holidays weren't too bad. We didn't have a clue what the problem had been the day before; the only thing we could think of was that there was some sort of stress caused by all the medicines. There had been no fits to speak of, she wasn't unwell and she had been to the loo on Christmas Eve, which we thought at the time was a bonus!

The steroids had done a good job. Her seizures had calmed down to a reasonable level and her chest had been very good. She was feeding well and had put on weight. We had bought her a little ring, a circle of hearts, for her birthday in April and although we had bought the smallest size it had kept falling off. Now that she was a little chubbier, it fitted perfectly.

The seizures that did surface were usually a salaam, a 'tree' or a succession of jerks, and they nearly always only appeared around a bowel movement. Dr Ramsay had given us a reprieve from hospital appointments as there was a nasty flu bug around, and the hospital had been full of it, so she didn't want Amberlie coming near the place unless she really needed to. We were due to see her next on 2 March.

By February, Amberlie's tree fits had slowly re-established into the routine again although they were very mixed in presentation and length. The last increase of sodium valproate had not had any significant effect. Her weight gain had slowed right down although she was still eating fairly well most of the time. We'd had to use the diazepam again from time to time, but thankfully not on a daily basis. The most worrying thing was her staring. This was not always preceded or instigated by a seizure and sometimes endured for so long you could do a full cabaret in front of her and she would not react at all – nothing – no lights on anywhere; then suddenly she would be back and alert with no ill or sleepy effects, just like she'd been there all the time. Now and again there would be some active times when she rolled on the floor to her music, enjoying a good giggle and swaying her head to the beat.

Amberlie's chest had begun to bubble again, which was more evidence that the fits were increasing. She was dribbling a lot and I could only assume that the secretions must have made their way down her throat and into her lungs where they would soon cause an infection. I did my best to keep her supported upright to avoid it settling in her chest and increased her chest physiotherapy to several times a day, patting away gently on her back and sides while she faced downwards over my lap. This was often enough to shift the fluid out.

We now also had to be more careful when she had a seizure, making sure she was well on her side, because the fluid collected copiously in her throat while her muscles were paralysed. The worry was that she would inhale the lot into her lungs as her breathing sorted itself out. It was also important to keep her tongue from blocking her airway. It was quite a worry when Amberlie slept because she didn't like sleeping on her side and no matter what support we put beside her, she always managed to get herself onto her back or wriggle off the pillows and cushions which supported her. She needed to be watched all the time.

The balance soon tipped when she got a slight cold – and it really was slight. It made her fit constantly for three days, needing regular use of diazepam. It was nearing the weekend and my nerves were on edge at that prospect. I decided to ring Dr Ramsay to see if there was any chance of temporarily increasing the steroids just to get her over the cold. Dr Ramsay was worried that if we increased them for three days we might not be able to get them down again, but left the final decision to me. I explained my worries about using the weekend doctor service and she said I was to ring her anytime I needed her. I was relieved and very grateful.

Amberlie did improve a little on the Saturday morning so I decided to leave the steroids well alone. She continued to improve and the cold subsided but she began to bring up a yellow fluid speckled with blood. I also noticed there was blood in her poo. I rang the health visitor and she said it was probably down to the cold and coughing too hard, and possibly she had overstrained when she passed the stool. It was unlikely to be anything to worry about.

The cold went but the fits and the staring did not. Another doorway had opened. A cold shudder went through me as I dreaded a similar repeat of last September.

When Amberlie was alert she was as on the ball as ever and seemed to make the most of her good periods, as did we. She still let us know when she did or didn't want something, and had even taken to letting us know if she had inadvertently pulled the bedclothes over her face in the night, by cooing in a certain way!

It was weird how she came and went. Whatever went on in her head seemed to stun her brain for a while then release. I didn't quite know what to make of it and the fear inside me didn't really want to analyse it. We were giving diazepam as and when she needed it, hoping to delay any increase in the steroids so we had them ready for an emergency.

27

It was getting near to Amberlie's sixth birthday and as usual we were racking our brains to think of something to buy her. She had every toy under the sun that she could play with or listen to. She had a wardrobe filled with beautiful clothes and every visual aid that she could desire. It was a problem.

Having always had an interest in alternative beliefs, I knew that an emerald is supposed to ward off epilepsy. I suggested to Bill that maybe we could have one put on a bracelet or something.

'You never know … it might help, mightn't it?' I said.

'Anything's worth a try,' he said, half smiling.

We knew such a thing would be virtually impossible to find so we would have to get it made as we wanted her to be able to wear it straight away. After a lot of ringing around we eventually found a gentleman locally who was pleased to help. We went along to see him and he showed us several different emeralds that he had in stock. He explained lots about them and where they were found and how they were cut. After some discussion and advice we decided to have a ring made in a simple design, which would not catch or scratch Amberlie. We chose an oval cabochon emerald and the jeweller measured Amberlie's finger and designed her ring there and then, drawing lots of sketches to fit in with our ideas. We decided to set the stone in the middle of an 18 ct yellow gold band, and have a kiss on each side in white gold from Mummy and Daddy.

We explained that we wanted the ring for Amberlie's sixth birthday and bless him, Mr Bailey had it ready for her within a week! It looked smashing on the middle finger of her left hand. Amberlie knew she had got something special and was all shy and smiley when we put it on her! It was obvious she was chuffed to bits! Bill and I were delighted – it just showed she really did have a light on somewhere! Then we couldn't bear to take it off her, so we left it, and I swear she poised her hand purposefully on the side of her pushchair so everyone we passed could see it!

Amberlie had a wonderful birthday. The weather was lovely (as was usual for her birthday) and she spent some time outside in the sunshine. My friend Gwen made her a gorgeous cake in the shape of a tree and she loved it, 'oohing' and grinning when she saw it! She had lots of visitors throughout the day and a little tea party in the afternoon, and got loads of cards and presents. She especially adored a Mickey Mouse balloon that had been tied to her chair. It was a super day and everyone enjoyed it.

I was so pleased Amberlie enjoyed it so much, I wanted her to love every minute so that somewhere deep in her little brain, she would remember it always.

Occasion days were often a sure sign that Amberlie was going to go off the rails. She generally had bad days at Christmas, Easter, and all the kids' birthdays. Looking back now, I think it was an emotional thing for her. She knew they were special days and I think found it difficult to cope with them and all the different visitors who appeared. The changes in routine unnerved her and made her tired but she was keen to stay awake in case she missed something. There was of course more excitement and more noise and although Bill was always around, I was often doing bits and pieces entertaining people and therefore couldn't spend as much time being with her as usual. It made her mixed up and unsettled and often disrupted her concentration when feeding. She still didn't appreciate being passed from pillar to post for cuddles and became uncomfortable and fidgety quickly if she wasn't held right. She liked to stay with her dad most of the day, sitting on his lap where she felt safe and secure.

28

Amberlie was now seeing Dr Ramsay monthly and this time I left her office feeling irritated, annoyed and thoroughly pissed off.

Amberlie had had three brilliant weeks following her birthday, hardly a flicker to be seen. It was lovely – surprising, but lovely. Then things cascaded into no less than bloody awful. Dr Ramsay was still determined to reduce the drugs and now wanted Amberlie to be rid of the lamotrigine altogether so that she could replace it with phenytoin.

It made no sense to me to try this drug again, which had failed Amberlie dismally when she was first diagnosed. It was an awful drug and rarely used for children because of its side effects such as constant sickness, acne and hepatitis. It was used years ago to treat people with epilepsy – because there was nothing else. It was also a nuisance in that it needed to be monitored very carefully with regular blood tests because any increase, no matter how small, could adversely affect the chemicals of the liver and upset the equilibrium of other drugs already in the system.

'No way,' I said. 'It never worked before, why should it work now? No. The risks are too high. I'm not having all Amberlie's other drugs upset and I do not think that feeling sick all the time constitutes a quality of life. If she feels sick all the time she won't eat or drink and she will be as miserable as sin. No … no way.'

Dr Ramsay agreed with me and said she was not sorry about the decision. Was I confused or what? She was apparently giving me an option!

Dr Ramsay seemed heartened that Amberlie was having a good day despite the last weeks and optimistically suggested that maybe we were in for another nice phase so we should leave things as they were. That didn't make me feel any better either. Just because I had refused phenytoin didn't mean I was happy to plod on regardless … and one good day meant what? It was sod's law that Amberlie was generally having a good day whenever we saw Dr Ramsay. It was always the same and totally predictable – a good phase, even if it was for only a day, was followed by an awful one. Why could the doctor never get past her eternal optimism? I just wished I had a videotape to show her how things were most of the time. The bad phases weren't just bad anymore – they were horrendous and worsened all the time – and yes, I could ring her any time, but …

A week after seeing Dr Ramsay, Amberlie developed an ear and throat infection culminating in a massive salaam seizure one evening where she aspirated (ie: inhaled something other than air into the lungs) the phlegm she produced during the fit. Her breathing deteriorated at a rate of knots and she was soon very blue and struggling for air.

I called the doctor and he called for an ambulance. They immediately put her on the in-ambulance nebuliser and this seemed to help a little. When we arrived at the hospital a doctor was waiting for us at the door and took Amberlie straight to the ward. They immediately put her onto intravenous antibiotics in case pneumonia was setting in and onto another nebuliser, which seemed to help most.

Amberlie was very poorly throughout the next twenty-four hours. Her breathing slowly sorted itself out and we were allowed home with instructions for a three-day booster course of steroids backed up with some oral antibiotics. They told us to put her on the nebuliser every four hours for a day or two, and to use it four hourly whenever we heard her wheeze until it disappeared. If Amberlie needed it more regularly then we should bring her back to hospital, keeping her on the nebuliser while we waited for the ambulance.

Amberlie struggled to get over this and she was ratty and unsettled. The increase in steroids, though short and effective, made her very stressed out. We were glad when the course finished so that she could settle down and recover properly.

No sooner were we back to normal than Clare came down with a sickness and diarrhoea bug. She was ill for two days, then Ben succumbed. His dose was awful and perpetual and after he threw up a load of blood we ended up back in hospital with him! He had vomited so much that he'd caused a small tear in his gullet. The nurses were astonished to see me back in with Ben. I was beginning to think that maybe I should start paying them rent!

Bill took time off to look after the other kids while I stayed with Ben. I hated leaving Amberlie but I knew she would be fine with Bill. Being in hospital didn't bother Ben – I guessed that was due to visiting Amberlie so much. He was an excellent patient and knew the routine! He quite happily gave blood and was fascinated by the blood-pressure monitor. Luckily the blood stopped and he had a good night. When he woke he asked the nurse for some toast and managed to eat a whole slice without chucking in back, so we were allowed home later.

Four days later I shot out of bed at 2 a.m. having heard Amberlie make the most awful noise as she threw up everywhere. She was covered in puke from her head to her waist, so off we traipsed to the shower to sort her out.

She settled back to sleep afterwards but woke with diarrhoea at about 8 a.m. I hadn't been able to get back to sleep, worried that she would vomit again and breathe it in. Understandably she refused to swallow any of her morning medicines and had a horrible, fitful day. We ended up using her diazepam four-hourly to get her over the worst. She slept most of the time, jumping and twitching, and she looked like the living dead. Luckily she wasn't sick again.

By Saturday she was brighter and on Sunday we took her out for an hour for some fresh air. She enjoyed her walk round the park and it put some colour back in her cheeks.

That evening Amberlie sat on her dad's lap and was working her way through a jar of orange and banana baby food when there was this awful single gulp, and I knew she had inhaled the food. Her breathing deteriorated fast and she was soon struggling and turning blue. I quickly suctioned away anything I could reach at the top of her throat and bunged her straight onto the nebuliser. Her breathing eased a little and ten minutes later she retched violently and threw up everything, shifting the blockage entirely. He breathing returned to normal and she settled again.

Within minutes her temperature soared to 39°C and like maniacs we laid her down on towels and stripped her off, dousing her with tepid water all over. The temperature was only in her torso and head – her legs, hands and feet were freezing cold. I risked giving her a dose of Calpol (paracetamol) and she managed to keep it down. After a couple of hours the temperature petered out and we popped on her pyjamas and she settled for the night. With the help of the Calpol, we managed the whole session without any major seizures. I made a mental note to ask Dr Ramsay for some rectal paracetamol.

The next day Amberlie went down with another tummy upset which lingered for about five days. At least it was coming out of her system. I was a bit concerned about how little medicine she was retaining throughout all this but there wasn't much I could do about it either. I think her slow bowels were probably the reason that her illness took different stages to come out. She wasn't able to pass the bug through fast enough. So bearing in mind that she only went to the loo once or twice a week, going once or twice a day was her way of having an upset tummy. The whole episode left her totally knackered.

Amberlie had terrible trouble recovering and was worryingly drowsy for days. I guessed her whole system was up the chute and the balance of her medicines had been upset. Somehow though, slowly, Amberlie's cast-iron spirit managed to drag itself out of the pits to give it another go!

As her health resumed so did the fits, which I always found pretty strange and upsetting. I supposed her brain could only deal with one thing at a time. When she was ill (apart from chest infections, which made them worse), it concentrated on other things so her fits either decreased or changed completely. Long mental absences dominated illnesses where there was no increase in body temperature and very rarely were there physical jerks or seizure positions. (Seizure poses were always disconcerting for me when they happened – they would be like mimes without the rest of the activity – just like practice sessions, or her brain letting us know that it was still trying to push the seizures through.) When she was better everything returned to its full-blown state. It broke me in two that she couldn't get a break either way.

There were always things that remained inexplicable and were so changeable that even when I thought I'd worked them out they would prove me wrong. It was almost as if her brain was playing games. Sometimes I wondered whether the seizure activity was helped or hindered by antibiotics, and if so, by which ones; and whether being ill and speeding up her waste disposal made a significant reduction in the drug levels, leading to the theory that the cocktail of drugs may have been causing rather than solving the seizures. If this was the case then it was natural and exciting to ponder the idea that drastically reducing her drugs right down could possibly help. So I ran the theory past Dr Ramsay.

She listened and said this was often the case, and she didn't know why either. She explained that some people had taken away all medicines from their children for similar reasons, or in the hope that they could start afresh, or so they could blame the drugs for the whole situation. The child then usually had two, three or four weeks of no seizures at all and a good quality of life. Then a seizure appeared, then another and another and before long they were in status … and then it was bloody hard to get them out of it … and some never did. It was a huge risk, and one not to be recommended.

'We all want these children to be on fewer drugs, but ultimately they can't live without them,' she said.

It was a nice dream for a moment.

At Amberlie's next appointment with Dr Ramsay she again talked about her drug schedule and asked me what I thought we ought to do. After all the shenanigans of the past few weeks I didn't feel it was wise to start the reducing regime again. She needed time to settle down a bit. Dr Ramsay was OK with that. I don't know why I even considered a total reduction in drugs – it was hell reducing even the tiniest amount. It was just me searching for a miracle again.

Dr Ramsay now had the 'resuscitation' document ready for us to sign. She asked me to take it home and talk with Bill again so that we were absolutely sure of what we wanted to do.

'It is better to make a reasoned and rational decision rather than having to make one on the spur of the moment in an emergency,' she said.

I asked her to clarify again what basic resuscitation with antibiotics meant and about respiration in general and she was happy to oblige.

'Let me have it back when you visit next,' she said.

The subject of Amberlie's education raised its ugly head again. Apparently the child psychologist had cautioned Dr Ramsay that there was nothing on paper regarding Amberlie's non-attendance at school. Irritated, I reminded her that the educational psychologist had visited me at home the previous year, and we had discussed it fully and agreed that Amberlie would remain at home. Dr Ramsay said she also did not think it was wise for Amberlie to be in school because of her low immunity, and that she would get something down on paper to keep the authorities at bay.

'It will also show that I have done my bit,' she said. She went on to say that the child psychologist had also pointed out that I could be sued. I said, 'Look, they can do what they like. It is a parental choice whether their child is educated at home or school. I provide all the education, physiotherapy, everything that Amberlie needs, and that is that. And for Christ's sake, this child is ill!'

'How far would you take it?' she asked.

'They can force it and get it back with jam on for all I care. I will fight to the death on this and let every daily newspaper in the country know about it. Go to prison … whatever … but Amberlie is NOT going to school.

Dr Ramsay said that she had heard on the grapevine that I was getting a little anxious about Raymond and Clare worrying about Amberlie lately, and suggested it might be a good idea if they had a chat with the child psychologist. (I remembered the first time I'd met her at 'playtherapy', when she had suggested I try to get Amberlie to hold her bottle during feeds…) I said I would think about it.

'How the hell did she know that?' I said to Amberlie when I came out of the hospital. I had only ever mentioned it to Eve, the physio. Damn, I should have told her to keep it between us. She was a lovely lady and anything she did was done with good intention and real concern, but I didn't like being in a position where I felt my arm was being twisted. It meant I wasn't in control and if I had been especially concerned I would have approached the problem myself. For now it was an observation I had made and I was keeping it on the burner for later on.

Of course I was concerned about how the future would affect the kids. They weren't daft, they knew all that happened and asked about it all the time, and Bill and I always told them the truth in a language they understood. It was important to keep them in the picture so that nothing was more of a shock than it needed to be. Things had worsened … but they had lived with the changes for the past six years and they were OK. They took things day by day as we all did. They needed cuddles and reassurance of course, because they loved Amberlie to bits. I wasn't sure counselling was a good idea.

I knew Raymond would be unlikely to want to talk to the psychologist. He only talked when he wanted to and would clam up if pushed. Clare would talk but she would ultimately be very upset. They were both sensitive children in different ways but were level headed, intelligent and well informed. I didn't want their normal lives being interrupted by having to attend little counselling sessions, which I saw as a risk that could potentially open up cans of worms that perhaps did not exist. It wasn't always wise to bring everything to the surface and if they needed to talk they did, and I often heard them having little chats about Amberlie together in their rooms. They were coping and living normal lives and we were all plodding along as best we could under the circumstances. I didn't want them to be upset before they needed to be.

Also life is life and shit happens whether you are four or forty and you just have to deal with it. I wanted them to grow up to be well-adjusted, normal people and felt vehemently that making them talk to a stranger wasn't the right thing to do.

Bill and I discussed it and decided that we would explain to them what was on offer and if they wanted to talk to someone they could.

It was too hard for me to stay neutral and democratic over this so I let Bill do the talking. He told them they should think about it for a while then let me know. They both said later that they didn't want to go. Bill and I had quite a chat with them about how they were feeling and whether there was anything they wanted to know that they weren't sure about or wanted to talk about, and we reminded them that we were always happy to explain anything, Amberlie-related or otherwise. Also, we reminded them that Uncle Ray and their aunties were there for them as well. We let them know we understood it wasn't ideal that they were sometimes left with others when we had to go to hospital, but they said they quite enjoyed it ... after all, they got spoilt!

'We're all right, Mum. You don't have to worry,' Clare said.

I was relieved and upset at the same time. I knew things weren't ideally as they should or could have been. They were so grown up ... so reasonable ... so understanding. I wished that we were just a normal family with four healthy children. Other people had that ...

I wrote a letter to Dr Ramsay thanking her for her concern and explained why I was declining her offer at that time.

Dr Ramsay was in a complete flurry at the next appointment. She was running an hour and a quarter late with all her appointments and was rushing every minute in an attempt to catch up. There was no time for any reasonable conversation or time to listen.

We talked about Amberlie's steroids because that was the worry at the forefront of her mind on that particular day, and she moaned about her still being on them. On another day she might have remembered our previous conversations. She wanted to retry reducing them again this time by 1 mg per week, which was at a slower rate than we had previously attempted. I was neither happy nor convinced it was the right thing to do because I knew Amberlie was right on the borderline. Wanting to establish a contingency plan, I asked if it was possible that we could give her a three-day boost to set her right if things got bad again. Dr Ramsay didn't want to know and as for as she was concerned the appointment was finished.

'What a fucking waste of time!' I grumbled to Amberlie as I straightened her in her pram. She smiled at me with those big beautiful eyes. 'Mmmm,' she went.

The next few weeks were, I suppose, pretty reasonable. Amberlie had a salaam once a day and a few tree tree fits, but loads of absences. There had been a lot of laughing fits mixed up with

299

some genuine laughter while amusing herself either playing or when out shopping. I was, however, starting to worry about Amberlie having too much fun. Lately when she had been very excited, merry and having a good time, a laughing seizure emerged. The difference was easy to spot because the laughter in a seizure was continuous and repetitive and didn't sound normal. It mostly happened when she was in the car watching her beloved trees pass by. The excitement was just too much for her little brain to cope with.

I seemed to spend most of my days making huge sighs, every one filled with total and unbearable pain. I loathed the fact that now her fun was being taken away from her. Amberlie probably wasn't aware of the interruptions as such, but when they were over she wasn't allowed to resume her fun because she was then too sleepy ... I hated it so much and there was bugger all I could do about it. She was slowly being robbed of everything.

I hardly ever walked to the school to pick Ray and Clare up anymore, always taking the car instead and waiting inside it. I didn't want to risk it ... there was too much for Amberlie to watch in the playground. She sat quite happily in her car seat and we had little chats that she responded to with smiles and dribbles. I watched her look around but mostly stare; I knew she could hear me but doubted she saw me. I had no idea what she was seeing – her eyes would move and roll around, fixing on nothing, and often be so far downwards that it seemed as though she was trying to look at the inside of her cheeks.

Sometimes something attracted her attention and she looked lovingly at whatever it was, but I couldn't make out what she was seeing, as there was often nothing there. She smiled lots and laughed after pauses as if in response to a conversation, she was alert and there were no tell-tale signs of a lingering seizure. Similar things often happened indoors when something would catch her interest and she would look straight ahead at apparently nothing then seem to follow it. She mostly did it when she was lying in the front room – she would look above her, talk and smile and go shy. It was as if something or someone was there. We always said it was my mum and dad visiting her as angels. I was sure there was something there because Amberlie was so different, always calm and chatty with no stress, jerks or twitches, or strange eye movements. It made her happy and relaxed, so to me it was a good thing. I wished I could have seen it too.

Amberlie losing a lot of her everyday awareness was punching very hard, and sometimes I couldn't help but be envious of other families' straightforward, normal lives with lots of normal children. It wasn't bitterness but a wish that things were different. I was bitter that it had happened to Amberlie – not that I would wish it on anyone else … I just couldn't see why it had to have been my Amberlie. People used to say to me that God only gives such special children to those who can cope. Well meant, but I could never work out whether I thought that was a good or bad thing, especially since he didn't figure in my good books anyway. There was no scientific explanation of why Amberlie had lissencephaly so I held him responsible. If 'He' was the all good, all powerful and almighty then why did he let children suffer? And of course theologically it wasn't his fault either but a deserved penance for something we did wrong as human beings, and he was just there to support us and psychologically make it all better. It wasn't any consolation to me. Bill's mum said to me one day, 'We have to thank God for looking over Amberlie and getting her through the bad times.' She was shocked when I replied, 'What? If I ever – and believe me, I don't give a toss – if I ever get up there, I'm gonna smack him one right in the mouth for what he did to my Amberlie, and I will never, ever forgive him.'

I felt so helpless. I wanted to make everything OK for Amberlie, I wanted her to have a life – a good life and I couldn't ensure that any more. It was so important to keep trying, though, because I didn't want any of her aware moments wasted.

Whenever she did catch sight of me she always smiled and cooed and I felt a whole sea of joy and pain sweep through me at the same time as she responded when I said, 'Hello darling!' Maybe she knew how I felt. I wished she could have told me something … anything. Twice in her whole life she managed to say 'Mum', and each time I dashed to her and she looked straight at me. I'll never know whether she truly said it or whether it was an accident. Those possible acknowledgements meant the world, and still do.

It wasn't long before Amberlie was back to being very stressed and extending herself backwards again. The seizures accelerated, and with no break in sight Dr Ramsay agreed to give her a three-day boost of steroids. The seizures decreased but Amberlie was constantly fidgety and agitated, crying and whimpering for no apparent reason. It seemed as though the temporary increase had totally stressed her again. It was questionable whether this was due to the steroids themselves of whether the seizures were occurring below the surface and the steroids were just providing a mask for them. Either way it was all getting too much for her.

I deliberated again over whether totally controlling the seizures was potentially such a good thing. Some of them obviously needed to happen to release the pressure in her head, and because the activity reverberated through her body via the nervous system, some were necessary to release the stress overall. When the steroids were taken away the stress subsided, so I felt it had to be worth a bash to try to reduce her usual dosage so that when we needed them to control things in an emergency it wasn't such a trauma for Amberlie.

I rang Dr Ramsay to say we were ready to try, and that evening the steroids were reduced down by 1 mg. Within a couple of days more seizures began to surface and Amberlie was very much in her own world. We reinstated the 1 mg again but it made no difference. Another door had irreversibly opened again, and I was devastated and racked with guilt.

We then looked at the lamotrigine again and gambled that it was now working in reverse, as Amberlie had been on it for so long, so we reduced it by 2 mg and the situation worsened. We reinstated that to no avail. Maybe it wasn't the drugs at all ... maybe things were just getting way out of control. We paused and sat tight, banking on the possibility that there was another bug in Amberlie's body and that she was brewing an illness. Nobody wanted her to be ill – we just wanted another, better, easier explanation.

I took her round to the GP to check her chest and ears and he found nothing wrong. I explained all that was going on and asked his opinion of the steroids. He agreed that they could well have caused Amberlie stress, and said they were a very powerful drug and probably better out of her system if we could possibly do it. Dr Jonathan wondered at her cast-iron constitution, saying that such a cocktail of drugs would knock both him and me unconscious.

Things then went from bad to worse to worse still and her seizures returned to more or less where they were before we introduced the steroids. My poor Amberlie was almost entirely engulfed in her own volatile, flickering world.

Dr Ramsay didn't know what to suggest and I could see by her despondency that there was no answer to Amberlie's problems. Some days were better than others and she seemed to be with us on and off for little times each day. It was very difficult to tell. She still seemed to hear and her sight came and went. When she couldn't see, she had no recognition, response or movement in her eyes even if we waved something frantically in front of her. She still laughed from time to time, usually at the kids or to music or something that had tickled her in that precise moment, and other times it was definitely a seizure and she would laugh hysterically; and sadly, to a point, we couldn't help but laugh with her, it was so infectious as she chuckled heartily away – but it was awful too, because we knew it was sinister. The kids didn't understand how

Amberlie could be happy and in a seizure at the same time, and they joined in her fun thinking she was playing a game of some sort. I suppose it could have been worse. I couldn't see the point in harping on about it to them – why take away what they saw as good? Dr Ramsay said, 'I hate laughing fits.'

I caught her gist. She didn't have to explain it.

Amberlie often sat slumped in her chair, leaning to the right and finding it hard to hold her head up for any length of time. She was also very, very floppy and it took all my ability to hold her comfortably on my lap. I would get her upper body sorted just for her lower part to go in another direction with her legs going all over the place at the same time. She was a weight.

Amberlie was due to see Dr Ramsay at the hospital one July morning and was sitting on my lap having her breakfast. Suddenly she choked and I felt something weird had happened. On the way to hospital she had a salaam seizure and I had to stop the car at the roadside to give her diazepam.

When we arrived in Dr Ramsay's office Amberlie was fast asleep in her pram. There was another doctor with her whom we had met briefly before when we were last on the ward. He was training to specialise in neurology and epilepsy. After much talk and bouncing around of ideas they admitted that there wasn't anything else they could suggest that would help Amberlie. It was Dr Ramsay's main concern now that we make Amberlie as comfortable as possible and advised that I should give Amberlie the diazepam whenever she needed it.

I didn't say anything. I knew. I didn't even feel the pain this time. I was empty of any feeling whatsoever. I had gone through my pain threshold – the punch bag was now well used to taking the hits. My brain was functioning at its usual rate though and I intended to keep it that way ... for Amberlie's sake.

Dr Ramsay asked me, 'At what times is Amberlie most upset?'

'She isn't really.' I replied. 'She seems quite content in all this mess at the moment, and doesn't seem to be distressed at all, apart from when she goes to the loo.'

The doctors asked whether she was having prunes and lots of fibre to help, and I told them that I found live yoghurt worked best. Dr Ramsay suggested giving Amberlie senna at night to try to lessen the difficulty; it would work in the morning. I expressed my concern at increasing her stool frequency because from past experience all this did was increase her seizures along with it and that would increase her bad days. I had to try though … didn't I?

The doctors also wanted to take away the nitrazepam and clonazepam (a) because Amberlie had been on them for ages, (b) because they were of the same family as the diazepam, and (c) so that the effect of the increased use of diazepam would not be enhanced by them, and this would therefore reduce the associated risk of respiration problems.

The nitrazepam was to go first; with the intention that it would be gone within a month. To compensate for its loss, Dr Ramsay wanted to increase the sodium valproate on a graduating programme over the next two weeks.

'The last time we increased the sodium valproate it didn't have any effect,' I said.

I needed Dr Ramsay to clarify the use of the diazepam for bad days. The usual dose was four-hourly, but sometimes Amberlie needed it again after an hour. Dr Ramsay said we could give her one dose per hour if necessary. I asked for the sodium valproate to be changed from a liquid format to tablets because it was becoming such a large amount for Amberlie to swallow along with everything else. I didn't want to upset her by keep making her swallow syringe after syringe of medicines, and she especially hated the taste of it. It was easier to crush up tablets altogether in a small amount of liquid and give it to her in one 5ml syringe.

'No problem, I'll do the prescription now. Please ring if you need me at any time,' said Dr Ramsay.

We made our way home. There were lots of times when I don't recall having driven home from the hospital. It was like I had pulled away from the disabled space at the hospital then suddenly arrived in our drive.

Amberlie continued to have fits throughout the rest of the day and some of them had quirks that I had not seen before. In one instance she rocked her head to and fro whilst on her stomach (which she normally did and which was a prelude to a salaam seizure), but this time her eyes were rolling in her head at the same time. She did go on to have the salaam, had diazepam and then passed out asleep twitching her arms and legs all the time. She half woke a while later into another fit where she was mouthing like a goldfish and making clicking noises, and her breathing was very irregular. This lasted a short time and then she launched full throttle into another salaam so I gave her diazepam again. She went back to sleep but was still twitching and jangling. After the small sign that morning I was expecting a change.

The senna worked like a dream and she went to the loo three times the next day with no escalation in seizures.

The next day, the seizures took over entirely and when Amberlie came out of the severe ones, she was constantly stuck in absence after absence and couldn't eat. I counted 120 different seizures that day, and they were only the ones I saw. I didn't even go out of the room for a wee. Persuading her to drink was a nightmare but worth the persistence. She woke during the night in a seizure and was very upset and had diazepam again. The next two days and nights were the same and every time she had a salaam she bit right through her tongue and blood poured from her mouth. The worst thing was that even after having the diazepam she was continuing to fit, and I noticed that in two different, though close together, episodes, she had stopped breathing for thirty seconds in each.

On the second night Amberlie's temperature soared. She was burning to the touch, pouring with sweat, and her breathing was noisy and laboured. I remembered a similar night when she had reacted terribly to the increase in lamotrigine. I had not seen any specific indications of infection at all and suggested to Bill that maybe she was having a reaction to the huge increase in sodium valproate. To date we had seen no improvement since the sodium valproate was increased and in fact we were shocked at how bad the seizures had become. What with this and the concern for her breathing, I figured we must be on the wrong road so I reduced the sodium valproate back to its former dose in the morning. I thought I would let Dr Ramsay know later.

By lunchtime Amberlie was still fitting but they were not so harsh and she seemed to be a little more aware. I took her out for a walk to the shops and she managed a whole hour, apart from some absences, fit free. Later on she calmly ate a little dinner and played for a short while on the floor. She wasn't twitchy or jangling and had not had any recurrence of the temperature of the night before. She woke twice in the night and was a bit jumpy, but went straight back to sleep without the help of the diazepam. The next day, she only needed diazepam once after a salaam.

Even though I knew that hell was on the brink of the horizon and that we had lived it so many times before, each new phase came and hit like a bolt from the blue. It wasn't a surprise – it could never be a surprise anymore – it was an expected total devastation that always turned out far worse than I ever imagined it would.

I became very used to things being bad on a certain level, adjusting to each change as it happened, and I could deal with any day-to-day trauma within that, especially if we had been through a similar scenario before. In the past we knew that when Amberlie started to fit for no reason there would usually be a chest infection brewing, but now we were playing a different ball game. This was her lissencephaly bulldozing its way through, saying, 'You can't control me anymore – here I am and this is what I do – I have returned as I first appeared, and now you have used up all your defences, so see if you can deal with me now!'

In that week Amberlie had changed beyond belief, and whilst we had made some way in returning her to having some quality of life, I felt destroyed and sick to the stomach as I realised I no longer believed we had any chance of saving her.

As soon as I saw her, every slight hope would drain away. Her eyes were so staring, her skin various shades of blue or deathly white. When she sat in her chair she leaned right as if she was trying to get out of the chair or trying to get away from having to be bothered with playing with her ball, which she still did intermittently between lengthy pauses. It seemed that she picked it up during the tiny breaks she had in seizure activity, but the noise of the ball as she banged it on the table was repetitive and predictable. My living thread of optimism kept saying that maybe things were not so bad, perhaps this was just the way lissencephaly children developed and learned to live, and maybe this was just another phase that would go away either by luck or by some miraculous change in her medicines. Perhaps a new drug would just appear from somewhere and put it all right. There was always a debate doing on in my head as to whether there had been a shred of improvement or not, whether I was seeing things or not and whether I should avoid jumping to conclusions either way. Amberlie was fighter, no doubt about that – she had won amazing battles one way and another – and of course she could do it again … if the seizures allowed. Then I wondered whether she now had enough consciousness to make that decision to fight, and did she still want to? I truly believed if Amberlie thought she could win then she would try. She was made of tough stuff, just like my mum was, strong-willed, full of fight and as stubborn as hell – before the cancer got her.

I felt locked inside a dark cloistered world, not only within my home but in my head too. There was nothing that mattered outside our walls and my only thoughts were of Amberlie. Much of the time it was like a dark abyss with slippery, slimy walls and every time I reached out to grab at a ridge it gave way, and down at the bottom was a deep, forbidding eternal sea of despair, as black as Amberlie's pupils and with about as much life within.

How did Amberlie live with all that happened to her? How did she manage to show her beautiful smile each time she had a trace of awareness? How did her physical body cope with all the beatings the seizures gave her? At the very least she must have had the sorest tongue imaginable. I knew she knew no different, but it must have been pure hell on earth. I didn't want to think about tomorrow or the next day, deciding to continue as we always had, one day at a time. I felt such an overwhelming love for her that I could barely cope with feeling it, but I kept alive my hope and determination to continue giving her all I could as her mother and her friend. I would do all I could to make her happy, comfortable and alive … until I had to let her go.

29

It was time for Ben to attend his induction days at school in preparation for starting full time in September. Parents were invited to stay for the first session and Bill took the afternoon off work to look after Amberlie while I took him. Ben knew quite a few of the children from playschool and happily played with all the different toys and activities. After that, once a week, there were several 'storytime' sessions lasting about half an hour, when Amberlie and I sat under a tree in the playground, which kept her amused amongst absences.

A couple of mums came over and introduced themselves and asked about Amberlie. I got off on the wrong foot with one of them, who came bounding over saying she used to be an occupational therapist and was used to disabled children.

On Amberlie's pushchair there were footplates fitted with straps that were intended to keep Amberlie's feel in the correct position, making her sit straight in the pram to keep her legs, hips and spine in the right shape. The problem was that Amberlie hated the straps passionately because they stopped her kicking her legs when she was excited. Eve had given up mentioning the straps ages ago because I insisted that Amberlie's fun was more important, especially considering that she was in such good physical shape anyway. Also, she was exercising her legs!

This mum decided to point out to me that Amberlie's feet should really be strapped to the plates. I don't think she meant to be quite so forthright but nonetheless I pointed out that whilst I was aware of the theory, Amberlie's happiness was the priority and she hated being strapped down so that was that. She immediately apologised and became one of the kindly few that were always ready to help if they saw Amberlie was having a bad day.

The summer followed, with each day presenting it own little problems. We did go out a few times but gave up in the end because Amberlie couldn't cope with the excitement and was launching into too many seizures. I mentioned to Eve that I didn't want to stop taking Amberlie out, but it was proving very difficult giving her diazepam without drawing attention to her, and said that her pushchair was no longer ideal for putting her back into when she was all floppy and sedated. Her head hung down heavily to one side and there was no support to stop her hurting her neck. After a long discussion, and bearing in mind that Amberlie wouldn't thank anyone for a pushchair that strapped her in from head to foot. Eve said she would organise an assessment for one that Amberlie could lie almost fully back in, so that she would be as comfortable as possible after a seizure. It was of course essential to maintain the support she already had in her current chair for when she sat up.

Amberlie and I had to attend a panel of doctors, therapists and technicians to plead our case because the pram would cost an awful lot of money. They had reports from Dr Ramsay and Eve, and did a full examination themselves to assess her general condition. They were concerned that all Amberlie's needs should be met for now and the foreseeable future, and agreed to supply it. I think the total cost was to be somewhere in the region of £1,750 and the health authority was to meet the costs in full.

September came and Ben started school on a 'mornings-only' basis. He seemed to settle well on his first visit although he looked a bit shell-shocked. When I collected him at lunchtime he stormed out of the door and kicked me hard in the shins! He then yanked at my arm, determined to get out of the playground as fast as possible.

It was obviously a huge protest statement and there was no point in getting cross. He didn't want to talk about it and I hoped he would be OK in the morning for the next session. Each day was the same and when I eventually did tell him off about the kicking, he shrugged his shoulders and said he wanted to stay with Amberlie and that was that.

Both Ray and Clare were at junior school now so it meant I needed to get to two schools on time. The stress was already massive in the mornings but I was determined we would make it somehow. There was nothing I could do about Amberlie's seizure on waking up – that was going to happen anyway – I just had to work round it.

Ray and Clare were generally really good and dressed themselves quickly and without fuss, although sometimes Clare threw the odd wobbly if her hair didn't go right. I made sure everyone was breakfasted and sorted before I woke Amberlie at around 8 a.m. Amberlie wasn't easily woken by everyday sounds – which was a blessing on those mornings. I dreaded waking her at all, so I used to start dressing her while she slept. Quite often I would have her fully dressed and her hair brushed and into a ponytail plait before she stirred at all. Sometimes I even had her strapped into her seat in the car before she surfaced.

When Amberlie woke she always gave me one of her beautiful smiles and a 'coo' because her natural way was to wake happily, but then within a few minutes or often seconds, she would start to stretch and nod in the tell-tale way and the salaam would hit like a ton of bricks. I loathed that it did this to her, and I loathed the fact that I had to put her back to sleep to get rid of it. Once she had settled I used to hoist her up into my arms and put my unconscious Amberlie into the car so the kids got to school. If she had stayed asleep while I sorted her she nearly always woke on the way or just as we arrived at Ben's school and would need to have the diazepam in the car. Ben used to wait patiently while I got her into the pram and got him in to school. On those days we used to make it to his classroom either bang on time or five minutes or so late. That wasn't great either because all his classmates would already be sitting at their tables doing worksheets, and I could see poor Ben felt self-conscious about going in when they all looked round. I would leave the school feeling dreadful and guilty, but there just wasn't anything I could do about it. I tried a different, earlier routine at home, but I found the seizure messed up getting the others ready and we were later than ever. On a rare good day I'd have all the kids in school and be back home before the seizure happened. It was a case of having to go with the flow and adapting everything else around it.

Occasionally the kids decided to be bloody awkward – as kids do – and then it was sheer hell. It was a very fine line between totally organised chaos and absolute bedlam, and Ben could be the most awkward little bugger if it suited him – and the noisiest! The fact that he didn't like school didn't help either. He did things at his own speed no matter how often I reminded him that time was ticking by.

Some days Amberlie had a succession of smaller seizures or prelude seizures that upset her, rather than a full-on salaam, and she would scream the place down, and then getting her dressed and sorted was a nightmare. She would make it as difficult as possible to get jumpers and trousers on, keeping her arms and legs dead straight so that I couldn't manoeuvre them. It would be impossible to do her hair because she tried to bash her face into the floor in an attempt to stop me doing it, so I often gave up. Ben made the most of all that: having sussed out from an early age that Amberlie developed ultra sensitive, well amplified hearing at seizure times, he would let out earth-shattering, decibel-busting screams and long monotonous sounds directly at her, driving her even more barmy. I couldn't bear it for long so I would shout at him to pack it up! That of course made him worse and in turn made Amberlie scream even louder … then I'd get two other voices whining that they were going to be late! Ray would have his coat on and be walking out the door with Clare following him stiffly and arrogantly down the path, incessantly moaning that yet again there hadn't been enough time for me to French-plait her hair. Sometimes I don't think they even realised Amberlie had or was having a seizure. Sadly, I suppose that showed just how routine it all was.

It was bliss once they'd all been dropped off and I felt my blood pressure drop the minute I got back in the car. Amberlie would have been soothed by the diazepam or the drive and would take another small nap before her breakfast. That gave me time to do a quick tidy up and get everything ready for when she woke.

When I look back now, I have no idea how on earth we ever got out in the mornings, let alone how we got anywhere on time!

Pick-up times were also stressful. Ben was at school all day now so I would bung Amberlie in the car, park it outside Ray and Clare's school, then put Amberlie in her pram to walk through to collect Ben from his. I used to wait until the last minute before walking so that I wouldn't have to stand outside his classroom too long. I used to hover at the back of the other mums, keeping my fingers crossed that Amberlie wouldn't fit. Ben usually came out pretty quickly, happy to escape from his prison sentence every day, and I still got a severe kick in the shin most days. Telling him off made no difference, so the television became out of bounds for a while until he learned that it was much nicer to say 'hello'. If Amberlie was asleep, I would chance standing in the playground until Ray and Clare came out, but most times it was straight back to the car, where I kept a look out for them. When I saw them coming I'd cross the road with them and we'd head off home. I was always relieved to get back indoors. If Amberlie had a really bad day, Christine would pick the kids up for me.

I felt pretty isolated at the time. There were my closest friends who always rang or knocked to see how we all were and were happy to help out whenever they could, but generally speaking I only had time to say hello to people and hadn't had the opportunity to get to know the mums in Ben's class very well. Ben would point out his friends so I was able to identify most of them that way, but I didn't know their names for ages.

Amberlie had missed her lunch following a large fit and a long sleep and was now hungry. I had just done the school pick-ups and rushed in to prepare her a meal. She ate all her food and drank her milk really well. I then sat her in her chair for a while in front of the television and she started to laugh. There were little pauses every now and again and the laughter gradually increased until she was hysterical. This went on and on until suddenly there was total silence and she disappeared into her own little world. Suddenly there was a huge crash and she sent her bell ball flying and her head lurched down towards the table. I struggled to keep her back in the chair to stop her hurting herself while I pulled on the straps to free her from it. I got her down onto the floor and onto her exercise mat and she salaamed like never before. It was ferocious and she screamed out in fear between the bows. There was blood pouring from her tongue and lip, and Clare, bless her, had dashed to get the diazepam and was standing there with it ready. I gave it to Amberlie and we waited for her to relax. She didn't. She carried on – it had not worked.

'Get another one!' I shouted to Clare.

She zoomed out of the room, poor kid, and brought back a whole box! She was as white as a sheet. I had to wait ten minutes between doses, and it was a terrible wait. I gave her another dose. There was a slight pause – and she started again!

'I've got to give it ten minutes,' I said to Clare. She had knelt beside me. She wanted to stroke Amberlie but I told her that it could aggravate her so best not. I held her hand and we both watched Amberlie, making sure she didn't hurt herself. It wasn't getting any better and I felt the panic surge through my body.

'I'll have to get an ambulance – stay there, don't move, just keep your eye on her'

I dashed to the phone and they said they would be with us in four to five minutes.

'Jesus, I've got to get someone her to look after you kids!' I scrambled for my address book and my friend Claire said she would be right with me.

She arrived one minute before the ambulance. My Clare stood outside on the kerb waiting for them, waving frantically to show them where we were.

The men ran in and Amberlie was still jerking but not so severely. Her eyelids were closing and I knew she was passing out. The men asked me what I had given her, and were devastated to find that I had done all that they were able to do ... apart from giving her oxygen.

'We need to get her to hospital to check her over,' one of them said.

'Yeah sure ... please,' I said.

They kept her in casualty for a while. She had settled into a long nap and the doctors left her to recover while they talked to the paediatricians. Amberlie was then gently moved to the ward, where they observed her for a while.

The nurses always greeted us as old mates and we were welcomed and fussed over. When Amberlie woke they talked lovingly and sympathetically to her, and she seemed to recognise some of them. She was always at ease on the ward and always gave them a little smile when they asked her, 'What are you doing here again? What have you been up to, sweetheart? We always like seeing you but ...'

I was so glad that this was our hospital.

By the time Bill arrived, Amberlie had settled really well and he gave her a nice warm bottle of milk.

Christine had taken over from Claire at home and had given the kids their tea and got them bathed and ready for bed. She was a real gem.

The consultant came around 9.30 that evening and said that if we were happy to take Amberlie home we could, it was up to us. She seemed OK so we said we would. He said if we were worried at all we could come back at any time. 'Just ring to say you're on your way.'

About half way home Amberlie began to twitch again and by the time we reached our drive she had salaamed three times.

'It might just be a reaction to leaving the hospital. We'll leave it a while and see,' I said to Bill.

We explained everything to Christine and she left saying if we needed her, just ring. Within the hour Amberlie was well into another run of salaams and had another dose of diazepam that also did not work.

'We have to take her back don't we?' I said to Bill.

'Looks like it,' he said.

'I'll ring Chris.'

'I'm so sorry to do this to you – I know you must be tired,' I said to her.

'Don't be silly, I'm fine, I can sit here and doze – it's no problem. The only thing is that in the morning I have to get my kids sorted out for school but I can always take yours over the road with me.'

I thanked her and said we would try to get Auntie Pat to come and stay with the kids.

It was very late so I rang her and explained that Bill would drop Amberlie and me at the hospital and then go and pick her up. I told her not to worry about rushing around in the morning if we weren't back, because I wasn't bothered whether the kids made it to school or not.

Once on the ward Bill dashed off to London. It was awkward that we had no relatives living nearby. I used to worry about him doing things like that because whilst we needed someone to care for the kids, he was worried sick about Amberlie and whilst there was no traffic at that time of night, I hoped he would keep his concentration.

Amberlie was put into a ward so that Pam, the sister, could look after her while looking after another very sick child. The doctors gave Amberlie more diazepam but it had still failed to work. They also gave her some chloral hydrate to sedate her in the hope that it might encourage her to sleep and/or indeed have a quietening effect on the seizures. The doctors were in long discussions as to what to do and contacted Dr Ramsay at home. The night continued very badly. The salaams were small yet consistent and they weren't allowing Amberlie to sleep. She didn't seem upset but was physically agitated. We managed to give her a drink although this was interrupted several times by little shoulder shrugs. It was 2 a.m. and Bill had just arrived back at the hospital and was worn out. We both sat watching and hoping all night long. As the morning approached the seizures started to accelerate again, and the doctors decided there was no option but to set up a phenytoin driver as Amberlie was obviously working up into total 'status' and they really didn't want to leave it any longer. I grumbled about phenytoin but they explained that it was the first course of action for status and that it would be administered in a very high dose, which should have an immediate effect. It was a short-term emergency treatment and the side effects were negligible compared to the risk to her life.

'We will assign Lucy to you for the day. She is a very competent nurse and knows her job – she will also explain everything to you every stage of the way.'

We were moved to a private room at the end of the corridor, which was set up for one of us to stay and even had an en-suite loo. They said if there was anything we wanted please let them know. They also gave us a menu for lunch and dinner and I said, 'Thank you but Amberlie doesn't eat normal stuff.' They smiled and said, 'No, no, it's just under Amberlie's name – we don't want you to go without anything to eat today. Please tick your choices and let us have it back.'

That was very nice of them. Despite not having eaten anything since lunchtime the day before we weren't really hungry, but thought if we ordered a sandwich each and a piece of fruit, we might fancy something later. When the food arrived we left it on the side.

Lucy had started to move all kinds of machinery into the room – the tall electronic blood-pressure monitor, a heart monitor, a saturation machine and the syringe driver. There were lots of syringes in many sizes and they were going to take some of Amberlie's blood as well. It all looked horrific and overwhelming. I felt so sorry for Ambams ... Jesus ... all the things she had to go through to survive.

The consultant popped in to see that all was going according to plan and said that Dr Ramsay would call in to see us as soon as her clinic finished at lunchtime. Lucy explained why we had all the machinery and how it worked. She told us that putting phenytoin in the system in such high doses and so quickly was not without risk, and that Amberlie's blood pressure could either soar too high or drop too low and either would have an effect on her heart. They would therefore be taking automatic blood pressure readings every five minutes and she would wear stick-on heart pads on her chest that would be read by the heart monitor. The saturation machine would keep an eye on the amount of oxygen being retained in her blood. She explained that she would stay with us throughout the infusion because of all the risks.

The phenytoin was measured into large syringes that would be attached to the driver and the driver would measure the amount of medicine entering Amberlie's bloodstream over a designated period of time. They were going to do two infusions – the first over two hours and the next one a few hours later over a shorter period – if the first went in successfully. It was all very tense in the room. I chatted endlessly to Lucy about Amberlie and all that had happened and she listened all the time, her eyes constantly checking the monitors and Amberlie. We did the same. Every time the blood-pressure monitor clicked in and pumped up the armband we stared at the figures on the monitor. Once or twice Lucy worried that things were nearing danger levels but they sorted themselves out after a few minutes. Generally Amberlie took the whole thing well, I held her hand and stroked her forehead, and twiddled with her hair. She had relaxed considerably. They expected this loading dose to knock her out … it didn't. I wasn't surprised – she had too strong a constitution for that. The second dose had a bit more effect. They also gave her some paracetamol in case she had a headache with all the changes in blood pressure and constant seizures, plus some more chloral and then she passed out. They had also set up a drip so that we would not need to feed her.

We breathed a sigh of relief, so pleased that she was no long fitting and uncomfortable. She looked a picture of innocence lying there out cold. The nurses carefully moved her onto her pillows and covered her up with blankets. They continued to monitor her every twenty minutes for a couple of hours then hourly.

Lucy made us a cup of tea and we sat in silence. We were both exhausted. I called home to see how the kids were, and Auntie Pat said she hadn't taken them to school but they were all fine and well and doing their usual thing.

'I'll call the schools and let them know what's going on,' I said. 'One of us will pop home at some stage to see them and collect a few bits.'

'I think I'll try one of these sandwiches – I'm feeling a bit peckish now,' I said to Bill, but they were all warped and warm, having been left for hours.

'I'll go to the shop, I fancy a can of Coke anyway,' he said.

It was so quiet in the room and I could only just hear Amberlie breathing. I was so chuffed that her seizures had stopped I was almost on a high.

I kept one eye on Amberlie and one out of the window looking at the boring flat grey felted rooftop like it was the most interesting thing in the world. Occasionally I glanced to the sky and into the distance but I had no thoughts except that I must get a new phone card from the machine – my brain couldn't cope with anything else – it was totally knackered.

Bill and I sat for hours talking, dozing and doing puzzle books that he had picked up in the shop. We decided that Bill should go home for the night to see the kids and have a rest.

'She'll be OK, I said. I'll call you straight away if there's a problem. I'm more used to being up than you … I can doze in the chair.

He hated going.

He rang about 11 p.m. and I told him there had been no change. Amberlie was having a really good sleep. He said he would be back in the morning after he had dropped the kids off at school. When he arrived in the morning he was amazed that Amberlie was still sleeping.

'Not even moved a muscle,' I told him. 'The nurses say she's fine and all her signs are normal and that she'll wake when she's ready.'

Bill said he had managed to get a few hours' sleep but woke at 5 a.m. and couldn't go back to sleep. He was as white as a sheet and looked disheveled. He said he had tidied up at home and put the washing in before he left and made sure Pat was all right to stay.

'She says not to worry about a thing. I've brought you a sandwich from home – hope it's OK,' he said.

'Actually … I could murder a cup of tea. The nurse bought me a lovely one at quarter to seven – do you think it would be OK if we went down to the café to have one?'

I went to the desk and asked if they could keep an eye on Amberlie as we were just nipping down for a cuppa. They said that would be fine and we weren't to worry.

'Go get a break and something to eat. Amberlie's going to need you in perfect running order!' the nurse said. We returned about forty minutes later and nothing had changed.

Amberlie slept solidly for over twenty-four hours. At about five o'clock she started to wake, opening one eye at a time. As soon as she spotted us she cooed and her wonderful smile lit up her face.

'Hello my darling,' I said as I kissed her cheek. 'Are you back with us? What a time you've had!' Amberlie looked up and grinned, sticking out her tongue and sucking it hard. She turned herself on her back and looked around the room.

'She's back, thank God!' I said to Bill, in utter relief.

At that moment Lucy came in and said 'Wow Ambams! What a clever girl!' Amberlie looked chuffed to bits!

The room was quite bland and there wasn't anything much for Amberlie to look at. I had seen a huge Mickey Mouse balloon in reception that she would like and I went off to get it.

On the way back one of the registrars on the desk said, 'Is that for Amberlie?'

'Yes! She came round a little while ago and she loves Mickey's face,' I replied.

'I'll tell you … that kid of yours is something else … a tough little lady and totally amazing!' he said.

'I know,' I said proudly, and slightly stunned, because reading between the lines, I knew they hadn't expected her to pull through.

An hour or so later Dr Ramsay came by with a paediatric palliative care nurse called Laura Symmonds, who specialised in epilepsy. It was to be a 'preparation for the future' session. Dr Ramsay talked about the last few days and we discussed Amberlie's medications and prognosis. We were over the moon that Amberlie had got through the status, but now we were being thrown into a reality that we really did not want to consider right at that moment. It was like being on a treacherous emotional roller-coaster. I took an instant dislike to Laura who had come across as pushy and determined. (I was later to revise my opinion of her!) She wanted to make us aware of a children's hospice, which was a fair way from us, where we could spend weekend breaks or longer with the kids and Amberlie, and where they would look after Amberlie while we ventured out and about. She wouldn't take 'no' for an answer.

'What?' I said. 'Why do we need to go to a hospice to have a break? And anyway, when we go out Amberlie comes with us. I don't want anyone else looking after her. She's never been in respite care and I'm not starting now. All I would do was worry … and apart from that, I am the best person to look after her.'

'Yes, but you will and do need a break,' she continued. 'It's very nice there and they make sure you are all comfortable and that Amberlie is well catered for. There will be other children there with their families and their facilities are excellent.'

'I'm sure. That's fine. I have nothing against hospices – they are good necessary places and I have nothing against them or families who use them. I just don't want to and will not hand over the care of Amberlie to anyone, not even for a short period,' I said.

'Yes, I can understand that, but your other children need your time as well and this will give you the opportunity to spend quality time with them,' she replied.

I let out a huge ruffled sigh.

'I think my children lead a good normal life, and yes, they also have a lot to deal with and understand where Amberlie is concerned. I really don't think they need to be faced with the realisation that lots of the children who will be there will not live for long. They will ask questions about them and why Amberlie is there and I don't want them upset. They are very sympathetic to disabled children and I am worried it will compound what they already feel about Amberlie. I don't know how long Amberlie's got – nobody does … but I'm not going to miss a minute of it – and from their point of view, they would hate being out without her – it is not our normal way. There will be plenty of quality time for them later. As I said, if we take a break or holiday or whatever, it will be with Amberlie, and not in a hospice.'

'Look, just let me get the details and if you change your mind, then I can go ahead and organise things,' she said.

'Whatever!' I snapped, dismissing her, and throwing my hands in the air.

Dr Ramsay changed the subject and said we were to use the diazepam whenever necessary and keep her informed. She was absolutely delighted and amazed that Amberlie had recovered and marvelled at her cooing and chatting to herself and her Mickey balloon.

We left the hospital the next day.

Amberlie was very upset for a couple of days as the medicines dispersed through her system and then she settled into a manageable period where she only needed diazepam two, three or four times a day. There were lots of sleepy days and days where she would be miserable because the seizures would not surface fully and niggled away at her.

I was soon to reach the big four-0 and a party was organised! It was at the village hall and everyone was invited. We took a huge gamble that Amberlie would be all right on the day, and she was. We bought each of the kids something new to wear and they were chuffed to bits. Amberlie had her proud expression on, knowing she looked fabulous, and she had lots of cuddles and attention and enjoyed the music, rocking and swaying every now and then in her chair. Towards the end of the evening she had a huge seizure and Bill and I managed to get her into the car to give her diazepam without causing too much attention. After that she dozed off and stayed sleepy for the rest of the evening.

Poor Ben had been so excited about the whole thing and had helped and been part of all the organisation during the day, that he was only awake for the first thirty minutes of the actual party then fell asleep, missing the entire evening! We tried waking him and keeping him going but it just wouldn't work. I felt so sorry for him, but he was OK the next day, if a little disappointed.

For several years I had been involved with the playgroup the kids had attended and I was finishing my last year as Chairman. Gwen, the playgroup leader, asked if I would like Amberlie to be part of their Christmas nativity play. I had my reservations but I thought this would be her one and only chance to be in a play and be what all little girls wanted to be – an angel. Gwen knew Amberlie very well and was very fond of her, snatching cuddles whenever she could, so she was well aware that I couldn't guarantee her health or tolerance on any particular day. She was willing to take the risk, so I thought, why not?

When the day came, Bill took the day off so he could see his girl, but Amberlie was indeed very edgy. She was very tearful and I knew it would be a miracle if she saw it though. Gwen and I dressed her in white with pretty wings and frills and put a tinsel halo on her head. There was naturally quite a lot of noise and excitement from the other children and lots of adults rushing about, but I could see it was starting to bother Amberlie as she was beginning to fidget.

The play started and within minutes I could hear her whimpering. I nudged Bill, who sneaked behind the curtain behind Amberlie. I knew she was in trouble. She had started to twitch and was rubbing her nose hard. Bill quickly picked her up and out of her chair and stood at the back cuddling and hoping it would be enough to settle her. As the children started to sing, Amberlie launched into jerks, tears and sobs and Bill quickly took her off the stage and outside. I followed and we took her home, where we rushed to get her normal clothes on before giving her diazepam. I sighed as I put her little halo into her jewellery box for safe-keeping.

The mums at the school were talking endlessly about the flu virus that had hit the area in the last couple of weeks. Luckily we hadn't seen it at home and I was keeping my fingers crossed. A few days later Amberlie showed signs of coming down with something and I thought we were doomed, but she managed to fight it off. However, it left her with some sort of odd vaginal infection that needed antibiotics. She then kept pretty well.

Laura Symmonds rang and said she would like to visit us at home to see how Amberlie was and if we needed anything. Groan, I thought to myself, dreading another hospice discussion, but I supposed it was just something I was going to have to live with every now and then. I agreed a time with her and she appeared. She never mentioned it. I sensed she knew I wasn't impressed with our first meeting and had dropped her 'pushiness'. I didn't mind that she was forthright and plain speaking so long as she realised she had to take 'no' for an answer. Laura had a lot of knowledge and information about medications and epilepsy and was interesting to listen to. She was aware that when Amberlie was poorly, feeding was often a problem and was quite concerned about the seizures affecting her swallowing in the future. She explained that should Amberlie need it, she was able to put in a nasal/gastric tube to save us having to go into hospital. She said that she was there to support us along with Dr Ramsay and should we ever need her we could ring and she would be right with us. I thanked her and she left. When Bill came home later, he said, 'How did you get along with pushy pants then?' I told him she was OK, very knowledgeable, and actually quite nice.

We plodded on in the same way until the week before Christmas, when Amberlie's chest clogged up. She needed lots of suction and antibiotics and was very jumpy with her seizures. Her feeding had gone entirely to pot and I couldn't get a drop of fluid down her. It was also awful and distressing for her having to take her medicines orally, so I decided it was time to call Laura. I explained what had been happening and she came within the hour.

The house was a complete tip, as we had just got the Christmas tree up. I hadn't had a chance in the last few days to even tidy up because Amberlie had been so ill, and the kids were all over the place, having finished for the school holidays. I apologized to Laura about all the mess and she said, 'Believe me, I have seen far worse!'

I said I thought Amberlie should have a tube so that I could at the very least get some milk and her medicines into her. Laura said she would have to ring the hospital to check that this was OK. One of the paediatric registrars immediately answered his bleep. Smiling, Laura replaced the phone and said, 'The registrar says that if Mrs Murphy thinks Amberlie needs a tube, then Amberlie needs a tube. They obviously trust your judgement, so let's do it.'

She explained exactly what the procedure was and how to measure the amount of tube to put into Amberlie's stomach. She then showed me how to put it in and do the litmus test each time before feeding and how to flush it afterwards. I remembered most of it from Great Ormond Street years ago. She also left me a spare tube in case Amberlie needed a change. She asked if I was OK with it all and said if I had any problems just to call and she would be there. I hoped it would all be just a temporary measure to get her over the worst and to get us all through Christmas without a trip to the hospital. I tried every day with a bottle so that she did not forget what to do. If she refused then I left her and continued with the tube feed. By Christmas Eve she was drinking well again and had taken some solids, so I withdrew the tube and threw it away.

Amberlie had a wonderful Christmas Day and Boxing Day, being both happy and well. Amazingly, there were no major seizures and she was fully alert and watching all that was going on. In the evening on Christmas Day, when it was dark, Bill crept away and dressed up as Father Christmas. We bought extra presents that year for all the children because at the back of our minds we didn't know how many more we would celebrate all together. The kids were already confused how Father Christmas managed to get into our house because we had a fitted fire at the bottom of the only chimney, so we racked our brains for a while on how Father Christmas would arrive. We decided that as it was tea time, it would be OK for him to ring the door bell as he was probably on his way home to the North Pole. They didn't notice Bill slip away and go out.

They were absolutely gobsmacked, and didn't recognise their dad at all.

'Ho ho ho!' he chuckled and walked in.

Ray and Clare stood motionless up against the wall and Ben looked up from playing with his toys on the floor with his eyes wide and mouth open. Amberlie sort of glanced at this splurge of red colour entering the room and looked away, then she suddenly looked back and over the top of her glasses to see what on earth it was! She looked him up and down and looked at me to see if it was OK for him to be there! There was no fooling her. As soon as he spoke to her, she knew it was her dad, and you could see the confusion on her face as she tried to work it out!

They were all delighted to have extra presents to open and it made a very special and exciting time.

Two days later, Amberlie's seizures started to emerge again and we were soon back on the diazepam run. That became the routine until about the middle of January, when she started to become increasingly distressed and made awful animal whining noises. We knew she was getting ill again. Her chest soon went under and we constantly had to suction her. Her seizures escalated alarmingly over the weekend and when the diazepam started losing its control again, we took her to hospital. There she developed a massive temperature and sweated profusely all night. The doctors took her bloods but they showed it to be viral. There was no sign of pneumonia on her chest and she didn't cough up any muck. I wasn't comfortable about their diagnosis but had no evidence to think otherwise. I felt that she should have had antibiotics even if it was viral because, knowing Amberlie, it would soon infect somewhere along the line. I understood about not prescribing antibiotics for viral infections and I knew that in many ways Amberlie needed to build up more immunity rather than have another course, but Amberlie was Amberlie and she didn't follow the same logic as the rest of the human race. As the temperature had subsided by the next day, the doctors were anxious for us to return home quickly because the ward was full of flu viruses at that time, and they said it was more likely she would pick up another one in hospital than at home.

Apart from her eating and drinking there was no general improvement. She was fitting and sleeping and feeding and fitting and sleeping. We assumed she had fought the virus and was in her own usual way recovering by sleep. Three weeks later it was still the same. Any stimulation caused a seizure – even saying 'hello' to her caused a seizure, no particular type of seizure, just whatever was about at the time. Occasionally she would have a day where she was totally stressed and unable to sleep, as the seizures would wake her the moment she dropped off with shudders and jumps and trembles. The trembles were pretty new and the jangling we had only ever seen twice, when she came out of status. These were mostly contained from the waist down. She had salaams, large and small, usually twice a day and repeated over ten minutes or so each time. Some fits were just a tiny upward movement in her jaw, making her top lip protrude, or there was the slightest bowing of her head. The tree fits were large and small, sometimes once, sometimes twice, sometimes loads following on from one another. Some were half trees, where Amberlie only raised her arms to waist level. They were similar to the first seizures that she had when she was first diagnosed. She intermittently laughed between them, but her grin was over-stretched and unnatural, and her facial muscles twitched. Her eyes would half open and bang relentlessly in their corners, looking either up or down, and they would often stay crossed for some while. Some of her jumps were huge and made her lurch forwards with her arms and legs forming a circular shape in front of her – these were massive in their intensity and very powerfully held her pose. Thankfully there was only ever one at a time, and guessed they had to be a variation of her salaams. I counted the seizures I saw in one day and was shocked to find that she'd had over seventy – I dreaded to think how many had gone unnoticed on top of that. I never counted them again.

When things were quieter, Amberlie had long absences and dribbled masses. She would often sit with her mouth wide open and sometimes she rolled her head constantly from side to side – it must have made her confused but she seemed happy enough doing it. The seizures all had the same thing in common, whether they were large, small or tiny – they all knocked her flat. The large ones had to be stopped with diazepam otherwise they just would not go away, and her dependency on that was now up to four or five times a day. Sometimes they wouldn't go away in the first ten minutes, which meant we had to give her a further dose, which luckily worked and sent her to sleep, but devastatingly, the minute she woke, the smaller ones took over again. On a few occasions we waited 30-40 minutes before the double diazepam worked and I knew it was fast losing its effectiveness.

Amberlie still seemed to hear us though and looked straight at me when I spoke to her, but responded only occasionally with a small, quick smile. Every now and then she would get excited to see us and oohed and cooed away, only for the mood to come crashing down as the stimulation spurred on a tree fit. It was heartbreaking.

Oddly in the evenings she would have a break of an hour or two apart from jumps and absences and she tried intermittently to play with her jingle ball for a few seconds. Her beloved music was now making her moan like an animal and in a way upset her. I think she knew that if she enjoyed it too much it would make her fit. I was so very, very worried.

After having a long talk with Dr Ramsay we reduced her steroids slightly, hoping that it would get rid of some of the stress. I found that when a part of her steroid dosage became ineffective it irritated her so I wanted it taken away in case it played a part in the seizure activity. Anything was worth a go.

It was Ben's fifth birthday and we had arranged for him to have a party with friends at Burger King. He was very excited and everyone was looking forward to it. I made sure Amberlie was fed before we went and she sat semi-consciously in her pushchair where she could watch the children. I could see she was struggling to stay awake to see what was going on but the seizures were making her jump and wince. I hoped she would be able to doze off, which she did for a while. I knew the party would only last an hour and a half or so and as much as I loved seeing Ben have a good time, I kept looking at my watch wishing the time would hurry up. It was such a huge relief to get Amberlie home, where I felt I could cope with anything. Ben's fun continued at home with relatives, while Bill sat Amberlie on his lap keeping her safe and secure while she enjoyed a nice warm drink.

At the end of January Amberlie had a shuddering and stretching seizure in the middle of the night, which made her sick. I called Dr Ramsay and she said that it sometimes happened in a seizure and the only real risk was from inhalation, so we needed to keep Amberlie on her side somehow through the nights.

I rang her again six days later because the seizures were speeding up and Amberlie did not seem to be able to cope with being awake at all. She was managing to get through sleepy bottles of milk and that was it. She was also going awfully white with pale lips and a blue centre to her face. Dr Ramsay was at a loss as to what to do and again hoped that things would settle down while she looked at her drugs again.

The weather was fairly nice if a little cold, and as Amberlie needed some nice trainers to wear over her thick totes socks, I took her on a trek to the local market. We managed to find her a nice pair and the man popped a £1 coin in her hand and told her how beautiful she was. She had a session of repeating tree fits and a single shout on the way back to the car, and no one seemed to notice her odd movements.

The following day I decided to take Amberlie out in her pram to collect the kids from school. We were out an hour and she never moved a muscle at all the whole time, although she was wide awake – eyes open but nobody in. It was like having a mannequin in the pram.

I always wanted her to experience the little but important things in life like raindrops on her head, the feel of snowflakes or gentle sun on her skin, and the breeze through her hair, and she had enjoyed them all with a giggle, a delighted gasp or a laugh. Now she wouldn't even notice them – her awareness had gone, unless it was something that made her jump or was too loud, and then all that did was upset her. I felt just a numb, because that stopped the pain. Amberlie had lots of shuddery fits that night.

30

Within five minutes of waking, Amberlie had one small tree fit, one small and one medium salaam, and then, after a brief interlude, a session of trees and salaams one after the other. I gave her diazepam but she only slept for half an hour and woke very distressed and upset. I thought some paracetamol might settle her and she then snuggled up for a sleep on her dad's lap. Later on she woke very twitchy and stretchy but managed to sort herself out enough to drink a bottle of milk and then went back to sleep. When she woke again there were more salaams, trees, twitches, shudders and diazepam that did not work. I gave her another dose ten minutes later and she drifted off to sleep but her breathing became very fast and the outward breaths were laboured. It started to ease a little but didn't right itself. I wondered whether it was related to one of her seizures or whether it was the extra diazepam that had affected her. I doubted it … that hadn't been the case before. It was more likely to be another chest infection brewing.

The kids had all had streaming noses that week but the colds in themselves were not responsible for the general escalation in Amberlie's seizures over the past weeks. I hoped Dr Ramsay would hurry up and come back with an answer, a plan or a suggestion … anything. The inevitability of having to go to hospital was looming in fast and I desperately wanted to avoid that and not go through another 'status'. I knew if it was her chest they could make her better … but what if it wasn't illness now?

'Oh please, Dr Ramsay, please come up with something.'

I also knew that I had to be fair to Amberlie and there was only so much she could take before I had to give in. Amberlie had such a fighting spirit – she had proved that before. I had to give her the chance to sort herself out – filling her up with more drugs would inevitably cause her damage at some stage, and/or knock her out altogether. I hoped and prayed that there was someone out there with an answer so that she could grab the chance before she was in trouble again. God, please don't let her have another chest infection as well.

During the afternoon, Amberlie's breathing started to deteriorate again and her outward breaths ended with a grunt. She was having difficulty dealing with her saliva, and was coughing and spluttering whilst drinking her milk, and she did not want to deal with her food at all. Soon her temperature rose and she was very agitated and trembling. I could hear rattling bubbly noises right at the bottom of her throat so I took her to the doctor's. He confirmed a chest infection and started her on antibiotics.

A pattern had begun to emerge: when she was ill and taking antibiotics, the seizures lessened off both in quantity and severity. I wondered whether there was a certain antibiotic that she could take permanently to improve her overall condition and made a mental note to talk to Dr Ramsay about it. This time her chest seemed to be fairly loose and she was managing to shift some of the congestion. Her breathing was still going awry form time to time and it seemed to be related to the seizures she was having, even though they were not harsh in appearance. There were lots of ongoing little ones and absences which were making her tighten her arms in different positions and made her bend and wriggle like a snake in discomfort. The diazepam's effectiveness depended very much on the type of seizure Amberlie was having at the time; it was certainly having immense difficulty controlling salaams or runs of salaams.

Amberlie was much more awake during the illness and actually managed to play happily with her ball for a few minutes each day. It was still hard to judge whether she was properly awake or whether she was in absences, but there were certainly some windows opening up from time to time. She had a lovely period during the evenings when she responded and laughed at us singing and rocking her. Generally, for whatever reason, she always seemed much brighter during the evenings, even when she had been through hell during the day. I couldn't fathom why. It was a mystery.

Amberlie had started to eat well again and was having three full meals a day even though they had the effect of leaving her a bit puffed out and panting. She was having two or three short-lived salaams before bed but usually fell straight to sleep afterwards without needing diazepam.

It was times like that when it was so nice to settle into a routine and enjoy Amberlie and what she did, and it was such a temptation to presume that she was over the worst and to look forward in the hope of brighter times. It was almost like living in two worlds – our ideal one and the real one. Bill and I knew deep down that everything was always temporary, so it was dangerous and upsetting to look beyond the moment or the next few hours because that stopped us enjoying what was happening that minute. We had to go with the flow but be ready and alert for sudden changes. It was always perilous to settle into generalisations that attempted to explain why Amberlie was the way she was at any given time.

Amberlie had a bad night with a runny nose that compounded some mucus left in her throat from some seizures she'd had earlier. Naturally this threw her breathing and I spent most of the night keeping her raised up and using the suction machine when necessary. Eve had taught me how to give chest physio and I laid her across my lap and rubbed and patted her back to help shift the muck. I also used her nebuliser to open her passageways to help disperse it all. Amberlie eventually had a nasty salaam at 8 a.m. and, despite diazepam, could not settle, so I gave her more nebuliser, physio and suction. Eventually she passed out into a noisy sleep, which was interrupted by a five-minute episode of shuddering. She did not want to drink when she finally woke, and I think that was down to the fear of more liquid going down her throat that she couldn't deal with. I tried again a little later and she managed 3 ounces and happily accepted a jar of pineapple and melon baby fruit – one of her favourites. As the day went on she took two-thirds of the next bottle and later another third and another jar of food.

The following day was quite settled despite lots of absences and wriggly sessions, but she had no big fits at all. In the early hours she needed diazepam, which did nothing other than make her stare straight ahead for forty minutes before falling asleep. She woke in the morning in a succession of tree fits and went straight back to sleep again. The rest of the day was fairly good but there were lots of seizures during her sleep, especially in the evening. Around 10 p.m. she needed diazepam after a nasty succession of seizures finally woke her; and after that she repeated the session every two hours until 4 a.m., and then slept till 8.30 a.m. when she woke, had a salaam followed by a small jump, drank a bottle of milk and went back to sleep.

The next day followed a similar pattern. I thought I would risk taking her out in the afternoon to meet the kids from school and she shouted and gurgled all the way there and back (roughly one and a quarter hours). When I took her indoors, she was foaming at the mouth.

It was very, very difficult taking Amberlie out – there never seemed to be a good time. Getting the kids to and from school was enough stress for me to deal with and to top it she now salaamed each time I put her in the pushchair to take Ben to his classroom.

If the seizure was in its first stages, I dashed through the playground and shoved him in the door so that I could get back to the car to give her diazepam. Unfortunately the first stage always included biting her tongue and blood ran from her mouth onto her coat without fail. It worked out better if I got Ben delivered first because that meant I didn't have to move Amberlie while she was unconscious. If I had to give her diazepam (which was usually the case), Ben was late and I risked disturbing her and causing another seizure by having to put her in the car seat to take her home.

Amberlie was extremely heavy when out cold and lifting her and placing her precisely was quite a feat.

I wished the new pushchair would hurry up and come – it would make such a difference to be able to position her comfortably, and maybe I could walk more often to pick the kids up, knowing I could administer the diazepam quickly and fairly discreetly. Amberlie was so drowsy that keeping her sitting totally upright just wasn't fair to her even on a short trip. It had been weeks and there was still no news of the pushchair's arrival. Eve said they usually took about three months to supply new chairs.

Laura had been keeping in touch by phone and monitoring the situation. The days were not improving – Amberlie was either asleep or fitting. It was Valentine's Day and I had got up that morning sensing it was going to be a really bad day. Amberlie woke up and there was something very different about her and I knew she had deteriorated. I called Laura to come and take a look at her. She was there within the hour and said she thought it was time to take her to hospital, so made a phone call.

I called Auntie Pat to come down and look after the kids and off we went, straight to the ward. They gave Amberlie some chloral hydrate, as that had had some effect then she was last in status, but this time it didn't work. They X-rayed her chest and said there were a few puffy bits on the right hand side so they started her on antibiotics.

The seizures quickly crept up in pace and the doctors decided to give her two doses of diazepam rectally and two intravenously with another dose of chloral. This knocked Amberlie out cold but didn't stop the seizures, which continued while she slept. During all this she pooed in her nappy, so I knew some of the additional seizures were down to her need to go to the toilet. I moved her a little so I could change her, and as I did so, her neck kinked slightly to one side and she stopped breathing. I hit the alarm button and everyone dashed into the room. Her face had ballooned and she was a horrid shade of blue. The registrar moved quickly and laid her flat with a pillow under her shoulders so her head hung back and she immediately started to breathe again. I stood there shaking and totally shocked. The registrar checked her over and sat with her for a while. He looked at me, paused, and said, 'Sandra, things are really bad … and I think this will probably be Amberlie's last admission to hospital. Her seizures are very bad even though we have her heavily sedated. Please do not leave the hospital for any reason … I am so sorry …'

I gasped and the sister pulled me down to sit on the bed.

Somebody said, 'I'll go and make some tea.'

The sister and a nurse sat with Bill and me for a while and talked to us about Amberlie and the situation and made sure that we were all right. Amberlie had settled considerably and we sat and watched her, frightened to even pop to the loo, and we painstakingly kept her as straight as possible in case she kinked her neck again.

That night she started to puff and pant a little and her throat was very bubbly. We were suctioning her every now and again but nothing was clearing. Amberlie's night nurse was very worried and asked the registrar to take a look at her. He said her chest was very noisy and that maybe another nebuliser might help to move things. It seemed to ease the noises but still nothing cleared. We were unable to give her chest physio because she had become touch reactive – every time someone or something touched her she had another seizure – so lots of rubbing and patting was out of the question. Things were no better in the morning and the registrar said he wanted another X-ray in case she had aspirated something. The X-ray machine was there within minutes and he confirmed that Amberlie had indeed aspirated on the left side. She was immediately started on intravenous antibiotics. Her breathing started to deteriorate and they wired her up to every type of apparatus possible in an endeavour to get her worsening seizures under control. Another phenytoin driver was set up. Her oxygen intake was gradually lowering, her heart rate was increasing and her temperature had started to rise. Bill and I sat biting our nails. We felt so helpless, useless, overwhelmed and desperate. It was hard to hold on to the tears. It was awful.

Dr Ramsay appeared in the doorway straight after her clinic and was clutching Amberlie's X-rays in her hand. Laura was with her.

'Oh Amberlie love ...' she said, as she moved towards her and squeezed her hand. She turned to us, 'Have you seen these X-rays?'

We shook our heads.

'They're something else you know ...' And she held them up to the light.

'This is the right lung and this is the left ... What do you think?'

I looked. 'Jesus Christ ...' I mumbled in shock. The whole of Amberlie's left lung was completely whitened out.

The sister had followed her in and said, 'It means the lung has collapsed and Amberlie has very severe pneumonia.'

Dr Ramsay said, 'Nothing is working – the fits are still coming despite everything, and now she has pneumonia. The next stage is to put her out completely on heminevrin – you remember she had this in the beginning?' I nodded. 'She should by rights now go down to intensive care but I want her to stay on the ward with you so that she is comfortable.' There was a long pause. She continued, 'This chest infection has to be our main priority and maybe if we can get this under control then the fits might sort themselves out. If we can, we need to give her a chance, and wait and see, rather than do the heminevrin now ... because we might not be able to get her off it once it goes in. If we can't sort the chest we must make her comfortable and perhaps take away all the medicines and let her go peacefully.'

The doctor's voice was wavering all over the place and it was hard to follow what she was saying. She was obviously doing what she normally did and that was to think out loud. It was a good job I knew her. She couldn't look at me and was desperately trying to hold on to her tears.

'I'm going to leave you for a while to think and I'll be back shortly.' She left the room.

I looked at Bill and I plonked down in the chair. I couldn't stop shaking. He stood rigidly by Amberlie's side.

'I guess this is it then ...' I said.

It took a while for us to sort and work out exactly what Dr Ramsay said and get it into perspective. We both agreed that Amberlie should be given the chance to get over the chest infection because that might well stop the ferocity of the seizures.

In the meantime one of the doctors tried to get a new line into Amberlie's foot because the phenytoin driver had needed to go into her hand and it had bruised and swelled severely. He was unable to find a decent vein because they had all shrunk away, and was conscious of not upsetting or distressing Amberlie any further, so he said he would try again later.

Laura had come back into the room and said she needed to explain things. She said that Amberlie was really poorly now and that there was only a minimal chance that she would pull through. She asked what we thought about stopping the medication altogether and letting her go peacefully with no pain or discomfort – because she was really suffering now.

Shocked, I had to go over what she said and there was silence for while. Bill said nothing either but his eyes were full of pain and tears. I couldn't understand why the situation had suddenly changed from trying to get her sorted out to this, and I challenged her about it. I felt angry now because I didn't know which way to turn. Bill and I had made a decision and now it was different.

'How can all that change in a few minutes? What the hell's going on?'

Laura apologised and explained more about the X-rays coupled with the seizures, especially as she had been in status for three hours at least, with the phenytoin not being as effective as they'd hoped. She said Amberlie was really was so poorly now that it would be much fairer to her to withdraw the antibiotics entirely. She said that she had no way on earth of surviving this infection and the antibiotics would just prolong her agony. I knew she was right but we were almost being asked to turn off the switch as such and I felt sick. Somehow I managed to sort myself out and I looked at Bill and then at Laura. 'I don't know how you do your bloody job,' I snarled. She paused and there was a pounding silence, she bit into her lip as her eyes filled with tears, she left the room.

'Shit,' I mumbled. Bill was looking at me. He didn't need to say anything – I hadn't meant to savage her – she was doing the worst job on earth. I sighed long and heavily, focusing my eyes out of the window and into the sky, searching for a way to escape the pain and refrain from making any decision.

Bill and I couldn't believe we had to now make such an unbearable choice. The tears wouldn't stop and poured and poured in endless torrents while we talked – mine dripping onto poor Amberlie, who was gasping for breath. We talked to her too – trying to explain, and I don't know, maybe even justify what we were to do … But how could we justify it? How could we make her understand that it was for her own good when she loved her life and all the little things that meant so much to her? She looked so innocent, so young; how can a child be in such a life-threatening state? It was not natural that as her parents we should be agreeing to withdraw her treatment because we would do anything to keep her well so that she survived. That's what I'd done all along. It was unacceptable.

In my head I heard two voices beating it out – one saying you have to let her go for her sake, and the other, to continue and fight and hope and deal with whatever is thrown back in the best way possible to restore normality. But there wasn't any normality – none at all. In my heart the bare truth said I could never make Amberlie's condition go away … and that her condition was what she had battled with all the time … and that it had deteriorated itself without any help from the outside world. The pain was deep and unending. We were destroyed … and the worst was yet to come.

The thing that worried me more than anything was whether Amberlie would ever be able to forgive her dad and me for making such a decision? I was also very worried about her suffering at the end. I knew I would never be able to forgive myself … I had never forgiven myself for whatever went wrong during the pregnancy to make her this way in the first place. I certainly felt I had no right or desire to decide whether she was to live or die.

Laura and Sister Jenny returned to sit and talk with us. We talked lots about everything to do with children dying and they reassured us that they would not allow Amberlie to suffer and would keep her comfortable. There were long periods of silence when all we could hear was Amberlie's struggle.

I wanted to know what would happen to her after she died, and they explained that we could stay with her for as long as we wished and told us their routine. I was also worried about the prospect of a post-mortem, because I couldn't bear the thought of someone cutting up my beautiful, precious baby. They said it would not be necessary because Amberlie had a known and monitored long-term illness. I was relieved and burst into tears.

Bill and I eventually agreed that the antibiotics should be withdrawn. I felt violently sick and I shot out of the door to the loo. I couldn't stop retching. Afterwards I pinned myself to the wall, and my knees buckled under me.

'God, I hate you!' I screamed. I took some deep breaths, swallowed, but still felt sick. 'Come on, pull yourself together, Sandra,' I said out loud. 'Amberlie needs you.' And I made my way back to her room. My body had slumped and I felt empty.

Laura said it would be a good idea to ask Ray, Clare and Ben to come to the hospital to see Amberlie.

Jenny asked the nurses to remove all the monitors and equipment from the room apart from the oxygen and saturation machine so that it no longer looked like an intensive care room and the children wouldn't be frightened. They said that the ward next door was empty and had seven beds available for anybody to stay and sleep if they wanted to.

It was very quiet in the room now apart from Amberlie's noisy breathing. Bill's mum had turned up to visit her and we had to explain what was going on. She was very upset and decided she was going to stay with us. The nurses brought us all a cup of tea.

I had seen a little black cuddly dog in the shop downstairs so I told Bill I was going to get it for Amberlie – a little friend to bring her all the luck in the world. I rushed straight there and back and put him beside her head telling her that he was there. I kissed her forehead and whispered, 'Come on my darling – you've got to give it all you've got. Please, please, sweetpea, you've got to fight for your life now. I'm so sorry, so sorry … please, my darling, forgive your mum … I so wish I could take your place … Please Ambams you've got to fight … you've got to fight …' I was on my knees begging.

When we had sorted ourselves out a bit and everything was calm in the room, I told Auntie Pat to bring the kids up to the hospital. I then rang their Uncle Ray to tell him. He said he would collect Pat and the kids and see us soon. Margaret rang Bill's dad, and before long, the whole room was full.

We explained everything to the kids when they arrived and we all cried for ages, especially Ben. It was so hard to be brave for the children. The nurses supplied everyone with chairs and tea and they said they would pop in frequently to see Amberlie.

Amberlie was completely unconscious, needing oxygen and suction all the time. In a way the kids kept us sane because after a while they needed something to do. The nurses said they were welcome to bring any toys and books in from the playroom or indeed watch the TV in there if they wanted to. They were free to come and go as they pleased. The nurses were in every twenty minutes or so, monitoring Amberlie carefully. The evening soon came and Uncle Ray took the kids to Burger King. When they came back there had been no change and Ben laid himself down on the bed after giving Amberlie a big kiss and went to sleep. The nurse's visits became more frequent until she was actually sitting with us. Amberlie's breathing was so noisy and laboured and her temperature was steadily increasing until she was literally burning up. The nurse gave her rectal paracetamol to try to control the temperature and keep her more comfortable. We had stripped her down so that she only had her nappy on in an attempt to cool her. I had not let go of Amberlie's hand for hours. It was now gone 11 p.m. The nurses had now made up the beds for everyone, and I told them not to feel bad if they wanted to sleep and that we would let them know if things changed. Nobody really wanted to sleep. Bill's mum and dad were in and out, unable to live without smoking.

It was now 3 a.m. and Jody the nurse was preparing us for the worst. Amberlie was struggling more than ever to breathe – her heart rate had increased and her oxygen saturation was low, hovering around the low 80s (it should be 98+). At 3.30 a.m. Jody had just taken Amberlie's temperature again and was having a good look in Amberlie's eyes. She looked at me, her eyes wide …

'What? What is it? Is she …?'

'You have an amazing little girl. Amberlie's temperature is on its way down and her signs are starting to return to normal. She's made it through!'

I gasped, dumbstruck. I couldn't believe it! Amberlie was visibly settling – her skin colour was returning to normal, and her breathing was much quieter. Jody covered her in a blanket, and rushed down the corridor to let the doctors and everyone else know!

'We'll still continue to monitor her through the night,' Jody said. 'Well done you – what a clever girl you are!' she said to

Amberlie. The relief was amazing and overwhelming. I didn't know what to do with myself – I wanted to scream and party, but instead I cried. Everyone was amazed and stunned into silence. Then I couldn't stop smiling. I was so proud of her.

'It wasn't her time!' I said to Bill. 'She is such a fighter, bless her ... and without antibiotics!'

Relieved, the others left to get some sleep next door. There was absolutely no way that Bill and I were going to sleep – all we wanted to do was stay with Amberlie and marvel at how wonderful she was. Jody came back in with some tea and we sat talking together for hours about all sorts of things. Jody explained she had recently lost her partner and was trying to put her life back together. I think we all helped each other that night.

Amberlie woke at about 11.00 a.m. the next day with her big beautiful eyes shining brightly as she gave me her usual gorgeous smile.

'Hello, my clever darling ... You did it you know, you did it!'

She cooed and oohed and grinned .... she knew she had been so clever!

The nurses all dropped by one by one to see her and say hello. Sister came in with Ros and said that they were going to give her a nice bath and wash her hair and make her feel good and fresh.

'Oh, don't worry. I'll do that,' I said.

'No, you have a rest ... we are going to do it. It will be our pleasure!'

They managed the whole enterprise in bed! They manoeuvred Amberlie to the top end of the bed so that her head hung over the edge while they poured water through her hair into a baby bath underneath. Then they towelled it and soaped her all over – there was water and towels everywhere! I cuddled her dry while they stripped the bed and put fresh linen on. I found her some clean clothes and they dressed her and sent for a hair dryer. Amberlie really enjoyed the whole experience and was relaxed and smiley all through. Once she was sorted they placed her on pillows and covered her. She settled straight away into another nap. She looked so beautiful, so sparkling clean and chilled – a sleeping angel.

We had to avoid Amberlie lying on her left side because that reduced her oxygen intake considerably. This meant she either had to be on her right side or slightly on her back facing right in a more raised position. Her poor little face had now filled with fluid and she had the most awful swollen eyes – she looked like she had been crying for a month. As her sedation wore off, things soon righted themselves and she looked pretty good again by the evening.

After her sleep she drank a warm bottle of milk and smiled and looked around the room. There were no seizures that we were aware of and she was comfortable and settled. Everyone was so thrilled that she'd made it through – she was the ward celebrity!

Dr Ramsay visited in the afternoon and told us she wanted Amberlie to stay in hospital for a further forty-eight hours to make sure she was steady and said she then thought it best we took her home and out of the hospital in case she picked up any further infection – unless we really wanted to stay! She did, however, warn us that now Amberlie's chest had been so bad it would be likely that another infection would not be too far away because that episode would have weakened her chest considerably, and that the residue muck would take a fair while to clear. She said Laura would be visiting us at home to keep an eye on her, and that she herself would be there for us any time we needed her. If we needed to bring her back to the hospital for any reason, we were just to ring the ward and say we were on our way because we were to have free access.

She walked over to Amberlie, stroked her arm and said, 'Clever girl!'

And left the room.

31

Bill and I were excited to be taking Amberlie home – something we thought wasn't going to happen. The kids were beside themselves, jumping up and down and wanting to grab cuddles with her as soon as we got in the door!

We felt very shell-shocked, as if we'd been caught up in some strange and surreal nightmare and had then been returned to reality to carry on as usual. It was like a miracle but at the same time I was anxious and scared and although home was the best place in the world, and I didn't want to be in hospital, we were on our own and the doctors and nurses weren't just down the hallway. Amberlie was out of immediate danger but she was still very poorly, and it was obvious that she wasn't the same little girl. She was very weak and had lost a lot of her sparkle. I knew that, along with the pneumonia, there was no way that she could have come through the three-hour-long status she had prior to that without killing off some brain cells - and that struggling for oxygen would also have caused some damage. We were so glad to have her home whatever, but we knew our poor baby was probably going to have to go through all this again.

It took me ages to sort everything out and get organised. I felt burned out with no energy at all, and I spent ages doing silly things like going into rooms and wondering why I was in there, putting things into wrong cupboards, totally forgetting what I'd done the minute before, and repeating what I'd only just said. I was all right all the time I was able to sit with Amberlie, but to cope with anything routine was beyond me. Bill made up Amberlie's bottles and we all eventually sat in the front room watching her sleep peacefully on her cushions in front of the fire. We all dozed off, shattered and exhausted, but I kept one ear open just in case.

Each day Laura came in to listen to Amberlie's chest and she steadily ticked by, slowly recovering and sleeping most of the time, but the seizures were starting to reappear.

One morning a different nurse came to see Amberlie. Hayley explained that Laura was ill and she would be standing in for her for a few weeks. I was disappointed because I was used to Laura now, and felt that I would have to establish a new relationship, and have to explain everything yet again. Laura had been there for both the last bad times and whilst I didn't like her at first, I now valued her support and I really wanted some consistency. Anyway, Hayley was very kind and gentle, chatty and obviously very experienced. Three days later when she popped into check Amberlie, I told her I was a little worried because I thought she looked more poorly and there had been some little rattles on her chest that morning. She had been a bit puffy, and although it had subsided quickly, I wondered if she would have a listen.

'She's got a hell of an awful chest infection,' she said. 'Her skin colour has gone and the bottom lobe of her left lung has shut down because the infection has inflamed the muck and damage left from the pneumonia.'

'Oh my God! Not already ... not again ...' I was shocked.

'We need to get some oxygen into her ... Have you got the small cylinder they sent you home with from the hospital? I'll call your GP and see if we can get her some powerful antibiotics so that you don't have to go back into hospital, unless you feel you want to.'

'No ... that's good.' I said. Hayley now had the oxygen mask on Amberlie.

The GP came straight away and left a prescription. Our local chemist did not stock the medicine because it was a 'last resort' antibiotic and was rarely requested. We managed to find one a few miles away but only because the person who it had been prescribed for had died in the meantime! We were lucky otherwise we would have had to take her back to hospital.

Anyway, it was no miracle cure. It didn't show any signs of being effective and we relied heavily on her nebuliser and chest physio to help her. It was a full and exhausting ten days before we saw any general improvement and Amberlie still sounded very chesty. We continued to work hard giving four-hourly nebulisers but by the end of another seven days, the infection had set in again, though not as severely. More antibiotics were prescribed and the infection started to clear quickly. We still could not get rid of all the bubbles and crepey (little snap-crackling) sounds, but there was definitely more air circulating in her lungs. We persisted with the nebuliser and physio to try to clear the rest of the muck and in the meantime she worryingly had some very odd temperatures which, apart from keeping us on full alert in case of another infection, appeared in strange ways, often presenting in patches and contained in the top or bottom or left or right side of her body, or they'd suddenly fly and then drop down too low, making Amberlie shiver. I couldn't work it out but presumed they were all to do with her chest.

Hayley visited every day – sometimes twice a day – and was always contactable by phone. She spent many hours talking to us and explaining what was going on, all the time endeavouring to keep Amberlie at home with us, which was where we wanted her. She also kept Dr Ramsay and the ward fully informed.

Amberlie now slept with Bill and me in our bed, where I felt I could monitor her better. Generally she slept fairly well, although I was not sure that her sleep was a natural sleep. Now she was over the infections, the seizures had begun to emerge again and the nights were full of trembling and shuddering, which we couldn't physically see but they shook the bed, and they naturally disturbed her sleep and upset her. I contacted Dr Ramsay and she prescribed some clobazam – another antiepileptic – which Amberlie was to take initially at night and then after a week, twice a day. This did not seem to have much effect and Dr Ramsay upped the dose a bit. After this Amberlie did have better nights –

not every tremble or jerk was eradicated, but they were not enough to wake her.

One Saturday morning Amberlie went into a succession of tree fits and managed to aspirate some of the secretions made from the seizures. The secretions she made seemed to amass from nowhere and were white, stringy and membranous, which made them linger and hard to shift. When we wiped them away from her mouth it was like pulling a continual thread. They also had the ability to bubble without bursting, like chewing gum, and the suction was the only thing that got rid of them – if I could reach them with the tube. These were not easy to shift with the chest physio either.

Amberlie automatically went blue and her breathing was terrible. I gave her the nebuliser quickly and her temperature shot through the roof. I put her on the oxygen and called the nurse. As it was the weekend, Hayley was off duty so another one came and said that her chest didn't seem too bad but she would have the Saturday GP come and listen. The doctor arrived within a few minutes and said that she too couldn't hear much and gave her some normal antibiotics just in case another infection was to start. I explained to her that the particular antibiotics she had prescribed were no longer effective on Amberlie, as she had taken them so many times over the years. She said it was good to rotate them and as she had not had them for a while, they might well be effective again. They naturally did not want Amberlie to become immune to the new one. I understood the theory but wasn't convinced.

Later that afternoon Amberlie started to throw sudden temperatures and she was clearly becoming very unwell. I persisted with the antibiotics for five days and then decided enough was enough, and took her round to see our usual doctor. He said her chest was badly infected and that she needed the stronger medicine again. I really hated dealing with weekend doctors and I moaned about it to the doctor. Time had been wasted and Amberlie had suffered unnecessarily because she hadn't been given the right stuff in the first place. I wasn't happy and kicked myself for not doing something sooner. I resolved that if Amberlie became ill again at a weekend, I would take her straight to hospital, so she would be seen by those I trusted.

Amberlie's chest cleared beautifully over the next few days and Hayley was pleased to find there was a lot more air circulating in her lungs again. Bill and I were delighted and relieved.

Again the seizures were establishing their menacing control and seemed to be gaining strength; and when they weren't making her jump and jerk all the time, they were manifesting under the surface, blanking her out entirely in her own world.

Amberlie started to panic every time food or anything was put in her mouth, and coughed and spluttered at the smallest amounts. I was terrified of her choking because I knew that the food would end up in her lungs. I now had to accept entire defeat with her swallowing and I knew we would never be able to get it back again. It was time to stop her solid food and Hayley said that there were specially formulated drinks that were nutritionally and calorifically enhanced, that served as full meals and were prescribed by the GP. This meant that everything Amberlie had could now go down her tube and the stress at mealtimes would be totally eradicated for her.

I had always wanted to avoid that moment, had always feared it, but now I could see there was no other way so it seemed the most natural thing in the world to do. Later I looked at the rows and rows of baby food jars stored in the larder and the pain and nausea rushed into my throat. I turned away and put the kettle on.

Amberlie no longer minded the tube – once it was in place. I changed it as quickly as possible for her about twice a week but sometimes she managed to pull it out accidentally and it had to be put back in again. Hayley got her some sensitive tape that didn't irritate her face while it held the tube in place.

It didn't solve all the problems because her inability to swallow also made it very difficult for her to control her saliva and dribbles, and they ran down her throat into her chest, which often sounded like a bubbling bowl of water. Hayley said there was a medicine that would dry up her secretions. I sighed.

'But she already has so much medicine … and what if it doesn't interact well?'

'It can be prescribed in a patch form which we just stick on her neck,' Hayley said. 'I'll talk to Dr Ramsay about it.'

Dr Ramsay wasn't keen – I don't know why. But Hayley pushed the point and the doctor agreed to try it.

We put a whole patch on at first but it made Amberlie very restless and stressed. We cut it down to a quarter to see if it made any difference and it didn't seem enough, so we tried half. This worked pretty well but had no effect on the amount of secretions produced on days when Amberlie had a lot of seizures. I also noticed that the day following a change of patch was an awful seizure-packed day – she had many more than usual and some really terrible ones. As the life of the patch wore out, so did a lot of the extra seizures.

Whatever we did, Amberlie couldn't win. I wanted to take the patch away but I knew that doing so would make her fill up with water again … but she couldn't afford to have any more seizures either, because that too increased the secretions. Hayley said that the increase in seizures was not a known side-effect of the drug. I said, 'That doesn't mean that it wouldn't affect Amberlie, and it was unlikely to have been test-tried with the other medications she took. Also any hyperactivity side-effect would make Amberlie stressed and that alone would aggravate the seizures. Apart from that, Dr Ramsay hadn't been keen in the first place, so she must have had her reservations for some reason.' I removed the patch from Amberlie's neck and stopped using them.

32

Following the rapid and significant deterioration in Amberlie's health at the beginning of the year, Bill had found it increasingly difficult to leave the house and go to work, and indeed felt totally unable to cope with all that being the branch manager of a fairly large high street bank entailed. He went to see our GP and was subsequently signed off work with stress. Unsurprisingly, Amberlie's near-fatal bout of pneumonia had compounded his feelings and he was frightened to leave the house for long periods in case something happened to her. I have to say that I was relieved. I hated the thought of having to cope with everything by myself, and I worried about routine things like collecting the kids from school or what I would do in an emergency if there was no one available to pick them up. Things changed so fast now in Amberlie's day that I couldn't say at any given time that I could guarantee anything. Even meal times were all over the place – the kids got their breakfast on time but the evening meal happened sometime between 5 p.m. and 8 p.m. The smallest journeys were a trauma and a risk, and it wasn't fair on Amberlie to keep dragging her in and out of the car when she was so ill.

It was such a support to have someone take turns to pick the kids up and go shopping, and to help keep the household chores going most of the time, because there was always someone with Amberlie. To have him around meant that I didn't have to worry about the mundane. He very much wanted to help me to take care of Amberlie, wanting to do his bit and have the opportunity to take time with her that he never could before. It also meant I had a friend, someone there to talk to whenever I wanted, and the same for him. The work element just didn't matter anymore to either of us. We would worry about that later.

We became very isolated apart from professional visits and the occasional relative. Auntie Pat and my brother Ray were often around. Bill's mum and dad came from time to time, but their visits were the most stressful because they found it all too difficult to handle and understand. They had their own opinions and largely exasperated us, so we never really bothered to say more about Amberlie than was necessary. Somehow they thought their love for Amberlie was enough.

Eve popped in twice a week or whenever we needed her to do chest physio, and to check her physical shape, but sometimes Amberlie was too ill or too touch-reactive for anything like that. June, her portage teacher, still came once a week just to see her. She was attached to Amberlie and didn't want to stop visiting, so we used to sit and have a cuppa and a chat while she sat by Amberlie, having little words in her ear.

Amberlie was always in the front room. She had always been in there so she was central to all that happened. We had adapted everything around her and made a bed right in the middle of the floor for her to be comfortable on so that she was with us all, all of the time. She would have hated being holed up in a bedroom, missing what the kids were doing, even though she was virtually permanently asleep. She always prised open her eyes when the kids came in from school and would smile and coo to let them know she knew they were there. They always came in with, 'Hello Ambams and how are you today?' and gave her big kisses.

I don't unfortunately remember very much about what the other kids did or where they went during that time. I knew they were safe and fed and cared for, but I don't remember much about their lives or things that happened to them at all. My whole world was Amberlie, she was twenty-four hours a day, seven days a week, and I thought about nothing else. Although I can't remember, I don't regret it either because that time was so precious.

It was all very strange really. We were cocooned in our own protective world. I wouldn't have the kids' friends round to play in case they brought in a germ – they didn't seem to mind and understood why. All the days seemed much the same – full of seizures, physio,, meal times, change times, cuddle times, Hayley times, and knife-edge times when we didn't know which way an event would go. There was no panic though – the bad had been so often that it had become the routine. The trouble was that even when something worsened, we just dealt with it, and it was hard in a way not to become blasé. It was such a closeted existence that I have absolutely no recollection of anything that went on in the outside world either, and nor did I care. Bill and I were both totally exhausted and barely slept at all apart from snatches, too frightened in case something happened, but we didn't seem to notice or worry about it, functioning entirely on automatic pilot.

As the seizures continued their savagery, Amberlie's breathing patterns changed. This was more noticeable in her sleep, when she exhaled hard and noisily. There were often pauses in her breathing, which, although lasting only a few seconds, were enough to worry about. She then seemed to remember that she had to breathe, took a deep breath and continued as normal. I asked Hayley about it and she said that it could possibly be another sign of deterioration and explained how gases exchange within the lungs.

Amberlie's fluctuating temperatures were now causing some concern and she was often hot and cold at the same time. Hayley explained that this too might be a sign of deterioration. She told us that the temperature of the body and many other basic functions were controlled by the hypothalamus in the brain, and that it was possible that the seizures were attacking and damaging that area. She said that it was not unusual for these children to eventually be unable to control their own body temperatures. The information was always a punch in the stomach but at least Bill and I were able to understand and reason what was happening to our baby.

One evening Amberlie became extremely cold and was icy to touch. No matter what we did we couldn't warm her up, so we took her to hospital where they wrapped her in silver foil blankets with other blankets on top and eventually she warmed up. The consultant said the same thing Hayley had … that maybe Amberlie's hypothalamus was now being affected.

One afternoon Bill and I decided to take Amberlie round to meet Ben from school as she was having an unusually good day, being more awake with no major seizures. It was sunny and breezy out – just the sort of day she loved.

As the children rushed out to their mums and dads, the teacher beckoned Bill and me over and said that she needed to talk to us. Apparently she was worried about Ben's learning and said she had not approached us before because of our circumstances at home, but now it was getting quite serious. Bill and I looked at each other and joined her in the classroom for a chat.

Ben had been having extra help at school for some time (which we were unaware of) because he wasn't learning his sounds and letters well, or indeed much else, and they were very concerned. Bill and I were confused. The teacher asked whether we had noticed anything at home. I told her that he was very lazy and had to be pushed into doing things, but generally I hadn't noticed anything odd. He always did his reading and handwriting practice at home. She said he was unable to read and identify even the basic sounds and that was why his reading books weren't changed very often. I wondered why he kept coming home with the same book.

I think they must have thought I was either round the bend or telling fibs or that I was so involved with Amberlie that it was taking its toll on Ben. The head teacher arrived to join our discussion. Bill asked whether they had a set of flash cards he could use. The teacher fetched them and Bill sat opposite Ben and said, 'Right Ben, what's this sound?' Ben looked at him and told him what it was.

'And what letter is it?' Ben told him. Bill went right through the entire alphabet and Ben got them all right. The teacher was amazed. She said, 'If I hadn't seen that with my own eyes I would never have believed it!'

I didn't understand why he read at home but not at school. I then remembered that he had told me he loved to play games with the helper and that it was great fun. The little bugger had been having them on and had nearly got himself on the road towards being 'statemented'. I couldn't believe he had taken it so far and got away with it! He was only five! The head teacher said that it could actually be an attention thing, spurred on initially by our situation, but now they knew what he was doing they would deal with it.

Ben obviously had a lot of catching up to do and needed to prove himself and show that he could progress. They told us they would keep us informed. We told him off when we got home and explained how important school was whether he wanted to be there or not – the latter also being a reason why he didn't feel he needed to learn!

I was quite devastated by it all though. I felt dreadfully guilty that maybe I just wasn't spending enough time with the other kids. Ben had been clever though, he read to me every night and I didn't have a clue that he was controlling a different situation at school. Ray and Clare seemed to be managing OK, but I thought I had better check, so we all sat down and had a talk about whether they were worried or finding anything difficult at school, and they looked at me as if I was barmy and said, 'No, it's the same as ever.' I also asked whether they felt that Amberlie's illness affected them at school, and they said that yes, they were worried about her when they stopped to think, but the rest of the time they were OK. They then quickly excused themselves because they were in the middle of a game when I called them!

Amberlie's seventh birthday was fast approaching and I was determined it was to be a fantastic day for her. We didn't really have a clue what to get her, so we settled on some new clothes – especially pyjamas – because she wore so many, plus T-shirts and shorts and stuff for the summertime. We braved a quick visit into town the day before so that we could look round the shops. Most of Amberlie's things were bought in the Disney Shop, so that was where we headed. On the way round we passed the cuddly toys and there was a huge 'Doc' from *Snow White and the Seven Dwarfs*. Amberlie noticed him and stared wide eyed at the huge black-and-white bespectacled eyes staring back. She shyly kept looking away and looking back, half smiling with her tongue out. I knew she liked him.

'Fancy having your very own Doc to have at home Ambams?' I said to her, and she cooed.

That was all I needed – I picked him up and plonked him on her lap in the pram. She couldn't take her eyes off him! I couldn't see the point in not letting her have him until her birthday. She watched and talked to him all the time and I could see her trying desperately hard to keep focused as the seizures bashed at her again. She had grabbed his arm and fell asleep holding on tight.

We popped into the supermarket to buy a birthday cake and couldn't decide on a chocolate caterpillar or a white one with a pink rose, so we bought both! We went and got lots of balloons and streamers, banners and anything else that caught our eyes, and her dad bought her a big bunch of pink flowers and some foil balloons.

Later that evening we bathed her, and marvelled at her beautiful fluffy mermaid hair hanging right down to her waist. We then decorated the front room while she watched totally amused and absorbed in all the colours above her. I hoped and prayed she would have a great day.

The morning followed its usual pattern, with nasty seizures on waking, but after some diazepam she settled into a nice sleep. The kids waited anxiously to help her open her cards and presents. Amberlie was brighter than usual although the seizures were attacking underneath and making her eyes wander a lot. She fought to see what was going on and played a little while with her bell ball, though this was short-lived because the combination of the noise of the bells and the physical activity needed to shake it was too much for her, and instigated some harsher seizures. It broke my heart that she could no longer do the things that made her happy. She kept her head leaning to the right most of the time and looked downwards as if she was trying to see better – maybe she was.

Later on relatives started arriving and friends called with cards and gifts. It was important to keep Amberlie as settled as possible, so she spent most of the day on either my lap or her dad's, or being carried around by us. Everybody managed a short cuddle with her but she soon became wriggly and unsettled, needing the security of what she knew. She did become a bit distressed at teatime, and I think this was down to her wearing herself out trying to see everything and fighting the seizures at the same time. We sat her in her chair later to light the candles on her cakes, and she watched for a while before more small seizures swiped her attention again. We managed to get lots and lots of photographs that day, and I was so pleased for her that she made it through without any major crises. Every now and again she got a little window through which she could enjoy herself a bit and show that she was still inside there somewhere, and I was glad her birthday was one of them.

33

One morning Amberlie woke into lots of seizures following ruthlessly one after the other, and her breathing was very laboured both in and out. It looked like she was going to be ill again. I called Hayley and she came quickly to examine her.

There had been a gradual escalation in seizures again over the previous few days and she looked as if she was bordering on status once more. Hayley said she thought it was time to take Amberlie to hospital and she phoned the ward. In the meantime Amberlie had also started trembling so much that we could actually see it. Sometimes when she was sitting on Bill's or my lap, she felt as if she was 'live' and we had to swap after a while because the sensation was too much. Dr Ramsay said she thought the trembling was down to the mixture of benzodiazepines (the family of drugs that diazepam, clobazam and nitrazepam belonged to) that Amberlie took, but I felt they were tonic-clonic seizures that were in some way prevented from surfacing.

Once at the hospital the usual tests were taken and Dr Ramsay came by. She said she was dropping the clobazam by half and wanted Amberlie to have no more than three doses of diazepam a day. At the same time she was going to follow the status protocol and give Amberlie another phenytoin driver. This time it didn't work. They had checked her chest and said it sounded pretty good considering and she certainly didn't have pneumonia. They could only assume that her laboured breathing was seizure related in some way.

The following day Amberlie seemed strangely odd and very quiet. She began to get progressively more agitated as the day went on and in the afternoon she had a nasty seizure during which she made a loud gulping sound and I thought she'd aspirated. She was given oxygen immediately and the stress dwindled away. They doctors said she should be OK now and left.

Yeah ... right, I thought, *I've seen this before ...*

'It will infect,' I said to Bill and the nurse.

Later that evening, Amberlie's temperature started to rise and I noticed a rash appearing on her trunk and called the nurse. The rash quickly spread all over her until she was lobster red in colour. No one seemed to know what it was and presumed it was viral. I had a sneaking suspicion that it had been the phenytoin, and that it had been just one too many drugs now; it wasn't anybody's fault – everyone was doing their best to help her.

Amberlie despite it all, was now quite sedate and restful. The nurse suggested I try to get some rest while they kept an eye on her. I was totally exhausted and the thought of some sleep was appealing, so I snuggled down on the bed next to her. As my head touched the pillow Amberlie made an awful noise and threw up everywhere! She then started at the other end with incessant diarrhoea. Her seizures took on another dimension under all the stress and she was given some paraldehyde, which they had managed to order in just for her. It did have some effect in quietening her seizures but it did nothing for her poor bottom, leaving her very red and raw, having taken the top layer of skin off. The nurse and I changed and washed her from top to toe and I used virtually a whole pot of cream topped with baby powder to help soothe and protect her bottom under her nappy. Finally, ages later, she settled and went back to sleep.

Dr Thomas, who had originally diagnosed Amberlie when she was a baby, was the consultant on duty the next day, and he said that after much thought and discussions with Dr Ramsay, they would be starting Amberlie on oral phenytoin. I did not agree that this was a good idea. I still didn't like the drug, it had had no effect on her this time even in a large dose on the driver, and I also now had my suspicions about its possible toxicity. It was sensible to me, therefore, than any smaller oral dose would be a complete waste of time. Dr Thomas said, 'You must understand Sandra, that we are up against a wall here and anything has to be worth a try.'

'I understand all that, but what's the point of her taking a drug that is likely to be ineffective, and that has awful side effects which will make her feel ill with sickness on top of what she already has to suffer? And what happens when she goes into status again – what are we supposed to use if she is already taking the drug that's supposed to be your one and only answer? No I am not happy for her to have it.'

Dr Thomas turned to one of the registrars and said, 'Perhaps you could arrange for the pharmacist to come and talk to Sandra about the drug and its side effects today.'

The pharmacist arrived within minutes and she sat and had a long chat with Bill and me. I explained that the last driver had not worked significantly in controlling Amberlie's seizures and that I wasn't convinced about its usefulness. She explained that I was quite right about the side effects, and said that if the drug hadn't worked within four hours of being put in through a driver, any oral dose would probably prove ineffective. I informed Dr Thomas again that I was refusing the drug.

I knew now that if Amberlie did go into status again, her chances would be less than slim. I wasn't going to give her anything that was going to make her feel worse than she already did. I couldn't imagine anything worse than having to live with feeling sick all the time.

Later on that night after Bill had gone home, the doctors visited again and said Bill and I needed to prepare ourselves for the worst now, and that morphine would be available if we felt Amberlie was distressed. I nodded.

At that moment nothing hurt anymore. It was very weird as I disengaged myself from the world and the only people in it were her and me; it was almost like I hadn't heard the doctors or I totally ignored them completely, and I sat talking and stroking her head in the lamplight, telling her how beautiful she was and how much I

362

loved her, and that she was a really clever girl to keep putting him with all this stuff. I know she heard me because even though her eyes were closed she gave a little smile and a tiny coo.

The next evening she became very upset and couldn't settle at all. The doctors took a look at her and said they would give her a small amount of morphine just to see if she would settle. I agreed saying, 'Just a little though ...' They knew it was a warning.

When they tried to put it in her tube they found it was blocked and Amberlie wouldn't let them touch it, flicking them away and putting the back of her hand on her face! I knew then she didn't want it, so I told them to take it away.

Amberlie's temperature had remained dangerously high at 39.9°C for three days now, and she had not sweated at all. That night it started to drop (although it was still fluctuating), and she began to visibly relax and settle and the colour improved in her face. This was not her time, and I smiled at her amazing ability to pull herself out of hell.

The next day Amberlie was wide awake, wonderfully relaxed, despite lots of interfering seizures, and responding well to Bill and me. She had been on oxygen for most of the time and her chest still sounded bubbly, but it had improved somewhat so the doctors reduced her intake a little. Dr Ramsay had been in several times to see her, and even left a barbecue she was attending with her husband on the Sunday afternoon to visit because she was so worried about her. In she walked that morning absolutely astounded that Amberlie had yet again made it through. I asked if it was possible to take her home and Dr Ramsay thought it was a good idea.

'Now ...' she said, 'Amberlie is going to need oxygen and I will get Hayley to organise that, and I also want you to have a saturation (oxygen) monitor at home. Hayley will let me know if you need anything else. And remember – I am at the end of the phone if you need me; and if at any time you want to bring her back, just ring and tell the ward to you are on your way. A room will be kept available for my Amberlie.'

The kids had visited Amberlie every day at the hospital but were still shocked when we arrived home with Amberlie wearing an oxygen mask attached to a small cylinder. They had been so used to her coming home from hospital 'fixed' and naturally assumed that this time would be no different. We explained that she was very, very poorly and that she would probably stay a bit like this for the moment. We told them that there would be some big cylinders of oxygen coming to help Amberlie breathe better, and as we settled her down there was a knock at the door and six huge ones arrived.

Within half an hour her temperature had gone sky high again and we had to tepid bathe her to try to get it down. She was already on four-hourly paracetamol to try to keep her stable. We managed to get the temperature down after about half an hour and that was the last high fly she had. We monitored her carefully and noticed many fluctuations that were obviously due to her deterioration. The diarrhoea persisted and Amberlie stayed on a salt-and-glucose mixture for another three days. Eventually the diarrhoea petered out, taking the rash with it. Amberlie had a few very stable days following that, although the seizures had resumed their full pelt and she was probably having at least a hundred a day. The reduction in benzodiazepines had released the previously pent up tonic-clonic seizures, and when they came they were bloody awful. As ever, nothing was predictable, and gradually the seizures changed again and most of the tonic-clonics were replaced by complex partial seizures, which led her straight back into status. There were breaks every now and again thankfully, but there was little we could do and all the time she slept peacefully, I could see no harm in it.

Amberlie had been constantly poorly for almost five months now and Hayley was with us every day, often for hours at a time. She supported us endlessly and was gently beginning to tell us that Amberlie was now suffering.

I couldn't actually face what she was saying and being a very persuasive and manipulative person when I wanted to be, I talked myself, her and Bill in and out of arguments for and against Amberlie's suffering. I always remembered Dr Ramsay telling me that where her seizures were concerned, it was far worse for us than for her because she wouldn't know anything about them – so I almost dismissed the status part. Every now and again Amberlie came through a little window with a knowing, recognising glint in her eye, perhaps with the odd half smile and that gave me all the overriding optimism I needed to stick to my theories. Most of the time though, her eyes were totally black and dilated, and I knew that she couldn't see anything.

She could hear though, and when Bill or I or the kids went to her she turned her head towards us and listened with a knowing expression on her face. It must have been so hard for her hearing us but not being able to see our faces. We didn't know how long she had been blind or whether it came and went so often that she didn't worry about it. It was obviously down to whatever type of seizure she was having at the time. There was so much going on that we didn't or couldn't see.

Hayley listened and understood and patiently waited days and days for me to realise that I was actually losing my arguments and that my reasons were thinning down fast. Bill had sorted much of it in his mind and was very quiet all the time I talked. I knew they were waiting for me to make a decision and I couldn't. No one was pushing me but I knew they were waiting …

Amberlie had always sorted it … she'd always pulled herself through before … maybe if she had a little more time …

One afternoon while I was out picking up a prescription for Amberlie, Bill had a phone call from work. He had been walking up and down carrying Amberlie in an attempt to settle her after another huge bout of seizures and still had her in his arms. The phone call was to inform him that when he returned to work he was not to go to his branch but to report straight to the area office, where it would be decided what to do with him. The full extent of what was said didn't sink in straight away and by the time I returned he was in a dreadful state along with Amberlie.

'You need to get back on the phone and sort this out,' I said to him.

They said that he would not be working in the same branch again due to the length of time he had been absent from work. Bill tried to explain all that had happened and that the bank was now causing additional stress on top of everything else. He said he had been covered by doctor's notes for the entire time and was disappointed at the lack of support he had received from the bank and would be contacting the union. After the call, he was very upset and said, 'It's obvious they think I've been swinging the lead all this time ... I just don't believe it.'

Later on his line manager called and tried to justify the decision they were making. Bill refused to accept it and said he had spoken to the union and was well within his rights, and that the bank could not do that while he was away on sick leave. The discussion rapidly became more heated and Bill was informed that he would have to go down the formal grievance procedure to make his complaint. The intimation was that Bill was not being truthful about his situation and naturally, that made him angry. He told his manager that he was very welcome to come and see how ill Amberlie was, and complained that during the whole time no one from the bank had bothered to ring or call or visit to see how everything was, and he was disappointed that after twenty years of working for them with hardly a day off sick, he was now being treated like scum.

I was pacing up and down the hall with Amberlie now getting very agitated. I shouted, 'Tell him I'll go to the Sun newspaper with this or any other paper that will listen.'

The manager said that he wouldn't advise me to do that, and I heard Bill say, 'I don't even tell Sandra what to do – so I don't see that you can!'

'What!' I shouted. 'Who the hell does he think he is?'

The conversation ended abruptly and Bill slammed the phone down in disgust.

About thirty minutes later, the phone rang again. This time it was a formal apology for all the stress caused and Bill was told that his job was safe and would remain so. He also asked Bill to apologise to me, to which Bill said, 'No, you can do that yourself.'

He apologised but I was unsympathetic.

'Nobody's bothered to come down here to see Bill or see the situation for yourselves, and all you've done is make things worse for him. You have no idea what everyone is going through at the moment. Our daughter is dying and you people are so up yourselves in your own little castles, that you have no thought, consideration or sympathy, let alone support for people who have worked their guts out in your bank for years on end without complaint or problem. Just you remember in your lives: what goes around, come around.'

I looked at Bill and said, 'Forget it Wills ... they don't matter.'

Bill told Hayley after and she was very concerned about all this on top of everything else, and couldn't believe the bank's attitude – after all, a paediatric palliative care nurse supports the whole family.

34

The sun had been shining gloriously in the back garden all day and it was warm and bright. Amberlie was having a really good day for some reason, and she was alert and happy, with only the occasional small seizure disturbing her peace. She had slept a fair amount while the kids were at school and now she was well awake so I thought it would be nice to take her outside where she could watch the trees. Clare laid out a blanket on the grass and scattered lots of cushions about so Amberlie would be comfortable. She was wearing her pale green T-shirt and shorts and she looked lovely and fresh. I laid her down and she happily kicked her legs and smiled and cooed to herself while Clare, I and the dog sat with her. It was so beautiful out there, the five o'clock light was meditative and calming and full of the colours of a real summer's evening. I went and got the camera and took lots of pictures of Clare and Amberlie together, and she took some of Amberlie with me. We stayed out there until the chill of the coming dusk moved us inside.

35

20 June 2000

I'm sitting here looking at Amberlie. She is propped up on pillows with duvets and a sleeping bag underneath her. She hasn't woken today. Her saturation monitor alarms every time she is about to go into a tonic-clonic seizure as her breathing pattern changes and her oxygen intake reduces. The alarm went off last night at 9.30 signalling the start of yet another assault of tree fits, and they have continued ever since in intermittent clusters. Her colour is barely better than the pure white blanket covering her.

22 – 23 June 2000

This is doing my head in. I feel lousy. I feel like my body's a void, but it hurts with the familiar, deep searing pain that burns pathways in different directions all the way through. My head is dull and it's hard to think – I don't want to think. Hayley keeps reminding me that Amberlie is suffering now … she's being as gentle as she can. I can't make a decision. Every now and again she wakes and looks around – little windows … She's still in there somewhere … How can I take that away?

Amberlie is 'live'. She is on the go nearly all the time she is awake. She fidgets in a stressful irritated way, arching her back amidst dozens of uncoordinated, involuntary movements, as if she is trying to make it go away. Her left arm keeps shooting up and her hand is bent forward like a submarine periscope. She frantically rubs her fist into her nose, which also seems to be irritating her no end. I hate it. And I hate it that I can't do anything about it. The diazepam doesn't seem to work anymore and the chloral, having already been increased, will knock her flat, but it won't stop the fits. She's exhausted. Bill and I do our best to comfort her on our laps, cuddling her as she drifts back off to sleep only to tree fit every three minutes. There haven't been so many full on tonic-clonic seizures today – only two, plus facial grimaces and constant shudders. She gets no peace.

Amberlie can't bear to be on her own, instantly crying if she is laid down. She needs her cuddles and I am so worried that she is frightened.

We had to put her back on the anti-dribble patches because she just couldn't cope with her saliva, and I think that they are responsible for the increased seizures. I know I'm looking for reasons, excuses … clutching at straws, anything to explain it all. The pattern is the same as before: initially more seizures then they slow up as the patch wears out and she gets almost a 'rest' day, but this time it's different. There is no rest day – she didn't get her day off even though the tonic-clonics were less. I have to try taking it away. Hayley said we could take her to hospital. I asked what they would do different there, and she said she didn't know, but that they would try again to bring the status under control.

'And do you think they would be able to?' I asked. She shook her head,

'Probably not,' she replied.

'Then that will be the end won't it? Because they will put her on heminevrin and they won't be able to get her off it because no other drugs work anymore. So they'll just increase it or add morphine until she's gone.'

Hayley nodded. I sighed with the pain and said, 'No, she stays here.'

Amberlie can't win. When the fits are reasonable, she gets a chest infection and that starts the whole circle rolling again … and every time the fits grow stronger and stronger and stronger. I hear Dr Ramsay's voice in my head telling me, 'That's because her brain thinks it is natural to fit … so it fights to fit instead of the other way round.'

The dribbling is back and it's worse. It is copious and incessant and she's swallowing every few seconds. She can't cope. A quarter patch is not enough so we are trying a third. Amberlie eventually settled and slept fairly well through the night, snuggled tightly between her dad and me in our bed. The seizures were still going under the surface and I could feel her trembles and shudders. When the bigger ones came, she held her breath and her eyelids slightly opened, and I could see that her eyes had gone up into her head.

At 7.30 a.m. the seizures surfaced again and the nose rubbing started and the tree fits appeared. Amberlie woke for a short time but soon got upset, wanting her cuddles so she could snuggle back down to sleep where she felt safe, even though the tree fits interrupted her every few minutes.

Bill fed her while she was in my arms. We don't want her to be hungry.

She had another bout of diarrhoea the night before last, which has now disappeared and we are keeping her on plain flavours of milk for the time being in case one of those didn't agree with her. On the positive side, Amberlie does seem to be a better colour today – there's a little more pink in her cheeks. I know it's probably only temporary, because her colour changes so fast and she is usually very pale with dark eyes, and occasionally she blues up all over. I was right. A while later the saturation monitor started alarming again, showing her oxygen was dipping and staying low. Hayley turned it off so it wouldn't keep disturbing Amberlie.

A special oxygen machine was delivered today. It was to avoid having to keep having cylinders delivered from the chemist, and removed the possibility and worry of it running out. The machine made its own oxygen when it was plugged into the normal electricity and could be easily moved around the house. In fact the man who sorted it out actually left enough tubing to reach from the machine to any room in the house so that Amberlie could have it anywhere without us moving everything. There was so much of it that we had to tape it to the walls to stop the kids getting caught up in it.

The seizures have caused an enormous amount of muck to collect in Amberlie's throat and I cannot clear it – it's too far down – and neither can she. She is having enormous trouble breathing through it especially after a fit, and we think that there might be some constricting happening in the base of her throat as a result of the seizures. Her laboured outward breaths show that her lungs are not working as efficiently to exchange gases, and again this peaks during high seizure activity.

Amberlie is as tough as old boots in her way, and I just don't know how she gets through it all. Her drug tolerance is incredible … What she takes would knock a dinosaur flat and they don't even touch her! She seems to want to survive and I wish there was a new drug that would stop all this and sort her out. But now there will be more damage to her brain because of all the seizures and what would that mean for her? More chest infections that will eventually kill her anyway. It is still hard to accept that she is technically incompatible with life, and without the modern anti-convulsants we wouldn't have had her for very long at all – ten to fifteen years earlier, she would have been dead at four and a half months. I asked Hayley what it is that makes her want to live when she has so much to overcome and put up with … what is it that makes her fight? And she said, 'Sandra, there is so much love in this house … and that is what keeps her alive and wanting to be with you all…'

I can't bear it – I can't stop crying.

I am watching her sleeping … and apart from her tube she looks so beautiful and so normal, despite her changing colours. Her hair is so strawberry blonde and in such pristine condition that it shines in the light, and her skin is still unblemished. She has the longest, curliest eyelashes I have ever seen and a wonderfully shaped mouth. How could anything be wrong with her? That bastard grey matter in her head is slowly destroying her.

If there is a God, I cannot for the life of me understand why he makes children suffer. Why do that to the pure and innocent? It makes more sense to accept that there is no God and that it was just nature 'gone wrong', as it does from time to time … and perhaps the result of a poisoned planet. I only have humankind to thank for my Amberlie's survival: evolution, intelligence and science is why I still have her, and why she enjoyed her life for what it was. God would have taken her back at four and a half months old. Maybe that was what was meant to happen – perhaps he makes mistakes too – not so perfect after all.

25 – 26 June 2000

Ambams was more awake yesterday and without being too distressed about it. There were a lot of awful trembles and batches of tree fits and one tonic while she slept. The diazepam actually seemed to relieve the trembles for a short time but I have noticed that if she is disturbed after it – either by noise or fits – they seem to return much harsher, as if they have unfinished business. The chloral seems to be working well at the moment, and having rectal paracetamol keeps some of her headaches at bay and maintains a settling effect on her.

There are still occasional little windows when Amberlie still seems to be aware of us, and I sometimes still get a coo when I tell her how beautiful and clever she is and while she is getting big kisses on her cheeks. The response if often fleeting, but so treasured.

When we put her in bed she was fairly settled and I thought she was going to manage to drift off herself without her usual chloral, but it was not to be and she soon needed it when she became restless. In the night she woke me, trembling hard and her breathing laboured. She was boiling hot and sweating buckets, and

373

the noise was worse in the base of her throat. It sounded like trapped mucus bubbling and cracking. I couldn't get a decent temperature reading from the ear thermometer so I couldn't see how high her temperature actually was. I gave her paracetamol, stripped her down and she started to settle. I assume that the rise in temperature was what made her tremble so badly. She went back to sleep and went right through until 1.30 p.m.

It wasn't long before being awake made her fidget and tremble again … she just couldn't take any sort of stimulation – opening her eyes was too much for her. I quickly washed and dressed her and brushed her hair, which seemed to distract her a little but she ended up having diazepam, which only gave her a few minutes' reprieve, and the seizures resumed their attack.

As the afternoon progressed, her breathing was awful again, it sounded just like her chest was filling up with water – every breath was bubbling. Hayley suggested increasing the patch slightly to see if it would help. Amberlie's temperature suddenly went sky high again and she was very hot and rosy red. I gave her some more paracetamol, which worked quickly and effectively again. We haven't needed the oxygen for the past few days as she has maintained her levels, but now she's back on it and it looks like we're heading for another infection.

It is soul destroying. The seizures are out of control and here she goes again with her chest. It's too much and I burst into tears again.

Hayley gently suggested that we ought to consider not giving her any more antibiotics again because they're not working effectively and are not clearing everything. She said most of Amberlie's infections seem to start virally and that meant the antibiotics were useless anyway. She was very concerned about the vicious circle Amberlie was living and said it was all prolonging her distress.

As usual I reasoned the point and said that I wanted her to have every chance – she had pulled herself through in February –

maybe she could do it again? Hayley nodded, she could see I wasn't ready.

'This way,' she said. 'Amberlie at least gets a chance to fight and build up some immunity of her own rather than having all her antibodies killed off by antibiotics that aren't working anyway.'

It was still a devastating decision to not treat her. Even though we had made it before, it was no easier now. It was all a gamble. Realistically things have changed since February, it's not the same situation now … her seizures are worse, and she is not as strong. I know if we sort out her chest again she will return to her world of seizures because that is what her normal is now. I just want someone to come and give me a miracle cure! … Please.

But I know my Ambams is frightened … And I have to make a bloody decision … and I can't bring myself to say 'yes' … because I'm terrified too.

It wasn't a good night. We went to bed at about 11.30 p.m. Amberlie's breathing had been bad all evening, struggling with the stuff lodged in her throat. Her chest was puffing and her nostrils flaring. The noise in her throat was awful and we tried two lots of nebulisers, suction, reluctant and careful physio because we were terrified of moving something into a fatal place now, and anything else we could think of that might shift it. She had her usual chloral but the breathing wouldn't let her rest and she lay there concentrating hard on what she was doing. We gave her some diazepam to try to ease the incessant trembling and turned the lamp to minimum to see if she would settle. Apart from the awful persistent noise from her chest, Amberlie managed to sleep through until 8 a.m. when she turned herself onto her left side and the noise vanished. She slept peacefully for a further couple of hours.

She woke again with the trembles and was an awful colour. She needed oxygen to maintain her saturations and the noises had returned in her throat. She looked bloody awful … in fact I would say she looked the worst I had ever seen her.

36

Hayley arrived at around mid-morning with news that Laura had returned from leave, and was now back at work and would be popping in to see us. I was pleased but we had now become so attached to Hayley that I panicked and said I didn't want to lose her visits. She said she would of course continue to look after Amberlie but that Laura would do some of the visits because of her experience in epilepsy, and that it might do us good to talk to her about all the seizures and drugs again.

Laura came the next day. I was glad and relieved to see her, especially as Amberlie had not woken that morning and her seizures were continual. Laura couldn't hide her shock when she saw how ill Amberlie was, and I tried hard to shrug her reaction away with a quick 'mmm ...' After observing her for a few minutes she said that Amberlie was definitely in some sort of complex partial seizure status and that we must do something about it. That was Laura – very definite – no mincing her words. She rang Dr Ramsay, who called her back a few minutes later. She was at a loss as to what to do and said the only thing she could suggest was to try the Topamax again. She thought maybe starting her on a small dose at night might enhance one of the other drugs. It was worth a go.

Laura said the medicine had to be sprinkled on Amberlie's food.

'So – is it supposed to go down her tube then?' I asked.

'We'll have to try a few bits at a time flushed through with water,' she replied, worried.

It took ages and ages each time, but it was the only way to get it into her. Anyway, there was no sudden miracle cure and in fact it didn't seem to do anything at all. I called Dr Ramsay. She said this particular drug worked better in smaller doses but I sensed there was also a fear factor playing a part due to Amberlie's bad reaction to the drug when it was first tried. Now, in hindsight, I felt that maybe I hadn't given it enough of a chance and that maybe Amberlie had been in a prolonged absence seizure that would have happened anyway, and it was just coincidence that it happened when the drug was introduced. I got upset. Bill said, 'We did what we thought was best at the time. It could have been a deterioration that happened anyway, but really it was too much of a coincidence to have overlooked it. And Dr Ramsay would have told us straight if she thought we had been wrong.' I didn't feel any better.

Laura had spoken to Dr Ramsay, and said gently, 'We really don't think that increasing the dose will make any difference now, Sandra ...'

Amberlie's chest was bubbling again and the patches were becoming ineffective. They had started to cause burn marks where they had stuck to her skin. Hayley suggested moving them around but wherever they were the same thing happened. They weren't easily treated with bathing and creaming either. I moaned and insisted they try something else. Hayley called our GP and he came straight away and prescribed a tablet version that Amberlie would have to take eight-hourly. These proved totally useless and her lungs continued to fill up. Hayley could not hear anything at all in the bottom lobe of her right lung and said that it had been worsening over the last few days, but she could hear air in the top lobe. Her left lung was getting quieter in the lower lobe but was changeable in the middle and upper lobes.

Amberlie's breathing was very changeable – one moment she would be breathing from her stomach and the next she was breathing from her chest in irregular patterns and there were lots of long, worrying pauses.

The nurses were continually preparing Bill and me for the worst and trying to get me organised enough to make a decision. But Amberlie kept managing to sort herself out and would return to normal breathing, and I thought that was because the muck was continually moving around in her lungs and throat, and that the seizures were controlling that – or rather, fouling it all up.

Amberlie had no peace from the seizures now. They followed one after the other hour after hour – hundreds and hundreds of them. We still persisted with the diazepam in the hope that it would give her the occasional break, and sometimes it did seem to take the edge off a few of the worst.

Amberlie was still filling up like a bucket and both Hayley and Laura were becoming increasingly concerned about Amberlie suffering. They sat down and fully explained to us about the medications that would make her comfortable. Hayley said that it was time to get the GP organised and to have the medicines here with us in the house ready for when we needed them, unless we wanted to take her to hospital.

'No,' I said. 'This is her home and she loves it here.'

The medicines were ready that afternoon. I put them high in the cupboard and out of sight. They were dangerous and I didn't want the kids getting hold of them, and I didn't want to see them around either. I pushed the driver machine to one side as well, ignoring its existence.

Amberlie was now becoming upset and was obviously very distressed. I could cope with it all when she was sleeping through and not bothered by any of it.

She had a terrible night with incessant seizures and she was boiling hot again. Her breathing was terrible and frightening and I knew I had to do something – she couldn't keep on like this … It wasn't fair. I said to Bill, 'I just wish she would go to sleep and not wake up again, and that way she wouldn't know anything about it.'

He nodded.

Laura came the next morning. Amberlie's seizures were more powerful than ever and her chest sounded dreadful.

'Oh Sandra, she is suffering so badly now. It really is time to make a decision. I know it's the worst thing on earth and no one can possibly understand what it is like … but for Amberlie's sake … You have done everything possible to make this little girl's life happy and comfortable and there is no more you can do …'

'Jesus Christ…' I mumbled through gritted teeth as I sat on the sofa rocking backwards and forwards, I tried to hold onto the tears but they poured anyway.

'Can't we just try little bits of the drugs … just to see if they would bring things under control?' I pleaded.

'No. They wouldn't touch Amberlie in small doses now – she's too resilient to them, and you know they won't hold the seizures. Her brain will fight everything to continue fitting because that is what it thinks is normal. Her heart is working far too hard and we have to consider what might happen if it fails … You also have her chest to consider … she's struggling to breathe.'

I still couldn't do it. Laura left Bill and me to talk about it and said, 'It's better I leave you for a while. When you are ready, just call me.'

We had talked it over for days and days. I could rationalise it, understand it and talk about it … but I still couldn't do it. I didn't feel it was anybody's right to end a life, and that all the time Amberlie was fighting, then she had to want to live. Deep down I knew that she probably wasn't aware of much at all and the little times that she was made her upset. I wanted to be able to ask her what she wanted me to do. I didn't want to do the wrong thing and make her hate me forever … And I also didn't want to hate myself forever either.

Bill had already made his decision but he never lost patience with me. He listened and at no time did he push me at all. I could see it in his face though. I was running out of my own arguments, and when I looked at Amberlie … I knew it was time.

I was still rocking in the chair. I hadn't moved for ages. I didn't have the power in my legs to get up, but as the sickness welled up in my throat, I shot out of the room, only making the bathroom just in time before I threw up and spent the next half hour on my knees beside the toilet, sobbing my heart out and violently retching.

I went back in the front room and said, 'I'll ring Laura.'

It was the hardest, most awful, soul-wrenching decision of my entire life. I had no option for Amberlie's sake. We had got so used to living on a bad level, adapting to each worsening one as if it was normal. This was the way it was, the way it had always been – we had just made the best of it, sorting out the worst of it as we went along. It was too hard to accept that we couldn't get her past this – it was like giving in. I had made the decision and I couldn't believe it – I felt as if I had two brains fighting each other over what was best. I desperately wanted to take it back.

It was Tuesday, 4 July and Laura was busy setting up all the equipment and medication. It took ages and ages and Laura explained what she was doing as she went along. Everything had to be logged and written down and the medicines were carefully measured and sorted. I had to witness them to agree that she had done as she had written, so that everything was accounted for.

After rubbing some local anaesthetic cream on Amberlie's leg, Laura put in what is called a sub-cut infusion, which is actually a tiny needle tucked just under the skin into the tissues. She explained that this initial infusion would take six hours to work and Amberlie should then start to settle down. She didn't though, nothing changed at all and in the night Amberlie actually managed to pull it out of her thigh, leaking the medicine all down her side. Her breathing was still awful and there was no relief from the seizures. I stayed beside her, watching her all night, terrified of falling asleep and terrified of what might happen. I didn't want to take her to hospital – as long as she stayed asleep she wouldn't be upset. As soon as the morning came I rang Laura. She came straight away and said that it would be better to re-site the infusion in her tummy.

'Oh no – that's awful!' I said.

Laura explained that it was actually quite comfortable and that a lot of children with diabetes inject themselves straight into their tummies. Amberlie didn't flinch at all and seemed quite comfy with it. Laura made sure it was all well stuck down this time. After talking to Matt, our other GP, the medicines were increased and a drug to control her secretions was added to the mixture and the tablets stopped. The bubbling and cracking soon improved in her chest but the seizures were still menacing their way through the medicines – Amberlie's drug tolerance was amazing. I began to get very fidgety and anxious that she still wasn't comfortable. They'd promised me that she wouldn't keep suffering and it all seemed to be getting worse and worse. My nerves were shattered and holding it all together was proving an almighty task.

It was another awful night. Just after midnight Amberlie had the most terrible, nasty tree fits imaginable, followed by lots of complex partial seizures that really upset her. We couldn't console her. Bill and I took it in turns to hold her, rock her, carry her but we couldn't calm her down. I felt so sorry for her. Her chest filled up quickly again and there was just no peace for her at all.

Hayley was now very worried that the morphine wasn't doing its job properly and asked Matt to come and see Amberlie. He said he wasn't surprised that the medicines didn't touch her and that she would now have to go onto diamorphine which was more powerful in smaller quantities. The medazolam was increased as well in the hope that it would control the seizures. I had already told them at the beginning that I was doubtful that this drug would be effective because it was related to the same family as the diazepam, and those drugs were useless to her now. It seemed I was right, but they hoped that the increase in the two powerful drugs mixed together would be more effective.

The next morning Amberlie aspirated her food and thankfully Laura was there. Somehow the seizures caused her stomach to eject the food formula, shoving it back up her tube and into her lungs. It was dreadful. There was already no room in her chest for an aspiration and as she desperately fought to breathe, the stuff poured endlessly out of her nose and mouth – she was breathing it. The poor little soul must have been in agony. As awful as it was, it wasn't time to panic – she needed help, and I crazily suctioned everything I could away, somehow managing to clear it from her nose and throat. After lots of oxygen and cuddles Amberlie's breathing settled down to, I suppose, a reasonable level. Laura said, 'You did well.'

It had shocked me terribly and now that everything was calmer I was shaking all over. I couldn't get the awful pictures out of my head.

The seizures kept coming and I was convinced we would have to end up taking her to hospital to have the heminevrin because this just wasn't working. Amberlie did settle quite a lot around lunchtime and we spent that afternoon snuggled up together on the sofa in the warm sunshine.

That evening the seizures took on another strength and Amberlie screamed horrifically in the pauses. We couldn't do anything to help her and were devastated by all her distress. I said to Bill, 'If she doesn't settle within the next hour, I'm taking her to hospital. This is just not fair to her – she's suffering and I can't stand it.'

I think she must have heard me because a few minutes later she calmed down. I decided not to take her to bed that night. She seemed quite settled and comfortable on her cushions and duvet on the floor so I was very reluctant to move her. I told Bill I would stay downstairs with her. Bill said, 'Me too.'

Apart from the usual seizures, she had nothing nasty and managed to sleep. I dozed on and off beside her on the floor all night, keeping my ears on full alert in case there were any changes.

At 6 a.m. I heard the doorbell ring. I looked at the clock thinking, who on earth can it be at this time? There was no one there. I went back into the front room, Bill was still asleep on the sofa and Amberlie hadn't moved.

'Strange,' I said quietly.

I carefully snuggled back up to Amberlie and closed my eyes. It rang again. I got up and as I did Bill opened his eyes. There was still no one there and I said to him, 'Did you hear the doorbell?'

'No,' he said and snuggled back down to sleep.

I went back to Amberlie and snuggled up to her again. Suddenly I felt as if someone was looking over my shoulder and I heard a voice say, 'I'm sorry.'

I opened my eyes and turned my head. There was nobody there. I looked at Amberlie who had woken and was smiling broadly at me and sucking her tongue between her lips as she always used to. But as I looked at her I knew that the voice I heard had come to tell me that I was going to lose my baby that day. I gasped and gulped.

Bill was looking at me.

'Did you hear that?'

'What?' he said.

'That voice – what it said … you must have done.'

'What voice?'

I told him what had happened.

'OK you probably think I'm barmy, and yeah maybe I am going round the twist, but I know what I heard, and I also know that we're going to lose her today.'

Bill looked devastated and he slumped back in the chair.

I wondered who it could have been and why say 'I'm sorry'? I was a great believer in the other world and thought it might have been my mum or dad who had spoken to me – but why apologise? There had only ever been one entity that I was angry with – and that was God. He was letting me know he was taking my baby away … and that's when he and I parted company.

Amberlie was more alert and not in the least bit sleepy! I gave her a drink and she drifted off for another nap. Hayley brought another nurse with her about mid-morning and explained that she would be taking over Amberlie's care for the weekend. I was in the middle of washing Amberlie when they arrived and she was watching me as I talked to her. Jen, the nurse, came over and said hello to her and Amberlie immediately turned her head towards her and looked her up and down, giving her the once over! Jen was delighted that Amberlie responded to her, and as Hayley looked over she said, 'Amberlie, you're awake! You shouldn't be awake!' She was totally stunned by her ability to override the medicines again!

Amberlie just looked at her, gave a little shrug of her shoulders, and with a smug look on her face turned back to watch me. She looked long and lovingly into my eyes and I could see that old twinkle she had deep inside. She then smiled and looked very chuffed with herself.

I was enjoying her. It was like old times and I forgot all that had gone before.

I changed her clothes and brushed her hair, tying it up as I always had. She looked beautiful.

Then she started to look preoccupied again and the complex partial seizures took over, and my heart sank as I was suddenly tossed back into reality with the most violent, sickening tree fit I had ever seen, which literally sent her sprawling off her cushions onto the floor, bending her over forwards, and then forcing her backwards into an arch. It was so powerful that it was throwing her around like a rubber doll. To top it all, she aspirated again and her breathing instantly deteriorated. The seizure wasn't giving up and in an attempt to try and stop it we gave her two doses of diazepam together. It soon took the edge off it but she was desperately struggling to breathe.

Hayley was shocked. We all were. She scrambled for her mobile phone saying, 'I need to get hold of Matt quickly otherwise things will become terrible.'

Matt arrived a few minutes later. They were going to give her the maximum dose but warned that it would still take four to six hours to work. He was stunned, and couldn't believe how much diamorphine Amberlie tolerated. Hayley said, 'This is a huge dose … What she has had already would be enough to kill an adult straight away.'

I closed my eyes and shook my head.

I watched as they put the medicine into her. It was nearly twelve o'clock and Amberlie went blue very quickly. It was a horrible blue – her lips were so dark, they were almost black. She was fighting for air.

The phone rang. Hayley answered it. It was Clare's school. Apparently she had been in the office with a headache virtually all morning and needed someone to come and collect her. Bill was all sixes and sevens – he didn't know what to do. I said, 'Go … Amberlie won't go until everyone is here. It's OK.'

He shot out of the door.

Hayley said she didn't think Amberlie would hang on much longer and asked for the number of Ben's school so that he could come home too. Ray was already home on an inset day.

Amberlie was getting bluer and bluer. Her nails and toenails were so black, as were her ever-darkening lips. She was breathing so hard. I picked her up so that I could hold her in my arms, hoping it would make her feel a bit better. As I cuddled her, some of the blueness faded away and she didn't look quite so bad. She started to settle a little and although her breathing remained noisy, it was less of a struggle for her, and she did not appear to be distressed. She was now asleep. After a while the noises lessened off and her breathing returned to normal. Her seizures had gone – there was no trace, and she slept peacefully in my arms. It was a relief to see them go. Hayley said, 'She's amazing you know, I thought she was going there and then. Perhaps she won't go until the kids are all here, maybe you're right – perhaps she has a purpose.'

I looked at her.

'Yeah ... maybe ... big Ray and Auntie Pat are coming too. They both called earlier to say they were on their way.'

Hayley continued, 'She wants everyone here who she loved. It's incredible how people hang on for certain reasons or until someone arrives ... It happens a lot ... They only go when they are ready.'

I smiled at her and nodded my head, holding desperately onto my tears. I took a deep breath. 'Well, knowing Ambams and her willpower, she's certainly not going until it suits her ... and that's fine by me.' And I chewed away at my lips as the tears stung and blinded my vision.

Ben's head teacher brought him home. She came in to say how sorry she was and offered to help in any way she could. I smiled, nodded and thanked her and she left. Bill had returned with Clare.

We all sat together in the front room. Ben asked why Amberlie was looking a bit of a funny colour and we told him, and the others, that she was so very ill now and that she was dying.

'Oh,' he said. They all sat quietly around her.

'Is it OK to touch her?' he asked.

'Course it is,' I said. 'She's fast asleep ... she won't mind if you're nice and gentle.' Ben bent over and kissed her. I looked away so he didn't see my tears. Ray sat and held her hand and Clare played with her hair.

Hayley said she would leave us all for a while and would come back later, or sooner if we wanted her. I nodded.

With Bill's help I moved Amberlie and myself up on to the sofa where we were both more comfortable and that's where we stayed. She was snuggled up close and tight to me and seemed fine. In the meantime big Ray and Auntie Pat came about 3 p.m.

Bill occasionally looked at the monitors but we decided to turn them off as her oxygen intake was slowly decreasing and I really didn't want to know.

The kids stayed close by and occasionally came up and stroked Amberlie's cheek or her hair. Her colour wasn't bad and she stayed sound asleep. I had no desire to move at all and wasn't about to put her down for anything.

At about 3.40 p.m., I noticed a change in her breathing. She had been consistently breathing from her upper chest and it had suddenly gone very quiet, and there were now little tiny breaths in a steady pattern ... but her chest was not moving any more.

'Bill,' I called quietly, and everyone else came too.

The little breaths got quicker and quicker until she started to pause between them ... Then there were three deep breaths and she slipped away ... no fight ... no struggle ... she just stopped.

37

The overwhelming, searing, burning, slicing rush of pain was too much to bear and I screamed, 'Oh my God! She's gone, she's gone…' as I rocked her in my arms, crying and screaming and crying. Amberlie looked so beautiful, asleep and calm. Everyone was crying and no one knew what to do, moving from one to the other cuddling and sobbing. I held her tight, she was safe … mine … I wasn't going to let her go … never.

Bill, Ray, Clare and Ben all had a cuddle with Amberlie while we waited for Matt to visit her for the last time. I swear that as she was passed into each pair of arms she smiled. Ben still had her cuddled close to him while Matt examined her. After he left, I took her again and Clare and I washed her and brushed her hair, and Clare fetched her prettiest vest, socks, T-shirt, pink cardigan and starry leggings to dress her in. She was very brave and wanted so much to help.

We tidied Amberlie's bed on the floor and laid her down, putting her favourite white blanket across her with her special cuddly toys. She looked beautiful. I then called Hayley to tell her.

Bill had noted that Amberlie died at 15.57 p.m. on the seventh day of the seventh month, aged seven years.

Hayley came and sat talking with us for ages and then made a call to the funeral directors. She said that she was going to clear the room and the house of all the equipment, as we really wouldn't want it hanging around. Bill and big Ray helped her load it all into her car. I looked around the room. It was so empty … just vacant spaces where it all used to be. It seemed as if it was showing the end, the no more … and it left me just as empty.

Dr Ramsay called and asked if she could visit. She came more or less straight away and was amazed at Amberlie so peaceful on the cushions on our floor, and how the dog walked round her and at one point even jumped straight across her. Hayley said, 'That's just the way it is in this house, Doctor!'

Dr Ramsay was very quiet and I could see she was upset and being strong at the same time. There were long periods of silence and she said to let her know when the funeral would be and that she would like us to come and see her at the hospital in a couple of weeks' time for a chat.

Later that evening the undertakers came and I followed them down the path as they took my baby away, and I must have stood on the kerb for ages after they had driven off. Bill and I went to see her the next day.

The kids also wanted to see Amberlie so we took them a couple of days later. They weren't fazed at all. They looked at her in her little white coffin and said, 'She looks just as if she's asleep.'

The lights of the chapel flickered all the time the children were there and I think that was Amberlie letting them know she was around.

When they touched her they were a little shocked at how cold she was, but one of the undertakers who had earlier introduced himself as Bob put his hands on their shoulders and said, 'If you stroke her hair, she won't feel so cold.' And they did.

On the way out Raymond asked if he could go back to see Amberlie on his own. We nodded and Bob said, 'Take your time – there's no rush. Just come out when you're ready.'

He obviously had something he wanted to say to Amberlie that he didn't want anyone else to hear. I have never asked him what it was - it was private to him.

What I do know is that he was much better in himself afterwards.

We had many strange happenings that week and odd coincidences. For example Auntie Pat had a couple of years back bought

Amberlie a big bubble lamp that changed colour all the time and was always on. On the day she died it stopped working. Bill changed the bulb and fiddled with it but couldn't get it going. Then one afternoon we were sorting out the music for the funeral, and as I turned the volume up to hear her favourite record the lamp suddenly came on!

Another thing was that I had a persistent, blinding headache for days from all the crying that tablets just weren't curing. I said out loud when I got into bed one night, 'Oh Ambams ... if only I could shift this headache.' That night, I dreamt of Amberlie rubbing my forehead with her thumb, and when I woke up it was gone.

Amberlie's Funeral

Bill and I decided that Amberlie was to have the send off of a princess. We arranged for her to have a white carriage drawn by four horses, followed by two white and black Daimlers.

I had asked for Amberlie to be brought home on the morning so she could be with us all for one last time. I was excited that she was coming home – it was like she had just been away for a while and I couldn't wait for her to arrive, and when the car pulled up outside I dashed to the door to welcome my baby inside. The undertakers brought her into the front room and she looked so beautiful. I kissed her forehead. They had put a little too much make up on her so I wiped some of it off. I picked a beautiful huge pink and white lily and some sweetpeas from the garden and put them next to her.

The kids came and kissed and stroked her hair and each left a little cuddly toy beside her. I also put in her black-and-white Skwish so she would have something to play with.

When the carriage arrived at 12.30 p.m. it was so beautiful. It was white with four carved pillars at each corner and was decorated with deep red roses and green leaves, with purple grapes cascading down the pillars. It had two Victorian lamps on the front and it was made of glass on all four sides. There were pink ribbons hanging down from each corner and at mid-points, which were gently floating in the breeze. The horses were as black as night, with long black feather plumes on their heads.

They were dressed to perfection and were so still and proud. The carriage master was in black with a top hat and a whip. The two cars had pink and white ribbons tied to all the door handles.

They put all the flowers on the roof of the carriage except ours, which were to cover her coffin. They were all delicate and white and trailed with greenery. Five pink roses were bunched on the top by a huge Mickey Mouse cuddly toy that had been nestled into the middle. It all reminded me of Snow White – a beauty encased in glass.

I stood beside her when it was time to go, and I watched them screw down the lid and carry her out of the house. There were lots of people outside silently watching. Even their children were quiet. I took a huge deep breath and felt the grief take over like an iced wind. I bit my lip. I had to stay calm.

The dog shot out of the door and positioned himself under the carriage. He wasn't for moving and actually went for Bill when he tried to get him out. Eventually he came, and I stroked his head as he came back inside. He turned his head up to look at me – I could see how much he hurt too.

Bill helped to carry Amberlie into the church for the service. We had all written a message to read but the vicar had to read my words and Ray's … the others were very brave and read their own.

We played her favourite songs, Edwyn Collins' 'A Girl Like You', Barry Manilow's 'If I Can Dream', Nicky Thomas' 'The Love of the Common People' and the theme so often used by Disney – 'The Sleigh Ride'.

The vicar made me smile on the way to the cars – he said, 'The kids are all very amused down there – the horses have peed in the car park!'

Bill and I greeted all the people, friends and family, who came to the church. It was lovely to see the nurses from the hospital, Dr Ramsay and Matt, June and Eve, as well as our health visitor, and especially Hayley and Laura. There were lots of people from the schools and many neighbours too. Even Bill's boss and two others from the dreaded bank were there to pay their respects.

The horses took Amberlie through the village, through the town centre, and out into the open countryside. It was a beautiful afternoon and Amberlie would have been delighted to watch all the green trees swaying her along. I could hear her giggling and cooing away.

At the crematorium, the Manic Street Preachers' 'A Design for Life' boomed out as Amberlie entered, and Bill, Ray, Clare, Ben and I each placed a single white rose on her coffin. Ben held onto his Uncle Ray's hand for dear life. The kids were all very brave. I was so proud of them.

Epilogue

The pain was enduring and unending. The devastation, desolation and odd sense of the unnatural consumed my whole being like a vulture ripping away at flesh. Despite all of Amberlie's problems I have never been able to accept that she died before me – children are not supposed to die before their parents. After seven years of concentrated love, care, nurturing and keeping her safe I felt as if my whole life had been slashed away, leaving me barren and broken. I spent endless days crying, wanting her back and wanting to be with her. If it wasn't for the other kids I might well be.

Years later the pain is still as raw as it was on that dreadful day. I'll never get over it and neither do I want to. I live with it, carrying it with me in a parallel to my daily existence. Amberlie is always there with me and I often talk to her. There are times when reminders or insignificant things bring it all to the surface again and I struggle to hold it back and put it back on its shelf, but sometimes I can't control it and the grief overtakes in seconds and the tears come in torrents. On bad days I find there is a very fine line between keeping everything controlled and having a total nervous breakdown. Thankfully, I have Bill, Ray, Clare and Ben who, by just being there, always keep me within the boundaries of sanity.

Strangely on the day of the funeral I didn't cry at all. I knew I had to cope that day because of the kids, and I think I psychologically blanked all the emotion from my body and I don't remember feeling a thing that day, either positive or negative, although I did grouch at Bill's brother for not contacting Bill at all since Amberlie died. It was like being on automatic pilot, I also did not want to say goodbye to her.

I wish Amberlie was still here and at the same time accept there is no point in such a wish – because she would still be ill, and I couldn't and wouldn't wish that on her for anything. She lived her lifespan and that was how it was meant to be. I miss her every minute of every day and sometimes I wonder the 'what ifs' (which I have found very self-destructive), but I can't change the past, and we always did what we thought was best for her at the time. She was such a character and a delight to have around and I miss her coos and giggles and little noises. But I do hear them sometimes, in a quiet moment or when we are doing something she would have enjoyed. The house still feels as though there is someone missing, a part of the jigsaw in our family, a part of the happiness that once existed, but I know she is with us in spirit. Sometimes, in dreams, I am allowed a cuddle and then I have to give her back.

When new people ask me how many children I have, I always think four but tell them three because I see no point in going into detail about what they probably wouldn't understand. Sadly, I find it is somewhat of a conversation stopper as well.

Amberlie's birthday seems to be more traumatic every year as I think about how old she would have been; and I try desperately hard not to think at all on 7 July. We always remember her special days with a bunch of flowers and a foil balloon, and I now have her name tattooed on my shoulder.

Life goes on though and we laugh a lot and remember all the great times. There are so many special memories and Amberlie taught me a lot about life and changed me for what I believe is the better. I have different views, beliefs and opinions now and I love more wholly and cherish what I have. We are indeed very lucky to be healthy and able to live full lives and I will forever wish that Amberlie could have had that opportunity, as I am sure she would have lived it for every moment with the zest and joy she showed when her brain allowed her to.

The bank gave Bill the rest of the summer off as compassionate leave (about time!), and big Ray treated us to a couple of weeks in Devon and Cornwall. Bill reluctantly returned to work the same day as the kids went back to school. That was such a hard day, and the first that I had been on my own since I could remember. I couldn't bear the fact that I was going to have to return to our house after dropping the kids at school without Amberlie with me to go through the front door. I shook as I stood outside and put the key in the lock. I opened it quickly and slammed it behind me. It was so quiet, a crushing silence – nothing but the dog snoring and I couldn't stand it. I stood with my back against the door, rooted to the spot and panicked. I told myself this was daft and I wasn't to be terrified of being in my own house, and that Amberlie was with me anyway. After a cry, I set about tidying up.

I was very much unemployed at home. There wasn't enough to do. Amberlie had needed twenty-four-hour care and I had nothing to fill my time and was unable to sit still for long. I still had her medicine and food times burned into my soul and the whole routine was difficult to let go of. I only slept minimally and found it very hard to adjust to a 'normal' day. I was in no mood to watch TV or paint or read books, and I didn't want to visit anyone either. I wasn't ready, and I didn't want to talk about how I was feeling. Everyone kept telling me I needed to rest but I just couldn't. I knew I was going to have to do something that got me out of the place otherwise I was going to go mad, and the kids had been through enough without finding their mother in a complete mess.

Ben's head teacher had suggested to me that if I wanted, I could always help out at the school. So that's what I did. I spent two weeks helping out nearly every day and was then offered a full-time job as a teaching assistant. I grabbed it with both hands and knew it was very much the right thing for me to do at the time. I spent a year full-time and then felt it was time to be at home alone so that I could start writing this book as I had always intended. I offered my resignation but they wanted me to stay part-time so I got the best of both. That, too, was the best decision because there have been many times when I have needed to walk away from my writing.

I have found that I'm no longer very good at coping with trauma, and if anything happens I instantly feel like a battered, worn-out old punch bag that can't take anymore. If any of the kids get hurt, my first reaction is to panic, and if they are sick I think the worst. Where children are concerned I am a huge softie. In some ways, though, I have become harder and less tolerant of the outside world. My resolution is very much to live for today and worry about tomorrow if I really have to. I don't think anyone can go through something like this without being changed somehow, but I wouldn't have had it any other way, because whichever way we had Amberlie was better than not having her at all.

Generally, the kids have all coped admirably with losing Amberlie and I have been amazed at their resilience. Luckily, Hayley and Laura were a huge support to us for weeks afterwards, calling in as regularly as they could to talk to the kids, sometimes individually and sometimes together. They listened to all they had to say and explained everything they were worried about or hadn't understood. They were truly amazing people who cared immensely for the welfare of our family. Naturally the kids have had bad times when they have been odd and behaved out of character, done something silly and got themselves very upset, but are now settled happily in their own lives.

Ben was the most affected by Amberlie's death. She had always been there with him and he found it very difficult to adjust to a world without her. It took a long time to pull him together at school and there were often tears and traumas at home as he tried to deal with his feelings. Ben still talks about Amberlie every day, and when he meets someone new, he says straight away that he had a sister called Amberlie who died. There is hardly a day when he doesn't say, 'I wish Amberlie was still here – I really miss her.'

He has just returned from three days away with the school and he brought home a little pink teddy for Amberlie to put by her box. We have Amberlie's ashes at home, in the front room, because that's where the kids wanted her to be – where she had always been.

I have learned never to underestimate children – they really are little people with surprisingly adult heads, and as long as they are nurtured, cared for and listened to, they won't go far wrong. The difficulty they have is in expressing themselves. Ours have been a tremendous support to us, and their refreshing attitude and black-and-white way of seeing things had helped us no end.

Bill is still working with the bank, and in time has been delighted to see his previous managers disappear out of the bank, which has helped him put his grievances behind him. He still finds it difficult to accept life without his Ambams.

Ray is now studying at university and Clare is doing her A levels. Ben is at secondary school and doing fine, but given the choice would still rather not have to go!

We made our final visit to the hospital to see Dr Ramsay a couple of weeks after the funeral and we talked for a long time about all the things that had happened. She asked if there were any suggestions we could offer that might have made Amberlie's treatment any better. We couldn't think of anything – everyone did their best and we would be forever grateful to her and her fine team for looking after our little girl so well. I later sent her a bouquet of flowers.

While we were there, Dr Thomas popped in to see us. He said, 'Amberlie was very lucky to have had parents like you who loved and cared for her so much. It isn't often the way and to have brought her to the age she was ...' and he shook his head and bit his bottom lip, '... is amazing. She was a very lucky little girl.'

My lips quivered uncontrollably and the tears poured down my face, 'You're wrong. It is we who are lucky, priviledged, honoured and humbled, to have had a daughter as brave and beautiful as she was.'

A HEADBANGER'S BALL

Also by Sandra Murphy

Withercraft: The Obsidian Box

(Fiction)

When chaos erupts in the Otherworld, the distraught, volatile Oak King appears in Ernest's cottage and forces him to find the child who can save him from extinction.

Angry at being ejected from his blissful wizardry, Ernest begins a perilous adventure through parallel worlds of magic and legend, where enchanted creatures, trickery and the opposing forces of good and evil will test his resolve and sanity, and ultimately change his destiny forever.

Inspired by British Folklore and the enigmatic Green Men of the woodland, this present day tale will appeal to all with a curiosity for the extraordinary.

ISBN-13:978-1499325201
ISBN-10: 1499325207